A
Mountain
in China

To Beloved Devika
I hope your adventures
in China will be as
wonderful as mine!
    Much Love
        Veena

Books by Veena Schlegel
A Vanished Road
Glimpses of my Master

A DVD of photographs to accompany
A Mountain in China
is available. Please see website for details

www.3books.co.uk

A Mountain in China

by
Veena Schlegel

ISBN-13: 978-1507824900
(CreateSpace)

The Shaolin Temple's symbol of Zen. Preserved on an
old stone stele in the grounds of the temple,
the image shows the fusion of Buddhism (Buddha in the centre),
Taoism (Lao Tzu on the right),
and Confucianism (Confucius on the left),
to form Zen.

Acknowledgements

I want to express my very deep gratitude to my three young friends, Ibo, Yujie and Andy, without whom my journeys to China, and this book, could not have happened. From the bottom of my heart I thank you all for sharing your life with me, for your endless translations, for all the information you have shared with me about Chinese traditions, history and ways of living, for organising expeditions for me, for finding me accommodation, for meeting me at bus stations, train stations and airports and for seeing me off at bus stations, train stations and airports – in short, for making this whole momentous time in my life possible.

I also give my heartfelt thanks to Master Wu Nanfang, his wife, Su Yufang, his daughter, Lijuan and his son Wenju, for so graciously taking so much care of me, for giving me insights into their very different kungfu way of life, for taking me on so many picturesque trips, for explaining the Zen and Buddhist traditions in the Song Mountain area to me and for telling me so many stories about local history and events.

I thank too the students at the kungfu school: Rende, Yaofeng, Chengeng, Hufei, Naomitsu, Ali, and little Rouyi and Tian De for so many happy and playful times.

Next I want to thank my lovely landlords, Mr and Mrs Shang, for providing me with such a beautiful and comfortable apartment and for so graciously accepting me into their family and taking care of me.

Then many thanks are due to other villagers in ShiLiPu: my first landlords, Mr and Mrs Wang; Chao Feng Lee, the convenience store owner, with his cheery 'Good morning, Weena', who so patiently tried to figure out what it was that I wanted; Liu, my buddha taxi driver; and all the villagers and the babies who welcomed me into the village and made me feel so at home here.

Then I want to thank Mr and Mrs Zhao, Yujie's parents, for inviting me to live with them in their homes on Hainan Island and in Inner Mongolia and for taking me on wonderful trips in these areas. I would also like to thank Professor Zhao, Yujie's uncle, for so patiently and informatively answering all my questions on Zen and Buddhism, and for taking me to visit the Linji Temple.

Many western friends are also due some heartfelt thanks. I would like to thank my editor, Dhiren, for his invaluable comments and critique, Nigam, a proof master supreme, and Bhagawati for all her support, Enormous thanks for your incredible help – without it this book could not have been published.

And last, but by no means least, I want to thank so many friends for their emotional, practical and even financial help in supporting and encouraging me to take off into the unknown East: Madhura, Mayavati, Yatri, Navyo, Amitabh and Vibhuti. Thanks are also due to Pankaja for being a wonderful travelling companion and to Carolyn for the very important task of taking care of my precious plants during the long months I was away.

Contents

Introduction

I fell in love with a mountain.... I would never have thought it possible to fall in love with an inanimate lump of rock, but that's what happened!

And I am not alone. Since before records began, people have been drawn to Song Mountain, the central sacred mountain in China. First it was the Taoists, then the Buddhists – and then in the sixth century AD, an enlightened mystic, Bodhidharma, arrived from India, sat meditating in a cave on the mountain for nine years, and then gave Zen to the world.

Emperors and empresses loved to visit and more recently, the Shaolin Temple, on the slopes of Mount Shaoshi, has become a centre for kung fu enthusiasts the world over.

Inspired by a BBC documentary I was drawn to this magnificent, primordial mountain in search of something I was not exactly sure what. I simply knew I had to go there. Not only did I find a certain essence of something unfathomable which took my path of Zen meditation to new depths, but I got happily involved in the lives of the local people living in the small village of ShiLiPu in the mountain's foothills.

I encountered the master and students of the little known form of Wugulun Kungfu, I met local farmers and villagers, and I became friends with some English-speaking university graduates who were able to tell me about local customs and traditions, as well as fill me in on the extraordinary changes rapidly taking place in modern China.

So many of the traditional ways of living are disappearing that I felt I wanted to record some of the stories my young friends told me about local people and their past histories, such as the cow helping to build a local temple or the rich young girl fleeing from an

1

arranged marriage to become a Buddhist nun living on Song Mountain.

Life in my village was not always easy; at times it was actually quite tough! Trying to function amongst people who rarely spoke English, wending my way through personal relationships in a very foreign culture, and coping with a climate of extreme weather patterns, occasionally took a toll. But the unconditional friendliness, charm and generosity of the Chinese people that I met, and the fascinating discoveries of the spiritual and historical heritage of the area, more than made up for the few uncomfortable times.

There is a Zen saying that the only Zen one finds at the top of a mountain is the Zen within oneself. I had ⊚ulfillme Zen for forty years under the guidance of my beloved Master, Osho, and it was his extraordinary insights and his apparent connections with this part of China that continually inspired me to delve deeper into the mysteries of this sacred place.

This book then is the story of my visits here, the people I met, my love for the mountain and all it represented, and the ⊚ulfillment I found in drawing on its subtle power to further my own personal path.

Veena Schlegel
March 2015

1
The Path to Song Mountain

Song Mountain

To return to the root is repose;
It is called going back to one's destiny.
Going back to one's destiny is to find the eternal law,
To know the eternal law is enlightenment.

LaoTzu: Tao Te Ching

The Inspiration

The only sounds in the silence of the pre-dawn scene was an intermittent sharp cry of a distant bird and the soft thuds of the feet of the only dimly visible figures as they practised their slow-motion movements. As the darkness faded into the hazy early morning light, the individual features of about twenty-five young men emerged – their faces still and softly focused as they moved. Slowly the outlines of silent mountain rocks, steep precipices and scraggy trees became visible…. I was mesmerised. I felt that I was being drawn into something deeply primordial, infinitely harmonious and somehow very portentous for me.

I was watching a BBC documentary and at the end of the hour-long program I disconcertingly knew, with one hundred percent certainty, that I was going to go to that mountain.

The documentary, one of three, showed the explorations of an English vicar into religions other than those of his own Christian calling – in this case, Zen Buddhism in China. His research had led him to the Shaolin Temple, home of Chinese kungfu, which apparently regarded Zen Buddhism as its spiritual heritage. Here it was that Bodhidharma, patriarch of Zen Buddhism, sat in a cave on the mountain – Song Mountain – for nine years after which he came down to the temple and introduced Zen Buddhism to the monks living there. The vicar was, however, rather disillusioned with what he found at the temple and decided to delve further by going to a monastery built high up in the peaks of the mountain to see if he could discover something more profound. At SanHuangZhai monastery, meeting two kungfu masters, Shi Dejian and Wu Nanfang, and their disciples, he did.

Knowing a little about Bodhidharma and his importance in

the heritage of Zen, the mountain, the masters and the disciples also touched me profoundly. Zen is my path and if I could journey to this place it would be a kind of 'returning to the source' for me.

But where was this monastery? How would I get there? Although there was a lot of information on the Shaolin Temple online, the location of this mountain retreat was not mentioned. My googling took me to a small town called Dengfeng in Henan Province in central China – very much off the beaten track, it seemed – but presented no other useful details.

I have always been a traveller but that youthful glow, strength and certainty which I used to have and which took me to unknown places with scarcely a blink of an eye, was now no longer so much in evidence. As a sixty-four-year-old pensioner, unable to afford the costs of guided travel tours, I was a bit more cautious and the idea of venturing off alone into distant mountains in China, destination unknown, was daunting, to say the least.

Further research tactics were necessary. I first called the BBC asking for more information. After being transferred from one department to another, I eventually ended up with exactly nothing – not even an assurance that there would be a repeat of the program. I had been so transfixed that I had not wanted to miss a minute by trying to video it, so now it was all just memory. There would apparently be no DVD made which I could buy.

I then tried googling the vicar – Peter Owen-Jones. This was much more productive because I found out there had been an article about his journey in a national newspaper, The Telegraph, and a local magazine in Lewes in Suffolk. The Telegraph article finally gave me the spelling of the Chinese names for the monastery and one of the masters.

Putting these words into Google threw up a website, yes, but it was all in Chinese! So that frustratingly provided nary a hint unless I could find a Chinese person to translate for me. I didn't know a Chinese person. So I next called the Lewes magazine and asked them if they could help me to contact the vicar. They were polite but said they couldn't hand out any contact details but if I wanted to write an email to them they would forward it. I immediately wrote an email asking the vicar if he could give me some information to help me find the monastery, and sent it off.

I then put the kungfu master's name into Google and eventually, after entering variations of spellings I found a reference to him on the website of The Chinese University of Hong Kong! Apparently somebody there had decided to do some tests on the master's brain to see the effects of meditation. The report, in English, was signed by a professor, Agnes S Chan, who had spent some time in the monastery. Her email was listed under her name. I immediately wrote to her asking if she could give me some guidance as to where this monastery was as I would like to go there to meditate. Within a few hours I got a terse one-line reply saying that visitors were not welcome there!

Somewhat deflated I tried to practise the art of patience – an art I am not at all good at – while hoping for an answer from the vicar. After a week or two and receiving no answer, I decided to write him a letter, figuring that the local Lewes Post Office could give me an address as the Rev. Jones was obviously a well-known person in the area. I called the Post Office and the post mistress said that, as he was a public figure, she could make public his address and so I immediately wrote and posted a letter to him.

Another few weeks passed but no answer came so I was pretty much stumped. I had of course tried Chinese travel websites, kungfu websites etc but found no reference to this place.

But this urge to go and find this mountain was a constant strong drumming in my heart so I finally decided I would have to somehow go alone to this small town, Dengfeng, near the Shaolin Temple and trust that someone would guide me to the place despite me not being able to speak Chinese.

But why this driving conviction that I had to go there?

Many years ago, in 1970, at the age of twenty-six, I had set off on the now well-known hippie overland trail to India. My vague idea was to follow the trail and eventually make it to Japan, a country which had fascinated me since I was a teenager. After many adventures along the way I eventually ended up sitting in front of an Indian mystic, at that time called Bhagwan Shree Rajneesh. I was initially a very reluctant disciple but, as the time I spent with him lengthened, I began to understand and experience the wonders of being with an enlightened Master and the insights and mysteries revealed by his guidance and meditation.

The death of my Master, who had now changed his name to Osho, in 1990, began a different kind of search: how best to continue on what I now thought of as my 'path' when I was no longer blessed by his physical presence and inspiration. The challenges of coping with the distinctly uninspiring everyday western world and its financial realities, and having to function while no longer supported by the commune in which we had hitherto lived for twenty years, were huge. I felt my grasp on all I had learned and come to understand, all that was vital to my life, slowly slipping away despite all my efforts.

Sixteen years after Osho had left this earth, after stints of teaching English as a foreign language in various countries around the world, including Japan, and a debilitating ten-year-long illness, I retired to a small cottage in Somerset hoping that the peace and quiet of the country would help restore that space which I felt to be the vital 'me'. But I found I had lost the ability to meditate deeply and got very depressed as I felt myself to be in a kind of limbo: not at all enthused about a rural lifestyle in England and yet not able to reach those spaces which made it okay to be anywhere on the planet, in any situation and still be on the path.

This, then, was the space I was in when, on January 4th 2008, I watched, with a growing excitement and a sense of enormous portent, this documentary featuring a mountain in China.

* * *

Three months had passed after first seeing the program and all my efforts to find some information on this place had come to nothing. The urge to go was, however, unabated; I could not let go of the feeling that travelling to this place was of crucial importance to me. And so one grey, wet, gloomy, infinitely depressing winter day I again resolutely attacked the internet, determined to find some clue as to where the mountain monastery was. This time I eventually arrived at a small amateurish website in *English* showing a small photo of the monastery with some young men doing the kind of kungfu I had seen in the documentary. I think the difference may have been that, instead of typing in the Chinese word 'gongfu', I had used the English version 'kungfu'. Or maybe the website had only recently been put online.

I excitedly searched through the pages of the website and there, in another small photo no larger than a postage stamp, I saw an image of Master Dejian and the other kungfu master, still nameless at that time, who gave such a beautiful talk on Zen in the documentary. Even more exciting was the name of a person, Meilin, and an English email address inviting people to write for information. I immediately wrote an email but my hopes sadly subsided when two more weeks passed and I received no reply.

I had noticed, however, a phone number on the site so I eventually decided to telephone and see if I could get any further. Because of the time difference I got up at 3am and made the call but could only reach a man speaking Chinese who rattled on about something and then left me hanging on in silence. Fortunately my experiences from living in so many foreign countries had taught me to be patient and allow the other person to arrange things and, sure enough, after two or three minutes an American-sounding young man came on the line. Finally, I could speak to someone! He was very kind and told me that Meilin was away at the moment but was due back in a few days and that she could probably help me. And, yes, he did know about the monastery and had been there many times and yes, he saw no reason why I couldn't go there. He said he would tell Meilin I had called and was sure she would answer me.

You can imagine my elation after this phone call – was the puzzle finally about to be solved? And then a few days later some very welcome Chinese characters appeared in my Inbox and I found a short letter in very good English from Meilin saying yes, she knew the monastery and both the kungfu masters and if I wanted to come to Dengfeng, she could take me to the monastery and introduce me to them.

The incessant drumming in my heart finally ceased and, hardly taking a breath, I immediately started searching for a cheap flight to China. I quickly realised that a complication was the Olympic Games being held in August and September and, on phoning a Chinese visa office, I was told that no visas other than those for the Games would be issued until after the Games ended. (The first encounter with the erratic Chinese visa story!) So I still had some time to wait, but anyway Meilin had told me that September was a good time to come to Dengfeng because the summer was extremely hot and uncomfortable.

With two or three flight options available I was making some lists when a friend called. Her name is Pankaja, Panky for short, and on patiently receiving my torrent of excited explanations she finally managed to interrupt when I was taking in some much-needed air, and say, 'Can I come with you?'! She went on to say she had also seen the documentary and had been massively inspired by it and would jump at the chance to go. This was the icing on the cake for me because I was still a little afraid of going all that way alone into the backwoods of China, even if I knew I would be met at the other end. As the reader will see, this travel collaboration turned out to be a truly wonderful happening.

After taking onboard her request and the happy implications of having a travelling companion, I told her the results of my searches for cheap flights and visas and she immediately said, 'Let's book a ticket now. I'll turn on my computer'. Together we discussed the various flights and eventually decided on one that left about two weeks after the end of the Games – on the 28th September. I told Panky I should quickly phone the visa office again to find out if visas would definitely be issued for that date. When they answered 'no problem', I called her back and then and there we booked the flights to China via our respective computers. Fastest flight booking I have ever made.

That done, I emailed Meilin back with dates and flight times. I think she was a bit surprised at the speed with which arrangements hadeen made, especially that now a second person was involved, but she replied in a few days saying that, if we liked, she could book us into a reasonable hotel and also arrange for a taxi to pick us up at the nearest airport which was in the city of Zhengzhou. We of course were enthusiastic to be helped in this way – and so the deeds were done and everything was now in place. And my heart was at peace.

* * *

After a few days had passed it slowly began to dawn on me that, despite my enthusiasm and excitement, I was in no physical state to climb that mountain! After more than a year of being imprisoned inside my cottage due to the ceaseless rain which had turned the whole country into a dark soggy mess, I was massively unfit and I needed to remedy this situation – fast! So I set myself a program of walking at least three miles a day – come rain, wind or sun – one mile of which was up a fairly steep hill which would hopefully prepare my muscles and lungs for mountain climbing.

I bought a Lonely Planet guidebook for China and found a vague plan of the area to which I was going. Neither the monastery nor the mountain walk featured in the documentary were, however, mentioned. But there were many other interesting facts about this region and, never having been too interested in China, my curiosity was now piqued and it seemed like a whole new world was opening up before me.

The Journey

Getting the visas presented no problems and soon Panky and I were boarding the plane for Beijing. After a pleasant and uneventful flight we arrived at the superbly designed Terminal 3 of the Beijing Capital Airport which had only been completed seven months previously for the Olympic Games. I had followed the construction of this terminal, the second largest in the world, and was looking forward to seeing it. It surpassed any expectations: it was a lofty, spacious, light-filled, almost delicately beautiful structure while at the same time being totally efficient. Stunning! As I walked through the various sections to catch our onward flight, I compared it with the ugly, jumbled, congested, inefficient Heathrow and reflected that this spectacular edifice was designed by the British architectural company, Foster and Partners, with the lighting designed by British lighting architects, Speirs and Major Associates. How come, I wondered, that our superb British talent cannot be utilised in our own country?

Arriving at our Gate to catch a flight to Zhengzhou, the

nearest airport to Dengfeng and Song Mountain, we got our first taste of the world we were about to enter – the majority of the other passengers on the plane seemed to be young kungfu guys, presumably from the Shaolin Temple which arranges tours around the world to demonstrate the often remarkable kungfu skills of their students. All of them had shaved heads, were physically loose and graceful, and had a very palpable energy despite the fact that they were obviously quite sleepy from much travelling. I was fascinated watching these quite different young beings.

Arriving in Zhengzhou we were met by a handsome man holding a card with my name printed neatly on it. Meilin had been really efficient! Liu was our taxi driver – a buddha in taxi man guise! Six years later, Liu is still our taxi driver. He is one of the people to whom we owe many joyful times in China. Centred, calm and charming, he would always manage to sort out all our problems despite not initially speaking a word of English. (Later I taught him some useful words and phrases and gave him a Chinese/English dictionary).

At this time, however, his English was non-existent but Panky had a secret device in her bag which proved to be a valuable aid as well as a source of great hilarity when meeting locals. While I had just a paperback dictionary, she had an electronic dictionary with a female voice pronouncing the needed word. Locals loved to listen to this and for many it was a good joke to work out what the voice was saying as their local dialect was often very different. Chinese is one of the most difficult languages in the world to learn because of the pronunciation. It is simple enough to learn a word but unless you pronounce it correctly, the Chinese person you are trying to talk to will not be able to understand. For example, the name of the city we arrived in is spelled Zhengzhou but pronounced Jengjo. And very often the pronunciations will differ markedly depending on the local dialect used.

Our first need was water to drink and Liu's laughing reaction to the electronic pronunciation was a hint of things to come. It was also the first Chinese word I learned—'shwee'.

As we journeyed along a new and well-kept highway we eagerly scanned the rather unprepossessing scenery along the way, agreeing that at times it looked as scruffy and as poor as India where we had both spent many years. I was interested, though, in what appeared to be a tree-planting project – thousands of young saplings, arranged neatly in rows, covered the land on each side of the highway. The vegetation was quite lush as here the rainy season, a bit like the Indian monsoon, is in the summer. We saw a few concrete high-rises in some parts but this did not appear to be a very populated area and the millions of Chinese inhabitants were not much in evidence. It actually all seemed pretty deserted.

After about an hour my heart started to beat faster because mountains started looming up in the distance. Almost exactly nine months after I first saw the mountains on TV, I was now seeing them for real. The name Song Mountain or, in Chinese, SongShan, is applied to the southern end of a long range of mountains which form almost a semi-circle: the range spreads from Shanxi in the north, southwards through Henan and then extends westwards a little into Shaanxi. We both lapsed into silence as the landscape changed and we realised we were coming close to our destination – perhaps also our destiny.

Finally we entered what the Lonely Planet guide rather aptly described as 'a tatty little town' – although the hotel that Liu deposited us in was actually quite posh with a large marble foyer, grand wooden carvings and tastefully painted hanging scrolls. Liu, possibly instructed by Meilin, took control and very efficiently facilitated the checking-in process and then went with us to our room to make sure everything was all right. He then took out his mobile phone, dialled, and handed the phone to me. It was Meilin!

She welcomed us and said she would come and see us that evening if that was okay. It was fine by us so we arranged for her to come at around 7pm because she told us that Chinese eat dinner early and the evening meal in the hotel would be served at 6pm, in two hours time. Liu then left after correcting my pronunciation of the second Chinese word I learned 'xiexie' – thank you. We were profoundly grateful to him for making our arrival such a smooth and enjoyable one.

Efficient hot showers perked up our now flagging energy and the evening meal was passable. The main problem was trying to find a vegetarian dish and here Panky's electronic dictionary was met with baffled stares. It seemed that vegetarianism was not a known concept.

Meeting Meilin was a memorable occasion. She was gorgeous! Despite all our correspondence, I had no idea of her age or what she would be like. Well, she was about thirty-years old, intelligent, alive, beautiful, charming and spoke English fluently. Both Panky and I were fascinated with her. We had discussed what kind of presents to bring her (having both lived in Japan we assumed that gifts were a necessary introduction in China too, and we were right) but knowing nothing about her made our choices a little difficult. In the end, we were successful. I had brought her a very nice cosmetic bag filled with all kinds of western beauty products and Panky had brought some gorgeous fancy socks and scarves.

After chatting awhile Meilin dropped a major bombshell on us!!! Tomorrow morning, she said, she would be taking some Dutch kungfu students up to SanHuangZhai monastery and there would be room in the vehicle for us if we wanted to come too. We were stunned at our dreams so immediately being fulfilled and of course we said a resounding *yes!* Sleep was now all important so we said our goodnights, Meilin left, and we were sound asleep as soon as heads hit pillows.

The Monastery

The day we arrived in Dengfeng had been rather cloudy and foggy but the next morning was bright and sunny. I could see the blue sky through gaps in the curtain as I lay awake for a short while contemplating the momentous fact that climbing the mountain, scene of my dreams for so long, was soon to be a reality.

We dressed quickly, tried to waive aside the early morning tea craving, and attempted to manoeuvre our way through the breakfast procedures which turned out to be a bit complicated as we had to get tickets in one place, have them checked in another and only then were we set free to choose from a rather strange assortment of food. At least the watermelon was recognisable.

We were still eating when Meilin arrived, all very efficient, and hurried us into finishing what we had attempted to eat. She also quickly picked up some napkins and stuffed them full of bread-like things to take with us – to eat as we climbed up the mountain, she explained! She then steered us into an eight-seater van and off we sped. We were to find that it was often hard to keep up with her when she was in tour-guide mode.

In the van there were four young Dutch guys and a Dutch woman, all attending Meilin's kungfu school. Quite what they thought of these two old ladies joining them I am not sure but they were rather charming and definitely as excited as we were to be going up the mountain.

Dengfeng is not very big and we soon reached the outskirts where we all collectively gasped at the panorama of the mountain range spread out before us. It is hard to describe quite what I felt but it was as if I knew a certain essence of this mountain and was hurrying towards a pre-determined place and meeting. This mountain has a magic and a mystery that I have never experienced anywhere else on the planet. That morning my heart and soul was captured and drawn into its magical web from which I have never escaped. I love this place like no other place on this earth.

* * *

Both Panky and I were momentarily daunted when we arrived at a parking area at the foot of the mountain, got out of the van and stared with dismay at the stone steps up which we were apparently going to climb. Staircase would not convey the right image; it was more like a ladder! That gentle Somerset slope on which I had been optimistically 'training' had not remotely prepared my legs or lungs for *this*! I had caught a glimpse of these steps in the documentary but then the vicar was going down them, not up, so it never dawned on me that I would be required to climb a ladder into the sky! Meilin, bless her, had considered the issue and suddenly presented an older lady which she detached from the crowd milling around the base of the steps. She introduced her as her mother, Lihua, who she had commissioned to look after us and to guide us slowly up the mountain while she went on ahead with the young, fit kungfu students!!! Meilin encouragingly told us to take our time and soon disappeared up the steps.

By a quarter of the way up I was gasping for air but with frequent rests the going actually got easier as my lungs were forced to expand and – way behind Panky, who was much fitter than me, being a TaiChi enthusiast – I did finally get to the top of stairway. Here, at a kind of resting stage, we were touched to find some of Dejian's students there to greet us with bottles of water. From then onwards the steps wound round outcrops of rock, and sometimes levelled out and had railings to hang on to to pull oneself up with, so the way wasn't quite so arduous. Still Panky and Lihua were managing better than me so I told them to go on ahead and I would take it more slowly.

This actually turned out to be an interesting move. We didn't know that that day was the first day of the big autumn holiday and thousands had come to the area from all over China. A good portion of them were climbing the mountain with me and I became quite a celebrity in a short space of time. Many of the younger Chinese were not very fit either so they joined me when I sat down to rest. This was the first time I had met the Chinese people en masse and I found that they were a very extrovert bunch and were delighted to stop and talk to me with their few words of English. I think I must have posed for souvenir photographs a least twenty times as we all laboured up the steps.

It was all so sweet and friendly that I was really spurred on and then, finally, I rounded a rock and got my first glimpse of the monastery I had come from so far away to find. It absolutely did not disappoint: on the contrary it far exceeded any imagined visions I had had and my eyes brimmed with tears at finally setting eyes on this amazing building in its magnificent mountain setting. Sometimes when one sees a scene or place in reality after seeing photos, one is disappointed. Not here. No photograph could ever do justice to this reality.

Meilin had come down to find me and together we climbed the last few steps and walked onto a kind of terrace where everyone else had already arrived and were having tea served by the young woman who had featured in the documentary. Standing on the steps to the entrance to a kind of temple were the two old ladies who had also been filmed. Strange to see in real life people you had gazed at so many times on a screen on the other side of the world.

It seemed that the gang was just waiting for me to arrive because very quickly Meilin rounded us up and told us we had been invited to visit Master Wu Nanfang, the master who had given the beautiful Zen talk, in his quarters. Master Dejian, disappointingly, was away in Hong Kong. (I think he was organising further funds for his project.) We now became aware of the scale of the building of this temple and monastery as we carefully picked our way – over rocks, round piles of bags of cement and past at least fifty men cutting stone and building walls – through what was a pretty huge construction site. When we stopped in one place to admire the stunning view, Meilin told us a bit about what was happening.

Just four or five years before, the only building here was a very small stone and wood temple in which the two old ladies we had just met had been living for the past fifty years. Their story is an extraordinary one which I will tell later.

Master Dejian had been a monk in the Shaolin Temple but had not fitted in very well with the life there. He came often to this small temple because it had been built on a fairly level piece of ground suitable for him to practise his form of kungfu – which was different to the forms practised in the Shaolin Temple. Master Wu Nanfang, a friend – or 'kungfu brother' – for many years, who had started a small kungfu school in the foothills of the mountain, often joined him here. Growing more and more dissatisfied with life in the Shaolin Temple, Master Dejian left in 2003 and, with the nuns' happy agreement, embarked on an ambitious project to build a large monastery and healing centre to further the traditions of ChanWuYi, the form of kungfu they practised, with an additional emphasis on herbal medicines and healing. The present construction was the result of his project.

We were impressed, to say the least. This was a monumental endeavour. Although the stones to build the buildings were cut from the rock on the site, everything else had to be carried up those steps from the valley below. I now understood something I had noticed on my way up: every fifty yards or so there was a man slowly trudging up the steps carrying a sack of what looked like either sand or cement powder. These were the building materials for the project!! And *everything* had to be carried up – like food, not only for the inhabitants of the monastery, but also for the hundred-strong labour force which lived there! The mind boggled. And all this had been built in about four years. Extraordinary – especially when one thinks of the extreme climate here: a bitterly cold winter and a fiercely hot summer! The mountain side would be very exposed to all these elements.

Pankaja, Master Wu Nanfang and Veena

In awed silence we now followed Meilin up a short, narrow but very steep stairway carved into the mountain side. We arrived at a gate and a beautiful small stone building and then gasped as we entered a small courtyard edged with a two foot high wall on the other side of which was a sheer drop of thousands of feet. Vertigo set in immediately and I had to take some deep breaths to steady myself. But there was one more short flight of stairs still to go and we then stepped onto the roof of the small building to be greeted by the gracious Master Wu Nanfang.

This was quite an extraordinary meeting! After listening to this man talking about Zen, and after watching him teach the rather ungainly vicar some very graceful kungfu moves in my living room in a little cottage in Somerset, here I was greeting him on the top of this spectacular mountain on the other side of the world. Meilin was a patient translator and we all had many questions to ask. While conversations were going on I moved to the side of the roof and looked queasily down to the jagged valley thousands of feet below. I recognised the roof as the place where Master Dejian had demonstrated his kungfu prowess to the vicar.

The air was so clean, the energy so pure, the rocks, trees, shrubbery and sky so overpoweringly beautiful, I wanted to stay there forever.

All too soon, however, it was time to leave and reluctantly we began the steep descent to the valley below.

This was definitely one of the best days in my long, varied and much-travelled life.

Out and About

We had discovered that Meilin was running a small kungfu school and was busy much of her time with her students, some of which we had met on the trip to San Huang Zhai, so Panky and I decided to do some exploring on our own the next day.

Liu, our buddha taxi man, was called and engaged to take us to another place recommended by the Lonely Planet guidebook: a wooded hillside area featuring the FaWang Temple, the Songyue Pagoda and the Songyang Academy. Dengfeng is bordered to the north and west by the mountain range, various peaks of which have names but they seem to differ depending on which snippet of information you are reading. I therefore am a bit hesitant to mention names! Mount Ta? Or Mount Taoshi? Even the locals give me only vague answers!

I was to find later that searching for factual information about Chinese history is frustrating and confusing – maybe because it is the result of the very dubious English used. Also it seems important that each place should be the biggest, or oldest, or most popular or the most famous etc etc so trying to sift out any clear or interesting information is difficult. It also seems to be obligatory to provide lists of boring statistics such as areas and heights and widths (maybe because they are easier to write in English!) instead of informative facts and stories to make the visitor enthusiastic about what he is seeing. I have often visited places about which I would love to know more – but no additional information is provided. The Lonely Planet actually often gives a lot of quite accurate details about the places they recommend, but sometimes the facts are quite sparse especially if the person assigned to write about the place is not enthusiastic about it. In the case of Henan Province, its important spiritual heritage is largely dismissed by the guidebook in favour of more dramatic tourist attractions in other provinces. But then it is a tourist guide after all, I suppose.

I digress. In our excitement neither Panky nor I were very interested in facts or figures that morning. Liu took us first to the FaWang Temple – the oldest, or maybe second oldest Buddhist temple in China, first built apparently in 71 AD. (The White Horse Temple was apparently built in 67 AD). As we entered the gateway of the temple we were very amused at the decorative artwork painted on the walls. They were absolutely Indian in style, not Chinese at all! Garish, poorly executed and in almost cartoon-book style, they resembled cheap pictures and posters printed in India. But, on the other hand, they were a reminder of the close early connections Chinese Buddhism had with India.

Venturing inside we found a lovely peaceful place with a few monks wandering around and some kungfu students doing their thing. The temple is built on the side of the mountain so each Hall is built on a level reached by a long staircase with wide views over Dengfeng which we could not see at that time because of the haze or fog which seems to perpetually blanket the city. The beauty of this temple is its isolated situation surrounded by the pine forests, the clear air and the silence. We loved it.

Next stop was the much more famous brick Songyue Pagoda which is the oldest of its kind in China. It seems it was once part of a larger temple complex which was as usual destroyed by one or other of China's destructive emperors or dynasties – the Cultural Revolution being one of the worst culprits. This is possibly one of the reasons so few facts are available; so much has been destroyed over the centuries that it is legends that exist, rather than historical facts.

The pagoda has, or used to have, at its centre a Buddha made entirely with jade, underneath which some important Buddhist scriptures are supposedly buried. The pagoda was built between 500 and 525 AD and according to a nearby sign:

> *'Comprises of an underground place, a base, a body and a top, the pagoda is a cylindrical brick pagoda with dodecagonal overlapped-eaves. The pagoda is nice and plump in looking, sturdy and erect in structuring, with a total height of 36.778 metres and nicely honored 'the Greatest Pagoda in China'.'*

Love these so-called information signs! We were entranced! But on the other hand, I had to search online in English for some more definitive informative facts about this place, and many others, when I later tried to delve a little deeper into the history of the area.

Driving back down the hillside we then visited the Songyang

Academy built alongside a river. This was rather disappointing because it has recently been rebuilt and nothing much of the original remains except for the two four-thousand-year-old cypress trees, supposedly the oldest in China, which are still alive. Amazing. The Songyang Academy was one of the four most important places of education in old China and is associated with Confucius. Although he didn't come here, some of his most famous successors did live here from about 1035 AD and gave lectures in the garden in a very charming little stone enclave sheltered with a tree. We took photos of each other here pretending to be rapt disciples of these scholars.

In the afternoon Panky decided she was really feeling cold and needed to buy a warm woolly hat. A hilarious few hours ensued because the Chinese word for hat is 'ma' which, however, has at least four different meanings depending how it is pronounced. The lady in Panky's electronic dictionary was obviously not pronouncing it in the way the locals understood – I think the way 'she' said it meant 'horse' so despite Panky's 'ma, ma, ma' and the insistent beating of her head, the shop assistants were totally mystified. That I was almost hysterical with laughter didn't help matters. After repeating the performance in five or six shops we finally had some success – in a shop window was a hat which could of course be pointed to. Panky also saw some sort of jogging pants which she decided to buy as well. She had paid for the two items before I calculated the price in pounds – just out of interest as this was the first purchase we had made – and was pretty shocked to find that the pants had cost £65 and the hat £14. Panky was horrified when I told her but by then the deal was done.

It was an interesting incident because, as I have subsequently found out, buying articles in China is actually relatively expensive because of the huge VAT mark up the government puts on manufactured goods. Many people ask me why I don't buy things, especially electronic goods, in China, assuming that, as they were made there, they must be cheaper. This is not the case. The same item is actually cheaper in the UK. So although food, petrol and rents are much cheaper in China, buying something is much more expensive. This enormous mark-up is one of the reasons why, Chinese friends tell me, the government has so much money and is able to spend so much on huge infrastructures like roads, railways and dams etc while the ordinary people remain poor.

In fairness, though, I should say that we had inadvertently gone into one of the most expensive and trendy little boutiques in Dengfeng (although it didn't look it) and the prices were considerably higher than those in most other shops.

We had invited Meilin and her mother to dinner with us that evening but they arrived unexpectedly early because, we were amused to discover, they wanted to use our shower! We of course agreed to the request and shared a grin with each other as we remembered early days in Pune, in India, when one friend would book into an expensive local hotel, The Blue Diamond, for a night and all friends would come and avail themselves of a dip in the private swimming pool and a nice hot shower afterwards!

During dinner Meilin sorted out the vegetarian problem with the waitresses and wrote down the Chinese characters for milk in my notebook which we could show to a local shop assistant and finally have some English tea. She also asked if we would like to go to the Shaolin Temple in two day's time with her and her students. She told us that she had studied for and obtained the government tour guide 'certificate' which not only gave her a lot of local knowledge but also allowed her free access to all the local tourist sights which we were already finding to be exorbitantly expensive.

Of course we were delighted to accept her offer but were glad too to have a slow day the next day as the jetlag and excitement was catching up with us.

The Shaolin Temple

For me, visiting the Shaolin Temple compound was as important as visiting SanHuangZhai – not because of the temple itself but because of the fact that on one of the mountain peaks within the compound was Bodhidharma's cave.

In his daily discourses, my Master, Osho, had spoken many, many times about Bodhidharma. In the first paragraph of his book entitled 'Bodhidharma: The Greatest Zen Master', he says: *I have a very soft corner in my heart for Bodhidharma. That makes it a very special occasion to speak about him. Perhaps he is the only man whom I have loved so deeply that speaking on him I will be almost speaking on myself.*

Just as a child is inspired by stories told to him, so I was inspired by Osho's many stories about Bodhidharma. Because my path is the path of Zen, Bodhidharma, as the person who gave Zen to the world, was of immense importance to me. I felt very much that this journey to China was really 'a returning to the source' and an essential part of my path.

Meilin arrived that morning at what felt like the crack of dawn but she explained that it was good to go early in the morning to beat the hordes of tourists. The temple is the number one tourist spot in this area and as the autumn holiday wasn't yet over, there would be a huge crowd. So off we went. I think always the Shaolin Temple is disappointing when you arrive. The entrance is a collection of modern buildings filled with shops all aggressively trying to sell as much tourist tat as possible. The gateway is plain and uninspiring and the queuing at every stage is off-putting – as are the crowds, even at that early hour. But the setting – a valley with a river running through it rising to high mountains on either side – is quite stunning. So I quickly learned that it was a good idea to keep your eyes turned upwards rather than ahead!

We took a little open vehicle to a place just opposite the

entrance of the temple, crossed the river and joined the thousands all taking memorial photos. Immediately people wanted Panky and me to be in their photos, which was both rather sweet and also a nuisance. The Chinese are very outgoing and not at all shy, like the Japanese, so as soon as they see you they come up and ask for a 'selfie'.

Meilin was an excellent tour guide and told us much about the history of the temple which has been destroyed and rebuilt many times. The most recent and most severe destruction was in 1928. Fire gutted most of the important building including one which housed many historical records and documents of Buddhist teachings.

I am not going to go into detail about the history of the temple because it is easily available. Just I want to touch on things which interested me. Perhaps one of the things which struck me the most was a stone stele with an image carved on it depicting the fusion of Buddhism (represented by Buddha), Taoism (represented by Lao Tzu) and Confucianism (represented by Confucius), to symbolise Zen. A stele is a commemorative stone slab covered with writing or drawings. Being stone it would not be easily destroyed by time or fire.

When Bodhidharma came to China in the early sixth century he is said to have sat meditating in a cave on Wuru Peak for nine years, after which he came down to the Chizu Temple, about two miles from the Shaolin Temple (which was in the process of being built), and started to teach Chan or Zen Buddhism which was a combination of the three current Chinese religions or philosophies. Zen proved to be very popular and so a new heritage was started. As centuries went by, however, Buddhism reasserted itself as the most popular religion in China while two schools of Zen, the Rinzai and Dogen schools, crossed the sea and took root in Japan.

Then again I was interested in the Damo Pavilion which is

built on the site of the original place where Bodhidharma (or the Damo as the Chinese refer to him) lived. It was outside this building that, according to legend, a man called Shenguang, later given the Buddhist name of Huike, cut off his arm to demonstrate his strong intent to be a disciple of Bodhidharma. He became the second Patriarch and carried on the lineage from which the two above mentioned Zen schools are descended.

As our group was also made up of the kungfu students, Meilin wanted to show us two special places. One was the Baiyi Hall, the walls of which were covered with monks demonstrating various kungfu forms. She described it as being almost a kungfu 'manual'. She pointed out two figures in particular which she said were a monk called Wu Gulun who was practising forms with his uncle. Wu Gulun, Meilin said, was the first Grand Master of the branch of kungfu which was being taught at her school. I didn't know at that time how much this kungfu master was to feature in my subsequent visits to China.

The other place she wanted to talk about was a rather imposing hall called the Thousand Buddha Hall which was of interest because it had a brick floor so ancient that there were a number of indentations caused by monks practising their kungfu forms over many centuries. Spending so long in various positions had worn away and indented the floor.

All this history was becoming a bit overwhelming so Meilin wisely ended her talks and took us out of the temple into the grounds where a few hundred yards further on she pointed out to us the peak on which was a rather ugly-looking statue depicting the Damo. Below the statue was the cave in which he had sat for nine years. This was of course where I wanted to go but the kungfu students were much more interested in seeing some kungfu demonstrations and so Panky and I privately decided we would come back here again on our own and explore further. There was too much to take in on one visit.

We also quickly visited the rather beautiful Pagoda Forest full of the tombs of past important monks and abbots – apparently one of the best preserved sites of this kind in China – before starting on the return path to visit a large pavilion in which one could see many demonstrations of the skills of the young kungfu students. Pretty impressive! Even to someone not particularly interested like me. I do remember the finale, though, when one young man thrust a needle through a solid pane of glass and burst a balloon held against the other side.

Despite the tourist circus and many negative comments by guide books, I felt that there was a real essence of history here in this valley. People came and went but the hills and land reverberate with an ancient energy. It is a known fact that ancient temples were built on energy places – ley lines if you like – where the fengshui was auspicious and I could really feel that energy here. I looked forward to returning when I was alone and could be quieter without so many people milling about.

Zhongyue Miao and the Gaocheng Observatory

We were now settling into life in our hotel and establishing good relations with the staff. Meilin's kind interventions had made them fairly comfortable with us and they no longer went into a panic when we tried to communicate something but attentively listened to Panky's electronic lady and tried their best to help. We were becoming the local rather eccentric but likable grannies!

One young man was particularly interested in practising his elementary English but his pronunciation was so bad that it was our turn to look baffled when he attempted to communicate something. Fortunately many years of teaching English as a foreign language had attuned my ear to murdered English so, if I concentrated, I was usually able to make out what he was saying. This was helpful as we needed to buy things like drinking water and he also directed us to the fresh food market which was phenomenal! So much fresh fruit and so cheap! Another thing that he tried to communicate was something about a theatre and he gave us some brochures showing some rather striking photographs. It transpired that he could get us tickets (no doubt getting a commission) so we decided to buy two and go to the theatre in China. Meilin was annoyed when she heard about it because she declared that he had charged too much and she could have got them cheaper (perhaps she was getting a commission too?) but she then arranged for herself and the kungfu students to go on the same night so we could go together.

Next on Panky's and my tourist list was the Taoist Zhongyue Temple. The young man kindly wrote its name and that of the Gaocheng Observatory in Chinese in a notebook which I had bought, and called Liu for us. We achieved more by having words or names written down in Chinese characters which we could show to a taxi driver or shop assistant, rather than attempting to pronounce them. Although we were happy to pay his entrance fee, Liu chose to wait outside the temple, so we went in by ourselves.

I immediately loved this place. Despite the Shaolin Temple honouring Bodhidharma and theoretically Zen, I found it very Buddhist. I can appreciate Buddhism but the worship of all the many gods and all the rituals makes me uneasy. My way of doing things is to sit silently somewhere, preferably outside in nature, and 'go in'. Doing all this worshipping and 'pujas' (ritual obeisance) to what seemed to me a huge number of gods of this and that, reminded me very much of Hinduism and Christianity and I had mostly rejected these rites and ceremonies. I did some of the bowing down so that I wouldn't offend – most of the people in these places were so gracious I loved them. I did appreciate the temples but just wasn't into the accepted rituals. Difficult to explain!

With Zhongyue Miao ('miao' is another Chinese word for a temple, most particularly including the idea of a very old or ancestral shrine) this kind of ritual seemed to be largely absent and I felt a real silence and peacefulness here. It seemed much more 'feminine' than the 'masculinity' of the Shaolin Temple. I am not a Taoist scholar, don't pretend to be, don't intend to be, but something in me intuitively responds to the energy in a Taoist temple – or perhaps to the fengshui of the position chosen to build the shrine or temple on. There does seem to be a feminine essence here somewhere. LaoTzu says in his Tao Te Ching:

> *The spirit of the valley never dies*
> *This is called the mysterious female.*
> *The gateway of the mysterious female*
> *Is called the root of heaven and earth.*
> *Dimly visible, it seems as if it were there*
> *Yet use will never drain it*
> (translation by D.C.Lau)

John Wu says it in an even more telling way, I think, in his translation of the last two lines:

> *Lingering like gossamer, it (the spirit) has only a hint of existence;*
> *Yet when you draw upon it, it is inexhaustible.*

The delicacy of gossamer – beautiful…. This temple had a delicate feminine energy.

It also had a few quirky things like the statues of the four officials whose bellies one should rub to be healed from various illnesses. And the toilet sign had the recognisable yin/yang (male/female) symbol printed on it! There is even less information in English about this temple than in the more visited Shaolin Temple but we assumed that the men walking around with topknots and black clothes were the Taoist residents – very different to the shaved heads of the monks in the Shaolin Temple who wear grey or yellow garments.

But for us that day the most delightful thing about the temple was that it was full of young kungfu students – both male and female – practising their forms. There is a lot of open space and many trees so it was ideal territory for them. And from their point of view I think we made their day because we were surrounded by youngsters intent on showing us their acrobatics: little boys with legs behind their ears, one-hand stands and quite amazing squats! Of course many photographs were taken and occasionally we were accosted by other youngsters again eager to practise the few words of English they had learned.

The whole morning proved to be a touching and heartfelt experience.

Reluctantly departing we again met up with Liu who then whisked us off to the Gaocheng Observatory after first investing in the now familiar Dengfeng fast food: the sesame bun. Just one of these filled one up very satisfactorily. A sesame bun is bought from a street vendor who pummels a big lump of dough before pulling off a bit, rolling it into a bun, coating it with sesame seeds and then roasting it on the hotplate or coals in his barrow. Once cooked, the bun is prised open and, depending on your choice, filled with some cooked tofu or a hot hardboiled egg.

To visit the Observatory we had to leave Dengfeng and venture into a rather desolate countryside – the reason for the desolation being, as we soon observed, huge coal mines which now filled our view. We had heard about the coal mines from a Swedish engineer who often breakfasted with us in the hotel. He had been brought over by the coal mining company to oversee the installation of more safety measures in the operation of the mines. He said he was very shocked at the lack of safety in the mines and although he was trying his best to introduce some measures, he expressed his doubt that they would be adhered to once he left and returned to Sweden. So we saw the reality of the unromantic side of China and the problems caused by the coal industry and its pollution.

But on that day we were doing the tourist thing and the Observatory quickly took up all our attention. Various different dates are given for its construction so I will just say it was built between 1267 and 1279 and is the oldest astronomical building in China and one of the oldest in the world. This is where, in 1299, the famous astronomer and mathematician, Guo Shoujing, after many long observations and exact calculations, was able to calculate how long the earth takes to orbit the sun and was in fact out by a mere 26 seconds. Astonishing when one remembers that, about 400 years later, Galileo was arrested and tried by a Roman Inquisition in 1632/33 for his declaration that it was the earth that moved around the sun rather than the celestial bodies that moved around the earth – which was the accepted Roman Catholic doctrine and not to be questioned. He was convicted of heresy and spent his remaining years under house arrest.

The Observatory and grounds were beautifully laid out and cared for and we were fascinated with the replicas of ancient astronomical instruments and indications of how they were used in scientific observations so long ago. We particularly liked a replica of an early invention of a water clock which still accurately kept time.

As we journeyed home we reflected that China was a land of varied nuances and many contrasts and it was unfair to make blanket condemnations about it – as is so often done – without taking a huge number of factors into account.

Evenings on the Mountain

That evening Meilin had invited us to have dinner with her, her mother and the other Dutch kungfu students at their kungfu school. It was a beautiful clear evening and the mountains were beginning to take on the pinkish hues of the setting sun as we arrived at the school in the foothills of the mountain. It was a rather shabby little complex and I could see why Meilin and her mother much preferred the comfort of our warm shower and clean western-style toilet as opposed this dirty concrete squat toilet and cold water bucket bath!

It turned out that Meilin had yet another talent – she was a very good cook, and the vegetarian meal she and her mother had made for us was excellent. It was so pleasant sitting outside in the fresh mountain air surrounded by the magnificent peaks still glowing with the rays of the disappearing sun. After the meal we were taken on a walk up a mountain road which soon proved to be quite magical as the stars started appearing. There was no moon and with no street lighting we were treated to a breathtaking panorama of stars in the clear sky.

On our way back we saw that a temporary barrier had been erected across the road to stop traffic during the night. The barrier was quite high and the young people climbed over it easily but Panky and I sought a way round. It was very dark and hard to see but on the other side of the barrier a Chinese man shone a torch at us and seemed to be indicating that we could walk around the barrier on the side of the road. So, half blinded by the bright torch light, I walked to the side – and fell into a three-foot deep ditch. He must have been warning us not to go there! One of those 'lost in translation' moments. The shock was tremendous and I felt a sharp pain in my ankle. I managed to haul myself out of the ditch but found to my dismay that I could not put my weight on my left foot.

Disaster! I instinctively knew that nothing was broken but it was clear that I had sprained the ankle. Perhaps not too badly because Meilin came rushing up and immediately started to rub the ankle and foot and soon I could hobble on it. A speedy return back to the hotel was indicated.

Despite bandaging it up tightly with a T-shirt, it was quite painful the next morning and Panky wonderfully managed to get hotel staff to bring some ice which we packed around the foot. It was very clear that I wasn't going anywhere that day.

Seeing that I was content to rest, and having ordered my favourite pumpkin soup to be brought to the room for lunch, Panky, who is a great walker, decided that she would go for a walk on the mountain. I was soon to find that I would not be alone, however. First Meilin flew in with food and fruit and a laptop so I could check my emails. Once she saw that I was okay and well taken care of with the laptop and my Lonely Planet guidebook as entertainment, she flew off again to take care of her students. Within a short time there was a knock on the door and the hotel manager, a very charming young woman who also spoke a few words of English, came in with some tea. Next, another young woman came in with a new batch of ice which she proceeded to pack around my ankle. And throughout the day I was visited regularly to be checked that I was okay and didn't need anything and the ice was regularly replaced! So sweet.

I was experiencing my first taste of the strength of the family in China. It seemed that in the minds of the hotel staff, I and Panky were now part of their extended hotel family and so all formalities went out the window and I really was being looked after as if I was a member of the family. There was also the refreshing respect that the Chinese have for older people. Whereas in the west older people are very often dismissed as no longer having any value, here older people are very much honoured. It was a strange but very touching and heart-warming experience.

I also had time to reflect on this whole experience. After spending nine long months trying to get here, how did I feel? The answer was an overwhelming feeling of coming home, of this here and now being absolutely 'right'. No reasons, no explanations were needed; simply, this was right.

By the evening it was obvious that my ankle was markedly better and I even made it to dinner in the hotel dining room with Panky. The staff were now very attentive – we could feel the subtle shift in their attitude to us – we were now more than just regular hotel guests.

Despite the improvement, I felt I still had to rest the ankle the next day and Panky also chose to stay in the room for a bit of a rest and a chance to catch up on emails on the computer. Again we were visited by various members of staff checking to see that all was okay and in the afternoon Meilin and her mother arrived to hang out and wash hair and shower in our nice bathroom.

It was important to look good because that evening we were all going to the Chinese theatre, including me. Meilin said she would get the driver of the van to take us right to the entrance and we were most impressed at how she managed to get us through all kinds of barriers, ending up in the VIP section so I didn't have to walk far. This was fortunate because there was a huge crowd of people and Chinese don't queue in the English way – to be precise, in *any* way! There was a lot of pushing and shoving so I was glad to be taken in through a protected VIP entrance.

Only dimly aware of our surroundings we finally sat down, took a breath and surveyed the astonishing spectacle. I know I will never be able to adequately describe this theatre and the performance – this is all I can say…. We were seated in an open-air bank of seats, as if in a football stadium, facing a 'stage' which was less a stage than a part of the mountain valley measuring at least half a mile in width. The backdrop was the mountain, the moon and the stars. Separating the audience and the actors was a small river running in front of the stage and in it were five huge rocks on which sat illuminated meditating monks dressed in orange. The river was fed by a waterfall on the right. We appeared to be looking at a village with a temple and houses and trees – all real. No stage props here. While the audience was being seated the various areas of the stage were subtly lit with coloured lights while soft music played.

I was already enthralled but once the show started I was spellbound. The performance was apparently about life in a village during the four seasons of the year portrayed through light, music, singing, dancing, and a lot kungfu. Here there were women washing clothes in the stream; there, there were people carrying water across a graceful, arched bridge. Then arrived a herd of goats and sheep that meandered around the stage – remarkably well-behaved! – and then it seemed as if dignitaries were gathering on their horses. After that, the scene moved to the temple where the monks were doing their meditations and important abbots or suchlike came to give their blessings to the villagers. This was all conveyed through light, music, dance and absolutely stunning kungfu movements. At times the mountain side was lit up with images of Buddha and an artificial moon waxed and waned behind the village. At other times there was snow and strong winds. And all the time the monks sat silently meditating on their rocks in the river which was fed by the cascading waterfall.

When it finally ended, Panky and I sat stunned. Un-equivocally this was the most extraordinary theatre performance I had ever seen, anywhere. I went home in a trance, small things like sprained ankles totally forgotten.

I dimly heard Meilin say she would pick us up the next morning after breakfast but didn't bother to find out why, so enraptured was I with what I had just seen.

A Kungfu Heritage

After a starry sky the night before, the next morning dawned cloudy and grey and as I lay in bed sipping my tea (we had now found milk to go with the English tea we had both brought with us) I wondered vaguely what we would do today. Going back to the Shaolin Temple and up the cable car as we wanted to do was not an option for another day or two with my still damaged, although almost healed, ankle. I felt bad about inconveniencing Panky but after her cup of tea she mentioned that Meilin had planned an excursion for the day which would not require much walking. We were really touched that Meilin had taken it upon herself to take so much care of us and we discussed suggesting that she recommend some really nice restaurant to which we could take her and her mother to show our appreciation. She had accepted contributions from us for travel expenses but wouldn't hear of accepting anything more.

After breakfast she 'flew in' announcing that Liu was in his taxi outside waiting to take us to Master Wu Nanfang's kungfu school. This was unexpected but sounded wonderful so we quickly got ourselves organised and were happy to greet our wonderful Liu again.

We retraced our journey to the Shaolin Temple but turned off the road long before we got there. Now we entered a rather shabby little village on a pot-holed dirt road full of women and old people chatting to each other, children playing around them and dogs roaming everywhere. Liu gently made his way through all this village activity and finally drew up at an ugly grey concrete building built in what we were to learn was a typical Chinese style which obviously dated from more violent times. The building looked fairly impregnable from the outside and one could enter only through a massive entrance which was closed with a metal door which could be pulled down and locked – rather like a garage door in one of our western houses.

It was, however, open now and as we entered into a kind of central courtyard we became the objects of great scrutiny by lots of young boys and a few older ones – the kungfu students who were milling around. Meilin told us they were having a break from their daily practice.

She took us up a steep uneven concrete staircase with the paint flaking off the walls and on to an upstairs veranda where Master Wu Nanfang was waiting to greet us. Up at San Huang Zhai he had impressed us as being a very gracious and charming man and that impression was now very much re-enforced. He was also taller than the average Chinese man and was very good-looking as well!

He took us into a kind of reception room which was rather poor and unaesthetic and invited us to sit on a very hard bench. It was autumn and not too cold but I thought it must be freezing in winter with no visible heating and a few broken windows covered with plastic. Master Wu Nanfang was, however, charm itself and we immediately plunged into conversation thanks to Meilin and her translating skills. Green tea was brought to us by a woman who, Meilin told us, rather surprisingly, was his wife. I guess I expected him to be a kind of monk!

After tea we went downstairs to an open space next to the building which was the training ground. The students were now all doing their kungfu forms and the master wandered off to instruct and correct.

This was our first look at this form of kungfu after seeing it on the documentary. Meilin gave us a brief explanation about what we were looking at.

This kungfu is a little known form of the more famous Shaolin wushu style, interest in which was rekindled after a Hong Kong movie was made in 1982 called *The Shaolin Temple,* starring Jet Li. The form of kungfu which we were now watching is called ChanWuYi and is practised by only a few people in the Dengfeng area, led by the two masters: Master Wu Nanfang and Master Shi Dejian.

Due to China's turbulent history, the Shaolin Temple, with its highly skilled fighting monks, was sometimes in favour with ruling dynasties, sometimes not. Around 1870 it was again in disfavour with the rulers of the Qing dynasty and the temple was in imminent danger of being destroyed yet again. The Temple Master instructed one of his foremost monks, Wu Gulun, to leave the temple and carry the traditions of the Shaolin culture with him to preserve them. He disappeared into the mountains to live in an isolated village, BaiYuGou, where he continued to practise and preserve the secrets of the Shaolin heritage.

As he needed to be able to pass on this knowledge, he married and had a son, Wu Shanlin, to whom he taught all the ancient secrets. Master Wu Shanlin became the second Grandmaster of the ChanWuYi lineage. Continuing to live in the small village, Wu Shanlin married and had two sons, Wu You De and Wu Tian You. To them and also his nephew, Qiao Hei Bao, and a young orphaned student, Zhang Qing He, he passed on the traditions. Wu Tian You had a son who sadly died when he was quite young. This son was Master Wu Nanfang's father. From an early age Wu Nanfang studied with his great grandfather, Wu Shanlin, then with Qiao Hei Bao and Wu You De and later Zhang Qing He. He is thus the direct descendent and inheritor of the Shaolin ChanWuYi and Wugulun tradition.

Chan means meditation, *Wu* means right movements of the body and *Yi* means taking care of the body with the right kind of food and natural medicine.

Having had a brief history lesson we were even more

interested in the graceful movements the students were practising. It seemed very meditative in comparison to the much more active and acrobatic wushu we had seen at the Shaolin Temple.

As we were watching the practice I noticed the sky was clearing, and turning round I was astonished to see the shapes of mountains looming out of the cloud. Within a further short space of time the sky cleared completely and we were faced with a panorama of mountain peaks so close I felt I could reach out and touch them. We had only been in this part of the Song Mountain range once before, when we visited the Shaolin Temple, but that day the mountain was also shrouded in cloud. Now it was revealed in all its awe-inspiring glory and maybe it was at that point that my life changed – I fell in love with a mountain!

We could see, though, that Meilin was getting a little edgy and, being aware of her responsibilities to her school and students, we suggested that it was time to leave. In answer to her call, Liu soon arrived and took us back to the hotel. Meilin was busy that night but we arranged to take her and her mother out the following evening.

A Discovery in Luoyang

Panky and I were really fortunate that our trip to Song Mountain had co-incided with the visit of the Dutch kungfu students because, at our very excellent meal the following evening, Meilin told us that she had hired a vehicle to take her students to see the famous Longmen Caves near the city of Luoyang, about an hour's journey from Dengfeng, and would we like to join them. As the Longmen Cave complex, a masterpiece of Buddhist rock carvings, is one of the most important tourist destinations in China, we of course jumped at the chance.

Crossing Song Mountain and going down the other side on a potholed, hairpin road filled with huge, scarcely road-worthy trucks carrying gravel and rocks was a pretty terrifying experience and I felt quite shattered when we got to the bottom of the pass. It reminded me of the pass on the western side of India crossing the Ghats between Mumbai and Pune. This was once labelled one of the most dangerous roads in the world. I think the statisticians didn't know about this mountain road in China when they made their calculations.

The rest of the ride was relatively uneventful and we arrived safely at what looked like a very beautiful scenic area although it was covered in the kind of fog that so often blankets places in this area. This, however, gave it a rather mystical atmosphere which, it turned out, was really appropriate for what we were about to see.

Luoyang was one of the ancient capitals of China – at different times, depending on which dynasty was in power. When the Northern Wei dynasty (386-534), which actively supported Buddhism, moved its capital to Luoyang, work commenced on an extraordinary project. Over a two-hundred-year period, more than one hundred thousand images and statues of Buddha were carved into a limestone cliff wall along the Yi River.

The word 'longmen' looks like an English surname but in actual fact it is Chinese for 'Dragon's Gate'. The word is in tribute to the Emperor Yu, who lived about two hundred years BC, and who is still famous for building checks on the Yellow River to prevent it from disastrously flooding the plains through which it flowed. The most famous of the 'checks' was originally called Dragon's Gate.

Although now a protected Unesco World Heritage site, the damage by vandalism to these carvings is devastating. From the beginning of the twentieth century, particularly, the heads of statues, or sometimes whole statues, were removed by unscrupulous collectors and sold to museums and private individuals all over the world. During the Cultural Revolution and earlier periods of anti-Buddhist feeling, vandalism on a massive scale occurred.

It was painful to see so much evidence of mindless destruction, yet the treasures that remained were awe-inspiring. The passage ways along the cliff have been sensitively designed to make the exploration of the caves and their carvings easy and exciting and we meandered our way along the cliff almost overwhelmed at such a huge artistic endeavour. There were also a few signs in relatively good English conveniently placed so at times we were able to get some explanations of what we were seeing.

Then, about a third of the way along the cliff, I stopped, astonished. Outside a smallish cave there was a sign saying 'The Ten Thousand Buddha Cave' (Wanfo Dong). Indeed there must have been ten thousand Buddhas – carved all over the walls and ceiling with most of the small, bas-relief statues being only about one and a half inches high. But this proliferation of buddhas was not what stunned me. It was the words. 'Ten Thousand Buddhas' was one of Osho's most favourite phrases which he used over and over again. When we sat each evening in meditation around him in our Buddha Hall in Pune, he referred often to us being a gathering of ten thousand buddhas. As there were nowhere near ten thousand people there, I just thought he was being poetic and imaginative, but here was more evidence of his connections to China – he was using a phase already in use about fifteen hundred years before. In fact, when I later did research on the use of this concept, I found that it originated even before the time that the Longmen Caves were being carved.

I had to sit down for awhile and contemplate this discovery. Osho had spoken at length about Lao Tzu, Chuang Tzu, Lieh Tzu, Sengcan (Japanese name: Sosan) and other Chinese masters, but in this Song Mountain area I was finding physical places which bore out his knowledge of the ancient spiritual heritage here and his connection with it. Again, I felt encouraged that my own yearning to come to this area was not just a fanciful mind-game but something deeply important for me.

Silently happy I caught up with the others who were all standing front of the magnificent seventeen-metre-high central Buddha statue called Losana, whose androgynous facial features are said to be modelled on the Tang empress, Wu Zetian, who funded the carving. This buddha statue touched me even more than my hitherto favourite, the Daibutsu in Kamakura in Japan.

The Losana Buddha was near the end of the two-kilometre-long cliff and we started our return journey by crossing the river over an attractive bridge which gave us a greater perspective of the cliff as it extended down the river. Picturesque small tourist barges painted red and gold slowly sailed up and down, adding bright touches of colour to the otherwise misty scene.

To get back to our vehicle we boarded the little tourist carts which we were amused to find had some of the best (in terms of quaintness) Chinese signs we had seen. We were instructed: *Please do not frolic in the car* or *Please contain your body inside the car*. While waiting for our vehicle which Meilin had summoned, we feasted on Chinese snacks – not chips and chocolate, but roasted corn cobs or sweet potatoes from heated barrows operated by charming, often toothless, old men or women.

A beautiful day. And my love for Song Mountain and my conviction that there was a mystery here for me to solve had just grown stronger.

Farewells

When we decided to book those plane tickets, Panky and I had no idea what we would discover or do here, but already the trip had far exceeded any expectations we might have had – thanks in large part to Meilin and her generous efforts to show us so many sights and to introduce us to Master Wu Nanfang and his students. Liu, our buddha taxi driver, and the hotel staff also played their parts in ensuring that our visit turned out to be one of the best holidays of our lives.

We both agreed that there was so much more here to discover and a much longer visit was needed. Panky, as a dedicated TaiChi student, wanted to spend time practising the ChanWuYi movements which she felt a strong affinity with and I was now deeply in love with this mountain and the Zen heritage it harboured. We were already spending many moments plotting our return.

One further surprise awaited us on the final day before we left. Having mostly packed our suitcases we were relaxing with a cup of tea when Meilin arrived to say that Master Wu Nanfang and his wife were in the hotel foyer waiting to take us out for lunch! We hurriedly got ourselves together and went out to meet them, registering quite a surprise to see the master dressed in normal clothes! He did look amazing – I whispered to Panky that he could have made a fortune as a male model! So much kungfu had given him a very fit body and his movements were very graceful. He took us to a small restaurant where we were introduced to our first 'hot pot' meal. On the table in front of one's seat was a hot plate on which a pot was placed and filled with boiling water or soup. A huge array of vegetables, noodles and tofu were then brought in and one dropped these into the boiling water to cook. Once cooked, they were picked out and dipped into a tasty sesame seed and soya sauce mix in a bowl and then eaten. Delicious and healthy.

Sad goodbyes were said but we assured the Master and his wife that we would be back soon.

We had a rest in the afternoon as we had a long journey ahead of us and in the evening Meilin and her mother arrived for a farewell dinner in the hotel.

Then very early the next morning Liu came to pick us up and I confess the tears rolled down my face as I said goodbye to the lined-up hotel staff and Meilin and her mother who had come to wave goodbye even at this early hour.

The flight home was comfortable and quite silent as Panky and I privately reviewed and digested all the wonderful things we had done and the special people we had met. And we were both, of course, already making plans for a return journey.

2
In the Foothills
of the Mountain

Bodhidharma's Cave

One has to become more aware than one ordinarily is.
To be a sannyasin means to enter into the phenomenon of the sacred.
For that more awareness is needed, much more,
because it is not something mechanical, something routine.
It is now every day.
It is moving from the unknown towards the unknowable.
It is dropping the known every day, dying to the known
and entering into the unknown.
It is an eternal pilgrimage, because every moment is so full of mystery
that one has to be very alert, otherwise one will miss.

Very few people know the beauty of the stars....
Very few people know the beauty of the mountains....

Osho: Is the Grass Really Greener?

Changing Homes

By the time I arrived home I was clear that life in the UK was going to have to change as I had no doubts that I wanted to return China as soon as possible for as long as possible. I was still a little surprised at the intensity of my feelings and yet, as a disciple of Osho, I had mostly learned to trust my inner feelings even if they seemed irrational and at odds with one's daily reality. But I simply knew that retirement in an English country cottage was not what I was about, so things had to change.

Existence appeared to be in agreement with my plans because, within a few weeks of being back, a friend, knowing that I wanted to move, suggested that we share a house together. She had been transferred to work in a nearby town and wanted to move closer to avoid long commutes. For me this would be perfect as I could take off for China without the worry and responsibility of leaving a residence unattended. I could not have left the cottage unlived in for a few months. As luck would have it, a suitable place was advertised almost immediately and after viewing the property we had no hesitation in renting it and moving in.

That big decision taken care of, I then found a reasonable flight to China with a Finnish airline. The Olympic Games had resulted in a rapidly opening up of China for both tourism and business, so it seemed to me that the airlines were all trying to jump on a bandwagon of lucrative new Chinese air routes – cheap air deals to get customers interested were being offered everywhere. Very convenient for me! The next hurdle was to get a three-month visa for China. The visa agency I had used before was very doubtful about getting such a long visa – the Chinese Embassy was apparently only issuing visas for a few weeks. I decided to take a chance, however, and paid the fee, then sat biting my nails while waiting for the verdict. Finally the young man at the agency called me, sounding extremely surprised that a three-month visa had been issued – but I was a bit ashamed that I had even doubted that I would get it.

I had been in email contact with Meilin throughout this period. Because the instructor at her small school had become too ill to teach, she had closed her school and gone to work with Master Wu Nanfang. She asked me to help her to design a new English website. Having had some experience with creating websites, I was happy to help her with this – she had done so much for me – and also with editing the reams of information in rather garbled English that she had collected about this form of kungfu which now seemed to be called Wugulun Kungfu. This work gave me a detailed insight into the heritage of this little-known branch of Shaolin kungfu and I found it incredibly interesting – especially because of the emphasis on meditation rather than the acrobatics of the more popular wushu currently taught at the Shaolin Temple and the three hundred or more kungfu schools in the small city of Dengfeng.

Panky was also planning to return because, as a budding film director, she wanted to make a film about Master Wu Nanfang and his Wugulun Kungfu. I was truly amazed at Panky! At the age of seventy-one, not only was she still travelling to out-of-the-way places, but she was embarking on a new career of movie-making. She told me she had done some study on making films when she was young but had never pursued her dreams because family – and then sannyas and Osho – had intervened. She planned to come to China a little later than me so that she could meet up with a tour that her TaiChi school in London had planned. She told me that she had already persuaded the organiser to spend two days in

Dengfeng as part of the tour, offering the tour-guiding services of Meilin (for a fee, of course) and some lessons with the kungfu master as incentives.

Arriving in Beijing's stunning airport I had an overwhelming feeling of coming home. England now seemed like a foreign country to me. Flying on to Zhengzhou, this feeling was registered even more strongly when a sparkling Meilin met me in a car, a small van actually, sent by Master Wu Nanfang. I was so touched. It was driven by one of the kungfu students, the beautiful Rende, who had featured very much in the BBC documentary as a kind of chief disciple.

As the mountains appeared on the horizon I had to swallow hard and blink a lot to stop the tears from falling and I felt filled with an indescribable joy at returning to this place.

Living Locally

On the way home Meilin told me that Master Wu Nanfang had found an apartment in the house of a local family in the small village of ShiLiPu – near his school – and that she and one other person was already living there. She was obviously not too pleased with the place and told me she had had to work hard to make it habitable. I was rather amused at listening to her grumbles but at the same time appreciated her efforts to make it fit for us to live in.

That day the mountain was visible and I was thrilled to find that I was going to live in such close proximity to it. Rende stopped the van in front of a rather forbidding concrete edifice with a big iron gate, and out we got. At the sound of the engine the family came running out to greet us, scattering a number of chickens in the process. We were led through one of those strong metal doors into a very ramshackle courtyard and then upstairs to our quarters. The family, including some neighbours, I think, all crowded in and excited chatter ensued. Meilin introduced me to Mr and Mrs Wang, their older son and his wife, their younger son, and the cutest ever little toddler whose name I later learned was Maiyen.

After telling them all to leave, Meilin then showed me around our new flat. It was a fairly new building, very spartan but spacious. The flat had never been lived in because, Meilin explained, it had been built as a home for the sons when they got married. I learnt that it was the Chinese custom for the new wife to live with her husband's parents so, as there were two sons in this family, accommodation had to be provided for them and their future families. There was apparently a daughter too but she had already moved to live with her prospective husband. I was a bit surprised at the number of children that Mr and Mrs Wang had because our western idea is that China has a one-child-per-family policy – yet here was a family with three children. I asked Meilin about this and she said that rural families are allowed to have more children, especially sons, to look after the farms and small family businesses. Anyway, she surprisingly told me, the law wasn't very actively enforced. She herself had a brother and her family came from a large city further south. This was news to me. I thought that the one-child policy was a very strict government rule. Later I found out that the policy is quite quickly becoming history because the youngsters, growing up with the whole focus of the family's attention on them, were buckling under the strain and a nation of spoilt, selfish, demanding, work-shy darlings was quickly becoming the norm. Not good for keeping the economy booming!

The flat had five really large, high ceilinged rooms complete with blue distempered walls and florescent light strips – just like places I had lived in India. But there was no water tap and no sink – let alone a toilet or shower or kitchen! So washing of any kind, cooking and going to the toilet had to be done downstairs which meant traipsing up and down the very uneven stairs for every water-related event. Really bizarre. The only exception was drinking water. As in India, one should never drink water from a tap in China, so each house has a kind of water 'machine': a returnable plastic water container is inverted onto a small sort of box which has two outlets – one for cold water and one for hot water heated to the right temperature for making green tea.

Meilin lived in one bedroom, I in another and a kungfu student from the school in the third. But I was rather horrified to find that the locked fourth bedroom was a control centre for a mobile phone mast which had been attached to the roof of the house!!! So I was going to be living within ten feet of radiation waves from a huge mast. This was *not* acceptable to me and I was surprised that the family was unaware of the dangers of living in such close proximity to this mast, especially as the older son's wife was pregnant with their second child. When I expressed my worries to Meilin she said that the control centre was not yet functioning and it would be some time before it was activated. Well, I hoped that it would be after I left!

But my room was beautiful because it had a panoramic view of the mountain through a huge window. The blind over the window was, however, rather a shock to the eyes. It was apparently the landlord's interpretation of Meilin's instructions to get something with blue in it – like the sea – to match the blue walls! It was definitely a marine-like scene with garish coloured fish and seaweed on a blue background!

Meilin had brought all the furniture from her kungfu school here so the communal living and dining room was quite well-equipped and she had even created a small shrine with some carved statues, some bowls and an intricately worked brass incense burner. A scroll with a picture of Buddha hung on the wall.

The Chinese concepts of a toilet differ radically from ours. There will be a few horror stories to recount throughout my tales and the first one started right here! When I mentioned that a visit to the toilet was necessary, Meilin's confidence faltered for a few minutes. She told me that the toilet was the worst aspect of the flat and she had worked hard with the family to make it more presentable. Poor girl, she had not chosen this flat herself so she had to be very creative about improving the facilities. The squat, concreted (no clean tiles) toilet, a communal one, led off the courtyard which is where family and friends gathered so when one wanted to use it, one was scrutinised by everyone – very public. The toilet was housed in a small room off a small storage room neither of which had doors, so there was a total lack of privacy. Anybody who has had to use a squat toilet knows that it is difficult to keep clean and usually stinks. This one was a prime example. The only saving grace was that Meilin had prevailed upon the family to frequently use water – from a bucket filled from a tap in the courtyard – in an attempt to keep it a bit clean and a bit less smelly. She even managed to get them to install a kind of 'valve' which fitted into the hole in the toilet and sprung shut after use, thus reducing most of the smell from what would otherwise be an open sewage drain. She supervised the installation herself while gagging all the while at the foul smell, she told me! Our Meilin was a very smart and resourceful young lady.

Very touched by her efforts I told her I had lived in India for a long time and although not exactly enamoured of the system, I could deal with it.

I was further touched by her efforts to make a shower! This huge eight-roomed house did not have any kind of washroom at all! Although things are changing now, in village houses in rural China a washroom is not common – people use communal bath houses as they did in Japan in older times.

Meilin had spotted that there was a storage space under the staircase and also a run-off hole to the outside for when the concrete floor was mopped with water. There was also a tap – meaning a water supply! So she had somehow found an ancient gas water heater with a rusty old showerhead, installed it above the tap, attached a hose to the heating unit and presto! Hot water ... sort of! When you could actually get the gas to fire up which usually required a strong whack with one's hand on the ancient contraption. Needless to say, showering here required a few adjustments. Yes, there was hot water but the water was just that, *hot*. Any attempt to make it cooler turned off the heater so you were suddenly deluged with very cold water! To avoid being scalded, I resorted to holding the shower head at arm's length to fill a basin, adding some cold water from the tap and then dousing myself with a plastic cup, Indian style.

Sometimes my shower was accompanied by the irritated clucking of a hen who had decided that a shelf just outside the shower was an ideal place to lay her eggs and once or twice I had to endure the vocal objections of another hen to having its neck rung in preparation for becoming the landlord's evening meal. No candlelight and soft atmospheric music here.

But compared to some places I had lived in during my travels, the house was palatial and, despite the inconveniences, the feeling was good and I was simply overjoyed to be here.

Other impressions of those first few days was the constant awesome view of the mountain from wherever one was, the incredible friendliness of the Wang family who never stopped wanting to feed me and the kindness of Master Wu Nanfang and his students who always welcomed me when I walked down to the fields in front of the village where the school was. The weather was clear but very cold! I had my first taste of the capriciousness of Dengfeng's weather system – something that would in the future be an influential factor affecting everyday life. I had checked the weather forecasts online back in the UK and the temperature was apparently a comfortable eighteen to twenty degrees so I selected clothes accordingly. But by the time I arrived, the temperatures had plummeted to close to zero degrees and I didn't have anything warm except my 'hoodie' which was only cotton. For nearly two weeks I was freezing cold and at night the only thing that saved me was a small electric blanket that Meilin gave me and a child-sized hot water bottle I found in a shop. I often went to bed at 8pm just to keep a little bit warm.

Another thing that was quite hard to cope with initially was the non-stop noise. The family and their friends all seemed to speak at a volume close to shouting. It took time to get used to the fact that they were simply chatting and not yelling at each other in anger. To add to the commotion our resident chickens were also very loudly vocal throughout the day, especially after laying their eggs. Then there was the noise of the nearby highway which was now much busier than when I had first come there only six months previously – and the prolific Chinese farm vehicles powered by horribly loud two-stroke engines made an exorbitant din. Even in this rural area there was a great deal of construction going on all around us during day – and, in the evening from about 7 to 9.30pm, blaring Chinese pop music was played at maximum volume in the open-air community centre behind our house. The actual reason for the music was rather sweet – all the local ladies turned out to dance the night away while their kids played on the swings and climbing bars etc. The modern version of doing TaiChi together, I suppose. I just wished it wasn't quite so loud and was more varied. The selection of songs lasted only about five minutes and so the same songs were repeated over and over for two and a half hours!

And so the first few days presented a sharp – but definitely interesting – learning curve for me as I tried adjust to such a radically different environment, to figure out how everything functioned and where to get what – while coping with jetlag and culture shock.

Meilin, having already lived in the flat for a few weeks, had more or less got the cooking scene together. It wasn't easy because she had to do all the cooking on gas or coal hotplates in our landlord's rather primitive kitchen downstairs, while storing all the food upstairs. This meant many trips up and down the uneven concrete staircase.

On the second morning Meilin announced that she wanted to go to the supermarket and suggested that I come too. I was excited about accompanying her as it meant a start on getting to grips with local life. We were fortunate that our area was well served by the local No. 1 bus which seemed to go every few minutes and took us into the town of Dengfeng about twenty minutes away. I was careful to note some recognisable landmarks so that in future I could do this by myself. Fortunately, near the main bus stop in town, there was a shop with a sign in English: 'Wedding Photographs'. Easy!

The supermarket was huge and I was of course fascinated by seeing all these different goods on display. I was also confronted by how difficult it would be to shop on my own as there was nothing written in English. Whereas in the west we might have one or two soya sauce options, here there was a twenty-foot-long shelf with all kinds of soya sauce for all kinds of dishes. Likewise for vinegar – which, being the same colour, looked just like soya sauce. I wouldn't know where to start! There was also a huge variety of cooking oils but these fortunately usually had a picture on them showing peanuts or vegetables or sesame seeds so oils were easier to select.

Where I was not at loss, however, was in the huge fruit section. I was overjoyed to see a wonderful variety of tropical fruit which no doubt came from southern China: papayas, mangos, pineapples, coconuts and those small 'finger' bananas which are much tastier than the bigger ones. Having lived most of my life in tropical countries this was the kind of fruit I liked and was deprived of by living in Europe. And it was all so unbelievably cheap. Meilin was somewhat taken aback at my enthusiasm and watched in surprise as I filled the shopping trolley with all this fruit. She was focusing on vegetables, many of which were strange to me.

There was a large bakery from which Meilin bought some little cakes, biscuits and bread. This was my first introduction to Chinese cookies which was a potential weight-gain disaster for me as they were absolutely delicious. The Chinese really know how to make cookies.

With far too much to carry on a bus, Meilin called Liu, the buddha taxi driver, to take us home and I was very happy to meet up with him again.

Breakfast was to become a delightful ritual. My role was to make a fruit salad as a starter while Meilin ran downstairs to make me some fried eggs and herself some vegetable. I could never get used to eating vegetables for breakfast but she adapted to eating fruit salad which she had never seen made in this way before. She was also inordinately proud of her toaster which an English kungfu student had brought for her from the UK. Now I understood the reason for the bread which, like Japanese bread, tasted to me like aerated cotton-wool but bore a closer resemblance to the real thing when toasted.

Another part of the daily routine was quickly established: going to the kungfu school which was about a ten-minute walk away. Meilin was working there. We invariably ate lunch there with Master Wu Nanfang. Joni, the young man I had originally spoken to when I first phoned China, was attending the school but, as a close friend of Meilin, often had his evening meal with us in our flat. The kungfu school food was not the greatest! It was mostly carbohydrates with a few over-boiled, tasteless vegetables floating in water. Meilin, on the other hand, cooked really well, so our evening meals were delicious. Many other students just happened to visit around mealtimes and were always fed – the Chinese way. At this stage, however, the third member of our household remained a shadowy reclusive figure and as yet I hadn't made his acquaintance.

To do my share of the chores, as cooking wasn't really something I could get to grips with, I offered to do the cleaning, vegetable chopping and the washing up. With the veggie chopping I was the subject of occasional criticism from Meilin. She complained that I discarded too much of the fruit or vegetable when I was preparing it. I slowly came to understand that she was prompted by a deep-seated concern for food, ingrained in her, I am sure, because of the terrible deprivation suffered by the Chinese during the Cultural Revolution when between thirty and forty million people died from starvation as a result of Mao Zedong's 'Great Leap Forward' policy. I heard from some people how the trees no longer had leaves as the people in desperation made soup from them or even the branches. Meilin's parents would have experienced these terrible times and no doubt the way they valued each morsel of food had been passed on to Meilin.

I later also came to notice something else related to this interest in food. In England, when meeting someone, after asking 'How are you?' we immediately mention the weather! 'Nice day today, isn't it?' or 'Looks like more rain this afternoon'. This is because the weather is so contrary and changeable in our country that it affects our moods and actions. In China, however, after asking 'How are you?', they immediately ask 'Have you eaten?'. At first I found this quite strange but then it was explained to me that the concern about not having enough to eat was so embedded in the psyche of the people that this question was an unconscious attempt to assuage those fears and to be assured that starvation was no longer an issue. And I assume that if you said you had not eaten, you would immediately be offered food – again as an assurance that those dreadful times no longer existed and food was no longer a compelling issue. Interesting. I was learning so much.

By the end of the first week our days had fallen into a happy and efficient routine allowing time for explorations further afield.

Meditation and the Mountain

The mountain was constantly in my consciousness. It was the first thing I saw as I woke up and, after making my early morning cup of tea, I gazed at it and communed with it from the comfort of my bed – a special meditation. My bedroom window framed the view beautifully and I started to become familiar with the mountain and its moods. Sometimes it was clear and tinged pink with the early morning light; at other times it was barely visible through misty clouds. At all times it spelled majesty and mystery.

Its call was strong and, as the jet lag receded, I started to try and figure out how to get much closer to it. Then one day, about a week after I had arrived, Meilin told me that a friend was coming that morning with a car and would take us to a valley in the mountain which she particularly liked. I was thrilled! I really wanted to physically be on the mountain and to touch it with my feet and hands. After driving for about twenty minutes we arrived at a small old and deserted village which was in itself intriguing – the more so as it was early spring and the place abounded with leafless trees shrouded in pink blossoms. But it was the mountain rather than the village that blew me away. Until you were right there you could not see that there was a deep cleft in the mountain, resulting in a valley through which a path wound. It really sent shivers up and down my spine as I was reminded of Osho's story of the man who, when faced with a picture of a path winding into the mountain, walked into the picture and disappeared. At the same time I recalled a photograph of the road Lao Tzu supposedly followed into the mountains – through the Huangu Pass – as he disappeared into Tibet. Could I disappear through this path into this mountain?

The friend, however, wasn't at all into mystical imaginings and took us off on a walk along the base of the mountain for about a mile until we came across another abandoned village, much more beautiful than the first. We explored the broken walls which still defined the dwellings and courtyards and I felt sad that such a precious heritage was being allowed to fall into ruin. Wasn't there a Chinese equivalent to our British National Trust? In China's maniacal drive to build more and more, it has tragically forgotten its heritage. Places like these should be taken care of, restored and preserved. I found myself wishing I knew of somebody rich who could buy this place and restore it and cherish it. This village was a place I would visit many times on my subsequent visits as it breathed a sense of past harmony of man and mountain where the people lived in tune with their natural environment instead of the artificial fabrication that so much of modern China is about.

Meilin's friend, called Liang, was in a hurry to leave because, it transpired, he and Meilin were hunting for some 'real' honey. Like many Chinese, although now mostly the older ones, Meilin was very aware of the value of different foods and was not content to eat too much from the supermarket shelves. I noticed this again when, on the return journey, she told Liang to stop, and jumped out of the car to examine something an old woman was selling by the side of the dirt road. She seemed very satisfied with her purchase as she got back into the car telling me that this was a mountain weed which, later checking in the dictionary I had brought with me, translated as a dandelion. She said it was very good for health. (I was to hear that phrase a few thousands times during my visits!) Actually, dandelion tea is popular in England for being good for the kidneys and as a blood purifier so I understood where she was coming from. But as a cooked vegetable dish it was really very bitter and I let her eat most of it.

Our quest for pure honey was unsuccessful that day but a few days later Liang arrived with a huge bottle – maybe three litres in size – of honey after he had successfully tracked down a farm on the outskirts of Dengfeng where the honey was produced. It took us a long time to get through so much honey.

* * *

Health and food issues were not, however, my focus, the mountain was – and now that I had some idea of how to get there, I was eager to start exploring as soon as possible. It was quite far to walk, so the next morning I got up at 6am and set off in the direction of the mountain. I had noticed a path past the school which appeared to go in the right direction so I decided to follow it, on the way waving to the kungfu boys who had just stopped their early morning training for breakfast. They seemed to be a bit concerned at what I was doing but, as there was no-one there to translate, I just waved and walked determinedly onwards. The path wound its way through some fields but eventually ended up at the road which I recognised as the one we had travelled the day before. I went further and eventually arrived at the abandoned village again.

Quite chuffed at myself for managing to find my way here, I retraced my steps as I knew Meilin would soon be awake and would wonder where I was. Before reaching the main road, however, I saw a water hole in a grove of trees invitingly glinting in the early morning light and decided to sit down for a few minutes as I still had a long walk home.

What happened then was totally unexpected. I sat on a rock facing the mountain, the pool of water at my feet, and immediately fell into a very deep meditative space – still and silent. My mind registered shock, but my inner being registered a profound 'rightness' and tears ran down my cheeks as I knew that my urge to come here was not just a whim but a real knowing that I was supposed to be here and that I had stepped back onto my spiritual path. This understanding filled me with a wild joy and I felt like I was melting into a oneness with this place.

How long I sat there I don't know but eventually I thought I had better return to the flat. When I stood up I looked around and realised I was sitting about three hundred metres in front of a small, ancient building. From Meilin later that day I learned that the building was well over a thousand years old and is thought to be the gateway to an old temple which, local legend says, disappeared into the sky one night! I didn't tell her what I experienced but wondered if I had been meditating on the site of the temple which could have accounted for the surprisingly strong energy I felt. The ancients all over the world built their temples, churches and other structures of worship on energy spots. I felt this was definitely one of them. And so, amid the disturbing concrete construction and modern chaos and noise of this country, I had found an ancient mysterious silence and energy into which I could tap to help me on my path of meditation.

Meilin was fortunately very preoccupied with getting a broadband connection into the flat and instructing some young technicians how and where to do it, so I could disappear into my room, sit silently and absorb what I had experienced.

To see if this was a fluke or not, I decided to go to this spot again the next morning at 6am. Sitting on the rock next to the silent water I knew that it wasn't a fluke. The energy was as strong as it was the day before. In anybody's spiritual search it is easy to play mind-games and to be carried away by imagination. Osho constantly reminded his disciples to be aware about this and to distinguish between what was really true and what was just a figment of the imagination and a creation of the ego. He says:

If you allow imagination, you can imagine all sorts of things: kundalini is arising, chakras are opening; you can imagine any sorts of things, and they will all happen to you. And they are beautiful – but not true.

So when you trust a person, in the very trusting you have to be aware of imagination. Trust, but don't become a victim of imagination. Whatsoever is being said here is metaphorical. And remember always, that all experiences are imagination – all experiences, I say, unconditionally. Only the experiencer is the truth.

So whatsoever you experience, don't pay much attention to it, and don't start bragging about it. Just remember that all that is experienced is illusory – only the one who experiences is true. Pay attention to the witness; focus on the witness and not on the experiences. Howsoever beautiful, all experiences are dreamlike and one has to go beyond all of them.

So, religion is poetic, one has to talk metaphorically. The disciple is in deep trust, he can fall a victim easily of imagination – one has to be very, very alert. Trust, listen to the metaphors, but remember they are metaphors. Trust – many things will start happening, but remember: all is imagination except you. And you have to come to a point where there is no experience; only the experiencer sits in his abode silently, no experience anywhere – no object, no light, no flowers flowering, no nothing.

As Osho was no longer here to give me a 'reality check' I had to do it for myself. I knew I had to try to bring as much awareness and as little imagination as I could to whatever I was doing – especially when considering things as intangible and often intellectually unfathomable as energy and meditation. Bringing as much awareness as I could to my being, therefore, it still seemed that this was, for whatever reason, a good place to meditate and I decided to come here every day to see what might happen.

That evening Master Wu Nanfang and two kungfu students came to visit. We had invited him to dinner but he had declined. He did, however, enjoy the shockingly expensive green tea I had bought a few days previously. Remembering the speciality tea shops in Japan, I had asked Meilin if there was a place where we could buy some good green tea so she took me to a picturesque small shop which sold very expensive tea and some beautiful tea pots and cups, some of which I bought.

During the conversation I asked Master Wu Nanfang about the place I had found in front of that ancient gateway. Had there really been a temple there or was the gateway building just a gateway to the mountains? And if there had been a temple, what had happened to it? Did it really vanish into heaven as the local legend states? He was very prosaic and said that there definitely was a temple there but that it had been washed away by a flash flood more than a thousand years ago. I then mentioned that monuments and sacred sites in the UK such as Stonehenge and Glastonbury were located on 'power places', often where ley lines converged. I wondered if this was too 'spiritual' for him but he was quick to respond with a word that I recognised: fengshui. He discoursed at length about this – which Meilin only briefly translated – but the conclusion seemed to be that my 'spot' could indeed be on the site of this disappearing temple because it was indeed likely that whoever built the temple would have checked out the fengshui.

Apparently the most auspicious fengshui for a building was where there was a mountain behind, to provide shelter, a river in front, and a flat space in between for the structure. My spot was sheltered by the mountain and I had noticed that I had to cross a small bridge over a dry riverbed to reach it. Master Wu Nanfang said that there used to be a river there but it had now been dammed up closer to the Shaolin Temple and that the dry bed was now a safety run-off area to prevent any occurrence of a flash flood and consequent damage to the land and buildings in the valley.

I was captivated by his comments and from then on I went every morning to my 'magic spot' to meditate.

A Short Trip into the Past

Two or three days after Master Wu Nanfang had visited us, I woke up from my afternoon nap and had just blearily taken the first sip of my afternoon cup of tea, when Meilin put her head around the door to tell me that her 'uncle', as she calls Master Wu Nanfang, would be arriving shortly. Apparently he wanted to go and look at the abandoned village in the mountain foothills because he thought it might be a possible place for the school to move to.

Rende was driving the van and took us up the road, past my meditation place, into the foothills. We passed some of the modern concrete atrocities built to re-house the villagers, then some older houses, and finally arrived at the picturesque ruins of the old village. Since our recent visit there I think Meilin's fertile little mind had been considering the village as a possible new compound for the kungfu school and had told the master about it. It would be a perfect place for the school – so aesthetic and atmospheric yet still convenient in terms of accessibility. Despite the million-dollar view, the current school was ugly, inadequate and uncomfortable.

Master Wu Nanfang was obviously very taken with the place and was doing some serious thinking when an old man appeared who invited us into his house. Stepping over the threshold of an old door in the stone wall was like stepping straight into a scene from a hundred years ago.

Here lived an ancient man and his ancient wife (both with no teeth) and their menagerie of animals. Chinese typically don't live in houses but in compounds consisting of two or three structures built round an open space which in the old days housed animals and the farm equipment but nowadays – as in the case of our compound in ShiLiPu – the motorbikes and washing machine. The extended family lived in various parts and shared smelly toilets and cooking facilities.

This place was really a ruin but one could see how absolutely charming it must have once been: beautiful old blue-tiled roofs and quaint doorways, steps here and there and the structures all on different levels.

The first member of the animal menagerie was a barking dog who soon calmed down, and then I saw a very large rabbit in a cage. He was very cute and happy to have his head scratched and then the old guy opened a door to a small building where there were about eight baby rabbits, all very friendly and curious and willing to be stroked. They were of course happily unaware of their future date with the cooking pot. Then there was a crowing cockerel and his lady hens and finally a tiny ginger kitten. The old guy had a woodwork table set up and was doing some carpentry with some ancient tools.

I presume this couple were too old to move to the modern concrete boxes nearby and no doubt would have been miserable away from their picturesque home in which they must have lived all their lives.

A scene like this was becoming a very rare occurrence in China's sad race to modernise and westernise. At least we in England have managed to preserve quite a lot of our heritage. If this place had been in England it would have had a preservation order slapped on it and kept as a slice of history. But China follows Japan in a race to destroy the old and build the characterless grey concrete boxes that are now the norm. Yes, a Chinese National Trust is sorely needed.

People

As the days passed I grew more familiar with my surroundings and the people I saw daily. The locals seemed to live a very outdoor kind of life and spent a lot of time sitting outside their houses and chatting with each other. The other favourite place to gather was the village community centre – from where the loud music blared at night. Each community in China seems to be provided with exercise machines so that the locals could keep fit. Our area had a variety of machines for stretching and running on the spot and also bars to work out on. There was also a basketball area for the teenagers to practise. And so each evening the locals gathered – all generations represented – to meet, exercise and socialise together. There was no drunkenness or violence.

Initially as I walked past the villagers, mostly women, old men and babies, they regarded me curiously – not exactly friendly, but not hostile either. Things changed when one day I went for a little walk with my landlady and her grandchild, Maiyen, who I adored and photographed as much as I could. Since Maiyen seemed to accept me, the local ladies felt free to encourage their own toddlers to say hello. Soon everything was all smiles and laughter and the children learned their first two English words: hello and bye-bye! The children were not shy, like western children, and were happy to play with me and to be passed over for a cuddle. I was a little dubious about the latter gestures. It was lovely to cuddle the little ones but I was well aware that this was rural China and the kids all wore the typical 'split' pants – with no crotch – which allowed them to squat and do their business whenever needed without nappies being involved. Little bare bottoms were definitely still a feature of the local scenery. But the cuddles were without incident and, as a psychology graduate, I wondered what the effect of this kind of toilet training had on the youngsters. Western methods of toilet training seemed to be so fraught with emotion and guilt. Here the toilet training process seemed to be entirely natural, free and without any guilt or tantrums. Quite wonderful.

And so I found my way into the hearts of the villagers by playing with the children and patiently answering the chorus of hellos and bye-byes which now arose each time I passed. And gradually I became an accepted member of the community.

* * *

Then two very important encounters took place which were to radically affect my whole time in China.

One evening I was sitting chatting to Meilin in our living room when our third flat mate, the young kungfu student, entered in his usual silent way and walked towards his room. I had just asked Meilin a question to which she didn't seem to have an answer and, before disappearing into his room, the young man stopped, turned around, and in three sentences answered my question in totally correct English including a whole sentence in 'present perfect tense' – one of the tenses all foreign students have great difficulty in learning.

I had no idea that this young guy even spoke English, let alone so fluently and accurately, so I jumped up and asked him to come and sit with us so we could talk. I learned that his name was Ibo and, despite talking rather slowly, his English was excellent. He kept apologising because he said I was the first western person he had spoken to but I was amazed at his accurate use of grammar and the extent of his vocabulary. He said he had only learned English in Middle School and had never had any other kind of lessons. But it turned out that he was a graduate in computer technology and was thus somewhat addicted to the internet where he accessed many western sites in English. He also loved music and listening to western songs.

I was pleased to have established a communication with Ibo as it meant that I now didn't have to rely solely on Meilin for translations. It must have been quite a burden on her to be entirely responsible for me.

Surprisingly there was soon to be a second young English speaker entering my life. Just a few days later, when I visited the kungfu school, I noticed a young woman standing on the side watching the boys practise their forms. During a break, Rende brought her over to me. She introduced herself in perfect English as his cousin and told me she was visiting for a few days. Her name was Yujie, and I was of course delighted to have yet another person to speak to. I was so curious about everything and everyone that I came into contact with, and longed to know more about what I was seeing and the people I was meeting. Yujie told me that she had a MA in English from an Australian University which had set up a branch in Shanghai, and was now teaching English in a language school. She was also teaching Chinese to foreigners.

It turned out that Yujie would also be a very important person in my life in China.

* * *

More people were to grace our little village lives…. Meilin told me that in a day or two an English TaiChi group would be visiting the school and that she would be looking after them while they were here. This is where I saw her come into her own: she was a superb tour guide and organised the group with grace and aplomb.

It was a beautiful day. I went early to the school and helped them make arrangements for the event. The boys brought out their school desks and chairs for people to sit at and nice tea mugs were set out for green tea to be served. The senior students all dressed in their special white outfits ready to give demonstrations of their kungfu skills. Both Ibo and Yujie were there and could fill me in on what was happening. Meilin, in the meantime, had gone to meet the group at their hotel, and soon the small coach arrived.

As in many situations when there is good feeling from both sides, the lack of verbal communication simply doesn't matter. In this case the TaiChi people were so friendly and respectful and eager to learn from Master Wu Nanfang and his students that the whole event flowed in a heartfelt communication – helped of course by Meilin's low-key but efficient organisation. The kungfu students demonstrated many of their forms and in turn the TaiChi group showed us some of their movements. The day was glorious and the mountain clear and imposing and many of the visitors told me that this was one of the best days of their tour in China.

* * *

74

Panky arrived soon thereafter. She planned to spend a few days in Dengfeng to make the documentary about Master Wu Nanfang and Wugulun Kungfu before going to Beijing to meet her London TaiChi group. It was great to see her again and to catch up. I was able to give her some of the information about the kungfu that I had so far gleaned. Our intrepid Meilin managed to arrange accommodation for her, at a massive discount, in a very posh new hotel not too far away. Being nearby meant that Meilin and I could shower and wash our hair there in the very elegant bathroom instead of at our flat where conditions were somewhat less luxurious. Bliss to have some efficient mod cons.

We spent two delightful days filming. Master Wu Nanfang turned out to have a very aesthetic sense of what would look good on film and took us up to the Songyue Pagoda near the FaWang Temple where we filmed three of the students doing a few forms in the picturesque gardens of the pagoda. I was put in charge of composing the minimal script which Meilin narrated, doing a good job of speaking into Panky's camera as she filmed. We then moved to a location on the mountain below the pagoda which featured a fantastic rock on which Master Wu Nanfang did some advanced YinYiBa moves. He then did some sparring with one of the students enhanced by a pink and white flowering tree forming a backdrop. The next day Panky took some shots of the students practising at the school with the master instructing them. I noticed her focussing her camera on Rende because she was fascinated – as I was also – by how he moved. I have never seen anybody who moved as if made only of liquid; there did not appear to be a bone in his body. It was almost hypnotising to watch him. Panky then said she was happy with her footage and was now ready to leave to join her group in Beijing.

Having become aware of how very talented Meilin was, and having seen her in action with the TaiChi group, I was beginning to wonder if simply being Master Wu Nanfang's assistant was going to be fulfilling enough for her. I felt that she was a leader and liked to do things her way and that her way was going to clash with the master's more traditional way. There was nothing I could put my finger on but I sensed something not really flowing in their working relationship. In a quiet moment, I talked to Panky about this and asked her if it might be a good idea to take Meilin to Beijing with her where she could meet the tour leader of her TaiChi group, a Chinese man called Tary, who now lived in England organising tours to China. Perhaps there might be some collaborative and money-earning possibilities there for Meilin. She was courageously supporting herself and I wanted to help her in any way I could. When we suggested the idea to her she was happy to go, and left with Panky. I knew I would be all right as I now had the translation support of both Ibo and Yujie and anyway I was really into doing my own meditation thing and actually didn't need much. Master Wu Nanfang invited me to eat at the school while Meilin was away so everything was working out well.

To each meal he invited either Ibo or Yujie – and Rende as well – so that I would have someone to talk to. During one of the mealtime discussions I asked for more details about the foundation of his form of kungfu – ChanWuYi – and suggested that it might be a good idea if he gave a bit of a talk about it and we had Yujie and Ibo translate. This would give me a different point of view to Meilin's one and I felt that to have a more 'rounded' picture would be good. Yujie had a broader vocabulary than Meilin, especially when it came to more abstract concepts and explanations already difficult to express in words. So one afternoon we all sat down and we got what I felt was a very comprehensive account. Yujie's academic approach was quickly obvious and she was meticulous in trying to get the master's exact words translated. She introduced words like 'awareness' and 'consciousness' which I felt more accurately labelled what the philosophy was about and gave me a deeper perspective than I had had before. After fully translating the talk, Yujie and I went over it and when it still wasn't clear enough for me she got Rende to come and went into more details with him. She then translated the text back to Master Wu Nanfang to get his approval, made a few more clarifications and, once I had done a final edit, I felt that I had a good explanatory text which could be put up on a website or used on a future marketing brochure.

As far as I could make out this was probably the first time that this philosophy had been translated into English. I just had a feeling that it was somehow important to record this small piece of local knowledge as accurately as I could so that more people could know about it. I had a sense, also, that many traditions and bits of local history were rapidly disappearing in the fast pace of modern China and I hoped that it might prove useful to capture and record some of them before they were entirely lost.

* * *

As it was now getting very light in the mornings (no daylight saving time) it was easy to get up early. One morning I set off for my magic meditation spot which I had not visited for a few days because it had been raining quite hard. Walking past the school, I stood for a few moments to watch the students doing their beautiful movements so silently. The whole ambience they created was so harmonious with that particular silence and serenity which reigned in the early mornings. Then on I went through a very changed landscape. The rain had turned everything green and I swear the recently sown wheat had grown at least six inches. The leaves on the smallish poplar-type trees, not much more than saplings, had got thick and turned dark green so my grove was quite a different place. As soon as I sat down I was filled with energy. I was aware of the sound of the breeze stirring the leaves of the poplar trees as I settled into an inner silence – but then a quite raucous sound started to disturb. I got a little alarmed, especially as the sound got louder and a quick peep all around me revealed nothing, but then I realised it was a chorus of frogs! The watering hole in front of where I was sitting had, until now, been not much more than a muddy swamp, but I realised it must have filled with water because of the rain and I guess the local frogs had decided to make the most of the wet conditions and spawn a few tadpoles!

After an hour of sitting I got rather chilly so decided to do a bit of meditative walking. I went over to the waterhole and sure enough it was full of water and frog activity. I slowly walked up towards the foot of the mountain, blissed-out with the beauty and energy of the place, and was greeted every now and then by some of the farmers setting off to do their work in the fields. I think they knew me now and accepted me as part of the landscape. I walked around for another hour surrounded by a cloud of magical silence and then wafted home and made myself a breakfast of tropical fruit.

Over the next few days I spent a lot of time walking on the mountain, getting to know it and using its energy to help me meditate. I discovered that it was a crystal mountain and found to my astonishment that almost everywhere I sat, I could pick up pebbles of crystal. I later learnt that it had been mined for crystals until it was made a UNESCO site and thus protected. Crystals have significant energies which are said to aid spiritual growth and meditation and I thought that this was perhaps one more reason why Song Mountain had been such a magnet for spirituality since the very beginnings of China's history.

* * *

After about ten days, Panky and Meilin returned with the London TaiChi group and another very delightful day was spent with the group and the kungfu students interacting. When the group went to the Shaolin Temple, however, Panky didn't want to go with them and, on hearing this, Yujie came up with a suggestion to which we were happy to agree because it seemed like quite a different Chinese experience. Apparently one of the great events in the Chinese tourist calendar was the annual Peony Festival in Luoyang which was taking place at that moment and Yujie arranged for Rende to drive us there in the school van.

Yujie and Rende with Luoyang peonies

I was looking forward to getting to know more of Rende as he intrigued me with his buddha-like face, his silence and his body-with-no-bones. When he did the kungfu forms I think it was maybe wrong to say he 'moved'; better to say he 'flowed'! I can't aptly describe it as I have never seen anybody move in that way. Even when he was still, there was a flow! Anyway, with Yujie around, he was much more animated and laughing – which made him even more intriguing as I now knew that the silence was simply a contented peace and that the smile was just in abeyance, ready to appear at any moment.

The landscape along the way was rather barren and uninteresting and Luoyang was a disappointing, big, modern Chinese city, but the flowers....! Incredible! We arrived at what seemed to be a park and once through the entrance gates our eyes were filled with a vista of acres and acres of pink, red, white and lilac flowers – as far as we could see. A peony is a large flower with beautiful wavy petals and I am sure every variety in the world was represented here in this large space. The flower is a traditional floral symbol of China and is regarded as the 'king of the flowers'. As well as the glorious floral display, there were lakes and rocks and fountains to wander around. Truly breathtaking.

Panky and her TaiChi group left the next day for England, Yujie left for Beijing and I came down with a bad cold so spent a few days resting until a further drama had to be faced! Meilin had bought some kind of flat bread and disaster struck when I bit into it – right onto a stone and out came the filling in one of my teeth. Well, it seemed like I needed a Chinese dental experience to add to my store of adventures here. Knowing how difficult it is to get a dental appointment in the UK I expressed my worries to Meilin who, however, seemed quite sanguine about the dental prospects. When I asked about making an appointment she was surprised. You apparently don't make dental appointments in China.

The dental experience was an eye-opener! The place was a spotlessly clean, pleasant clinic with big picture windows filled with dental chairs and you just waited for your turn – which in my case took about two minutes. A charming young woman, completely unfazed by having to treat a western person, very competently assessed the damage and put in a temporary filling in about ten minutes, for which the charge was six English pounds. When I told Meilin that I travelled two hours to see my dentist and had to wait for up to three weeks for an appointment and that a filling like that would cost about sixty pounds at least, she was astounded.

Damo Dong

It was now time for me to do what I really wanted to do: visit the cave of Bodhidharma (Chinese name: Damo) on Wuru Peak in the Shaolin Temple compound. When I spoke about it, Master Wu Nanfang kindly suggested that Rende should take Meilin and me by car to the temple, so a few days later Rende arrived to pick us up at the crack of dawn – 6am – although Meilin and I had been up much earlier to prepare a picnic breakfast.

We went early for two reasons: firstly, Dengfeng's capricious weather was at its best and clearest early in the morning and secondly, if we entered the temple compound that early, the guards at the temple gates were not yet on duty so we could drive in without being stopped and asked to pay the exorbitant one hundred yuan (ten English pounds) per person entrance fee.

That early the weather was indeed glorious: a clear blue sky against which the various mountain peaks were etched in sharp relief. We passed loads of kungfu students (some so young) doing their early morning training and then a small nunnery, the Chuzu Temple, where there was a group of three westerners looking at the very ancient building. Built in about the twelfth century AD it was one of the few buildings not constantly destroyed – perhaps because only nuns lived there and they were not seen as a threat.

The earliest building on this site was apparently built for Bodhidharma to sit in meditation with, and to give talks, to his followers. It is just below the cave (*dong* in Chinese) where he sat.

One of the westerners started talking to us. He was Russian so I jokingly mentioned that he was following in Putin's footsteps. (Putin had visited here about three years before – a big event in local annals.) We were surprised to hear from him that actually he was Putin's translator for the event as he spoke fluent Chinese – as well as English, French and German.

Passing the nunnery a young nun came out of a back entrance and set off up the mountain path ahead of us. We took it slowly and, as the path became a staircase, I started to use the kungfu students' way of climbing steps. This worked extremely well and I climbed up endless steps without even having to pause to breathe for more than a few minutes. Also the legs didn't complain at all.

It is difficult to explain this method in words but, very briefly, it involves developing a slow rhythm as one propels one's body upwards with the leg that is on the lower step, rather than pulling one's body upwards with the leg on the upper step. This requires much less effort. You breathe in as you propel yourself upwards and breathe out as you rest briefly on the next step – so you are taking in sufficient oxygen to provide energy for each upward movement. In this way you don't get breathless or tired.

On the way up, with all my awareness focused on the next step, I was greeted by a youngish monk who accompanied me part of the way and who tried to teach me to say a few Chinese words. I obligingly repeated the words because he was so full of smiles it would have been churlish to refuse. (Later I found out he was teaching me to say 'I am tired'! I wasn't actually!)

As you can imagine the views in all directions were stunning in the fresh, clear, early morning light. When I first arrived in Dengfeng everything was brown and dry but with the heavy rain a few days previously, the trees and bushes had turned green and were comparatively lush.

Finally the gateway to the cave in the rocky mountain face appeared and I stopped to savour the moment. This is where Zen began – mind-boggling to try to conceive of the huge importance of it all. And I thought of the many, many times Osho had told the story of Bodhidharma sitting in this very cave.

On passing through the gateway I was amazed to find that actually the door to the cave was not padlocked but was in fact wide open – it was often closed, apparently – and the young nun who had gone on ahead of us was meditating inside. I cannot describe how I felt as I entered the cave and sat down next to her. Meilin and Rende stayed at the entrance and I told them I wanted to sit here for a while. As they left, the monk who I had met on the way up came into the cave and sat down on the opposite side – the cave was small, about ten feet wide and twelve feet high.

What happened next can be encompassed in one single word – Osho! I felt flooded with his energy; it was as if I was again sitting in front of him as I had done for so many, many years. This was the strongest I had felt his presence since he died nearly twenty years previously and before long I was in tears – those tears we all used to shed at the wonder of his presence.

I wished I could have sat there longer, preferably forever, but I was aware of Meilin and Rende waiting outside so all too soon I left, promising myself I would come back again – alone, so I could spend more time there. We went up to the very ugly statue quite recently erected at the summit and ate our picnic breakfast, although it was hard for me to act and talk normally so strong and overwhelming had been the experience I had just had.

On the way back down I wanted to visit the cave for a few minutes one more time, and as I left again, the monk followed me out. I really wasn't into talking but he started interrogating Meilin about me. (She had to put up with a lot of this kind of thing and was graciously patient as well as skilful in her translations.)

But then things took a strange and interesting turn. I heard the words Chan (Zen), Damo (Bodhidharma) and Indu (India) so could guess what was being discussed but the monk didn't appear to be satisfied and seemed to want more details and I heard Meilin say the word Osho. I watched the monk take a sudden sharp breath, look intently at me and then start talking quickly and excitedly. When Meilin translated I learned that he had been reading Osho's books in Chinese and thought that Osho was, in Meilin's words, 'a very successful spiritual leader'.

How surreal can things get?! Here I was just outside Bodhidharma's cave, suffused with Osho's energy, and the young monk who had been meditating at the same time as me (whose silent presence I also felt quite strongly) was telling me he had read as many of Osho's books that have been translated into Chinese as he could find! Needless to say the questions poured forth.

Apparently he was an itinerant monk, called Zhongzheng (pronounced jongjung), following his own path which had taken him all over China and to Singapore, Indonesia and the USA although he spoke no English. He had tried to go to India on three occasions but was disappointed to be refused a visa each time. He seemed well-educated and from a well-to-do background and his questions and comments revealed an intelligent, enquiring mind with perceptions based very obviously on his own real experience. He was the first person I had met here who shared my kind of 'spiritual experience' – my kungfu 'family', although understanding and tolerant about my meditation, were on a very different path.

Zhongzheng wanted to know all about Osho and his kind of meditation techniques and what my experience of being with Osho was like and what I experienced during meditation. I told him how Osho had called Bodhidharma 'the greatest Zen Master' and how I cried because I felt the energy in the cave so strongly. (He must have heard me.) Of course this was all very difficult to talk about in any normal situation but having to communicate via Meilin made things much more difficult. I think his questioning was a bit too much for Meilin as they seemed to have an altercation of sorts – but I could sympathise with her as all this was way out of her experience and I thought she did very well. It must have been quite exhausting for her to keep translating as he didn't let up!

How I wished we could have spoken directly. He was so alive and knowing, it was a rare treat to communicate with him.

And then, as he was leaving, he really stunned me when he turned back and looked at me and said, 'I think you were not crying because of the energy you felt in the cave but because you felt your Master. Even if he died twenty years ago his energy is still here.'

I was deeply touched at his understanding. And I remember Osho saying:

> *If you loved me, I will be with you forever. In your love, I will live. If you have loved me, my body will disappear but I cannot die for you. Even if I am gone, I know you will search for me.*
>
> *Yes, I can trust you will hunt for me in every stone and flower, in every eye and star... And I can promise you one thing: if you hunt for me, you will find me – in every star and in every eye – because if you have really loved a Master, you have moved into eternity with him.*
>
> *The relationship is not of time; it is timeless. There is going to be no death. My body will disappear, your body will disappear – that will not make any change. If the disappearance of the body makes any change, it simply shows that love had not happened.*
>
> *Love is something beyond the body. Bodies come and go, love remains. Love has eternity in it – timelessness, deathlessness.*

That evening, while lying on my bed still feeling blissfully full of Osho energy, Meilin came into my room to say that Zhongzheng had just sent a text message – a poem. She said it was difficult for her to translate so I asked her to send the text on to Yujie. A few days later Yujie replied with this:

> *Although the cave of meditation is as cold and lonely*
>   *as the rock in heaven,*
> *The Dhamma, like a vast ocean, enlightens with no sound.*
> *Although the space of the cave is small, it is like a universe –*
> *as boundless as a void,*
> *The Dhamma, embedded in the rock, is passed from heart to heart.*

I had told Zhongzheng that one of the meanings of Osho was oceanic. The Dhamma is the Buddhist scriptures.

Meeting this unknown, itinerant monk, who knew about and loved Osho, at the top of Song Mountain in China was one of the most extraordinary experiences I had in this country.

Huashan and Xi'an

It was becoming hotter and hotter and, never good with heat, I found myself wilting with the weather and, for the first time, my thoughts turned to England's cool green fields and huge shady trees. And insect-free nature! I could no longer go to my meditation place because a million midges had taken up residence there and sitting still had become an impossibility. But there were still three weeks to go before my flight back.

Meilin was also feeling the stress of this inconvenient flat – constantly running up and down the stairs for every need was taking a toll even on her seemingly boundless energy. She told me to come with her one morning to a house in the street behind this one. Construction mostly completed, it was now at the stage of interior design. Meilin told me she had negotiated with the owner – at present there from Shanghai – to rent it. When I saw air conditioners being installed I wanted to move in immediately! Sadly, the utilities had not yet been connected and there was no chance of moving before I left.

Meilin then had a brilliant idea. Joni, her kungfu friend, was soon to return to the west and had been talking about going to Xi'an to see the famous terracotta army, so between them they started to plan a short holiday there. As Meilin assured me it would be cooler there I was keen to go with them. And so plans were made to coincide with a visit from a mutual friend of theirs, Jasmin, who would travel to Xi'an from Beijing.

Within two days we were off – by taxi to Luoyang where we caught a train which travelled inland roughly parallel with the Yellow River. One of the places we went through was Lingbao. If one alighted here it would be possible to find the so-called palace where supposedly Lao Tzu wrote his famous Tao Te Ching. According to legend, Lao Tzu was on his way to Tibet to spend his last days there when he was captured at the beginning of the Huangu Pass by order of a Zhou Dynasty emperor who wanted him to write down his wisdom before he disappeared. Lao Tzu was reluctant because he said the truth cannot be put into words, but he had no option but to comply with the emperor's demands. He however started his much treasured book with the words: *The Tao that can be told is not the eternal Tao.*

One thing that I didn't know – and I don't think is, in fact, commonly known – is that until about 800 AD the Tibetan border reached as far east as Xi'an, so it was easily possible for an old man like Lao Tzu to journey there. It would not then have been the Tibet that we know today. After Lingbao, small mountains started to appear which, when I checked later on a map, were really the very beginning of another mountain range which eventually becomes the Himalayas.

To my surprise it turned out that our destination was not Xi'an, but a town before it: Huayin. Apparently it was here we were to meet Jasmin and she was right there, waiting to meet us as we got off the train. She was a very beautiful and vivacious young woman who also spoke good English. Apparently she was keen to climb the mountain I had already glimpsed from the train window – HuaShan, another of the five sacred mountains in China, and revered for being the ancient centre of Taoism.

Meilin had connected with a local tour guide who directed us to a small hotel. I was relieved to find that, although cheap, it was clean and had an en-suite shower and western toilet – and air-conditioning.

Sadly, on the next day, the day of the next great adventure, it was pouring with rain but my friends were determined to climb the mountain anyway. The experience was quite unreal. We all bought brightly-coloured plastic ponchos before boarding a bus which would take us to a cable station at the base of the mountain. With the mist and rain it was an ethereal journey until we reached the station. This was unreal in another way! There were hundreds of people, all wearing these different coloured ponchos, lined up for what seemed like miles, waiting to get onto the cable cars. I thought we would be there all day but the queue moved surprisingly quickly because the cable cars were huge, each one taking ten people. This was high tech in comparison to Song Mountain's cable car system.

The ride up must be pretty spectacular but unfortunately we couldn't see much through the mist, and the experience was the same when we got to the top and started to walk along a narrow path cut into the mountain side with the steep, vertigo-inducing sides a misplaced footstep away. One shuffled after the person in front in a long, long line and by the time we reached a wider area, drenched to the bone, I decided that this was not for me. At this resting place there was an arrow pointing to a way down, and, having confirmed with Meilin that this was indeed the way back, I told her that I didn't want to go any further but would return to the hotel for a rest. Naturally the three pals could continue. Caring as always, Meilin was unsure that I could make it by myself but I was confident that I could, and I knew she wanted to continue with her friends. And so we parted and I easily found my way back to the hotel.

The three returned in the evening glowing with excitement at what they had achieved and when I saw their photos I was extremely glad that I had opted out. I could never have done what they did.

The next day we went to the huge museum complex in Xi'an which houses the Terracotta Army. As my story is about Song Mountain, I won't go into detail about it here – information is available everywhere – but I can say that the place is extraordinary and no photograph or video can ever capture the sheer brilliance and enormity of this historical find. It has to be seen.

Jasmin was to accompany us back to Dengfeng and listening to her on the train journey back, I made another discovery. She was discoursing at length to Joni about sexuality and relationships, in English of course, and I smiled to myself, thinking that this sounded quite like Osho's ideas. But then she said something that I really recognised, so I asked her if she had ever heard of the Indian mystic, Osho. She stopped, surprised, and said yes, she had read three of his books, in English, which her husband had brought home from abroad. She said Osho had changed many of her ideas about the world. I just couldn't believe that here was Osho appearing once again in the most unlikely circumstances. If, in my short time here, I was already encountering instances of Chinese people being interested in him, despite his books being banned by the government, how much further had he already permeated the Chinese consciousness? I was overwhelmed. There was much here for me to contemplate and understand.

A Walk in the Sky

When we got back to the flat there was chaos! The landlord had somehow decided that our absence would be a good time for the technology necessary to operate the still dormant mobile phone mask to be activated and when we arrived back there must have been at least six men in our flat working in the control room and playing loud music and smoking. Cigarette butts and rubbish were strewn all over the living room floor and our tea and food supplies had been raided. We were incensed at having our space invaded like this. (Fortunately both Meilin and I had locked our rooms.) Meilin called Mr Wang who came up and heated arguments ensued. The Chinese have little concept of privacy so he did not seem to understand why we were upset. Of course my being there was an excuse for the men to stop and stare and I did not much feel like being so intruded upon in my own home. Like many Chinese they worked long hours so they were there from about eight in the morning until nine or ten at night.

In the end there was not much we could do. Meilin told Mr Wang that I was leaving soon and she probably threw in that she was leaving as well and asked him to delay work for a few days but he was not interested and walked off.

With the temperature now having rocketed to close to forty

degrees, this invasion was really the last straw for me and I followed Meilin as she flounced out of the building and stormed over to the new house where Joni and Jasmin were staying. Meilin had arranged for them to sleep in the new house where some electricity and one of the toilets was now functioning, although there were no cooking facilities and the workmen were still there doing the final touches. The idea was that they would eat with us. After a bit of a conference we all went into town to shop for some supplies, have dinner and discuss things.

I told Meilin that I really couldn't deal with this situation (these guys were all using the communal toilet which was now absolutely disgusting) and could she help me to go to Beijing. It was only ten days now until my return flight. She decided to come with me although Jasmin said she would like to stay in Dengfeng for a few more days.

I asked Meilin to call Yujie for me because I wanted her to find a place for me to stay in Beijing. Between them they finalised travel plans – we would leave in three days – and having satisfactorily concocted our escape plan we returned home to find our place relatively quiet as the workmen had mysteriously disappeared.

Then Joni came up with an idea. I had expressed a regret that I couldn't see San Huang Zhai one more time so that evening he suggested that we go there from the Shaolin Temple side, rather than the steep shorter route I had used previously because, he said, the walk was quite spectacular and I should experience it before I left. He told me that the steep parts were interspersed with flat parts making the climb easier to manage. To do this would be cutting things fine but I figured that if I packed everything the next day, we could do the walk the day after.

It would be a six-kilometre walk across the mountain and I wondered if I could do it, but, as I did not know if I would be coming back to this wonderful place, I felt I could not miss this opportunity. And being so high up in the sky it would be cooler so maybe more doable. Jasmin said she wouldn't go because she wanted to do some kungfu training with Master Wu Nanfang, but when Ibo came in and heard about the plan he decided to come too. This was all very fortunate because, having now done the walk, I know I could never have done it alone.

The next day I packed as much as I could and when we went for lunch at the school, Master Wu Nanfang said he would go up the short back way to the temple and meet us there, possibly with Master Dejian. This was interesting for me as Master Dejian kept away from visitors as much as he could and it was considered a rare honour if one could meet and talk with him. Master Wu Nanfang also suggested that Rende take us early in the van to the Shaolin Temple to avoid paying that high entrance fee.

So Rende picked us up at 6.30am and drove us to the temple grounds, easily entering via the side entrance without being stopped. At that time of the morning the place was cool, beautiful and quiet without the tourist crowds. The atmosphere was very different and one could feel something of how it used to be before it became the commercial establishment that it is today. Meilin and I had packed a picnic breakfast and we found a picturesque little pagoda to eat in. Then Rende returned to the school while Joni, Ibo, Meilin and I floated up the mountain on the cableway. But I really was full of trepidation. Could I manage this long walk and climb on my sixty-five-year-old legs with my sixty-five-year-old lungs? My travelling companions were in their twenties and were all fit kungfu students!

This early in the morning we were the only people on the path and it was beautiful – clear, serene, mystical and majestic. I felt like I was in touch with something very deeply primordial – I have no recollection of ever feeling so at home on the earth as I did then.

The first part of the journey was okay on the legs but after about four kilometres the steps started to get longer and steeper – we were climbing up to the highest point of the path which is actually where San Huang Zhai is situated. At many places we could stop and look back down to see where we had come from. I would never have believed I could have climbed so high. Now, sadly, as it was about 10.30am, we started to meet the tourists who had climbed up the back way. So the shrieks and yells to evoke echoes, and the transistor radios blaring out Chinese pop music, started – rather spoiling the ambience.

The only thing that got me up those steps was the kungfu walk previously described. I don't think I could have kept it up but my three companions went in front of me so I could copy their rhythmical movements which made things much easier. Finally we made it to the suspension bridge, featured in the documentary. I had so wanted to cross it and it didn't disappoint. It gave a feeling of being suspended in space, but vertigo sufferers would have had a pretty hard time.

By now there were many tourists and, as some of the places were very narrow, a lot of spatial negotiations had to take place. At least Joni was there to share the honours of being another tourist attraction and to answer the incessant 'hellos'. The last half kilometre was very steep and I was pretty exhausted – being so high up the air was probably a bit thin – but finally we made it though the gate of the dramatic monastery. Master Wu Nanfang came out to greet us and, after being provided with a simple but tasty lunch, we were introduced to the legendary Master Dejian. I admit I was disappointed because he simply ignored Joni, Ibo and me and spoke only to Meilin. I felt that there was certain arrogance and a real lack of courtesy here: that he was everything and that we were nothing and simply warranted no attention at all. Maybe he felt that we were not going to add significantly to his coffers!

Before departing we greeted the lovely old nun, Yonglian,

whom I had met briefly on my first visit. In contrast to Master Dejian, she was intensely interested in us and recognised me. She told me she was happy to see me because this mountain was a special place to be so it was good that I had come back again. When she heard I was leaving the next day, she asked when I would return. I told her I wasn't sure but I would try to come as soon as possible, to which she replied that she was growing old and her body was growing weak, but she would wait for me to return so I

Ibo and Yonglian

had better make it soon. She was so innocent, sincere and beautiful that I had tears in my eyes and couldn't speak – I just took her hands in mine and smiled silently.

The view as one went down the very steep back way was also spectacular – we could see for miles into distant parts of Henan.

Coming back to a still undisturbed apartment was a relief and, after a quick shower, I collapsed into a very deep sleep which efficiently readied me for the departing journey the next day.

And then Goodbye

The bus to Zhengzhou and the train to Beijing were both air-conditioned so the journey was comfortable if uninteresting. We passed through huge areas of food cultivation and the land was flat as far as one could see. Even the Yellow River didn't add much to the scenery.

It was great to see Yujie waiting for us at the exit of the frighteningly busy Beijing South-West train station – supposedly one of the biggest and busiest in the world – and she took me to a Youth Hostel while Meilin went off to visit her friend. Yujie had booked me a simple little single room that I found charming because it had a view of the 'Hutong' tiled roof tops and in the evening faced the setting sun. The 'Hutong' areas are the old original parts of Beijing as yet not ploughed under to build high-rises which I could see from the room, but only in the far distance. At the time of the Olympics there had been much controversy over the destruction of these old districts with their tiny houses and narrow streets and picturesque human lifestyle. The government wanted them all destroyed because it was felt that they did not reflect the new modern China. Many were destroyed but fortunately not all.

The last few weeks in Dengfeng had been pretty challenging – here in this little room was at last comfort! As it was now evening I told Yujie I just wanted to rest and we could meet the next day; she any way had to teach some lessons later in the evening.

I had heard some negative things about Beijing but, as a visitor, I loved it! It had that 'buzz' that many iconic cities have and it was fun just walking through the streets. Yujie turned out to be a good tour guide too and with her brother, Renzhen, we did all the usual tourist things such as going to the Forbidden Palace, the Temple of Heaven, some other temples and parks. I loved it all. We also went into an area where 'old Beijing' has been reconstructed and wandered around small streets and funny little shops and ate interesting street food which I would never have dared to touch without assurance from my companions. One of the old silk shops had been rebuilt and I wanted to buy everything in sight – the silk fabrics so colourful and exotic left me gasping in delight. We also visited the Olympic Stadium. It had looked so impressive in the TV coverage of the Games and in reality it stunned even more.

How reluctant I was to leave, but soon I had to board the plane for the journey back to England, knowing full well that, no matter what existence threw at me back in the west, I would return here just as soon as I could make it.

3
Accepting the Unexpected

BaiYuGou Village

The Great Way is not difficult
for those not attached to preferences.
When not attached to love or hate,
all is clear and undisguised.
Separate by the smallest amount, however,
and you are as far from it as heaven is from earth.

If you wish to know the truth,
then hold to no opinions for or against anything.
To set up what you like against what you dislike
is the disease of the mind.
When the fundamental nature of things is not recognised
the mind's essential peace is disturbed to no avail.

The Way is perfect as vast space is perfect,
where nothing is lacking and nothing is in excess.
Indeed, it is due to our grasping and rejecting
that we do not know the true nature of things.

Live neither in the entanglements of outer things,
nor in ideas or feelings of emptiness.
Be serene and at one with things
and erroneous views will disappear by themselves.

Sengcan, the third Zen Patriarch: XinXinMing

An Island in the South China Sea

Despite the challenges of my spring visit to China, I had left my heart there and England was not an interesting place for me to be now. I longed to go back and experience more of the country and, in particular, the sacred Song Mountain, but further travel naturally meant money was needed, so I set about finding as much work as I could

I was in touch with both Meilin and Yujie who had teamed up in Beijing to start their travel company. Talking to Yujie one day in late October, she told me that she and Meilin had decided to go and stay in her parents' house in Hainan Island, in the South China Sea, to do all the groundwork necessary for setting up their new company, and would I like to join them to celebrate Chinese New Year with her family in mid-February? Panky was also welcome to come. Needless to say I was thrilled at the prospect. To go to Henan in February would be far too cold but Hainan Island was warm, even hot, at that time.

Hainan Island is just off the coast of south west China and, in fact is closer to Vietnam than to the Chinese mainland.

Panky was predictably excited at the prospect. Her first documentary about Master Wu Nanfang and his kungfu had already won some awards in some amateur film festivals and she was keen to make a more in-depth documentary about the subject.

As I was working hard, the time fortunately flew by and finally all was ready, the visa for three months was again surprisingly issued and off I flew, this time to Hong Kong instead of Beijing. From there I flew to Sanya, the biggest city in Hainan.

I was very happy to see Yujie's charming face at the airport and immediately felt I had come back home. My heart, left behind when I returned to England, now reinserted itself into my body and I felt alive again! After my intense few months in the UK, the life and energy of the people here was a welcome change for me. Such a contrast -- for me an exhilarating one.

I spent the first day and night with Yujie in her family's home in Sanya and the next day Meilin and four of the young university students now working for her, came down from the mountain house to see me and spend an afternoon at the beach. The youthful exuberance of so many lively young people was infectious and my jetlag disappeared sufficiently for me to enjoy the long trip to a beautiful beach outside of the main city. Being a bit of a connoisseur of beaches around the world, I judged this one to be up there amongst some of the best: clean white sand and crystal clear water with interesting coves and islands all bathed in a bright, but not too glaring, sunlight.

The next day we all took a bus up a steep and twisting mountain road, bounded on each side with luxuriant tropical trees and undergrowth amid lots of rice paddies carved into the mountain sides. The Zhao's mountain home was gorgeous; silent and isolated, it was built on the edge of a large river with mountain views as far as the eye could see. Meilin and her friends were staying in another place so off they went and I collapsed, still rather jetlagged, in my lovely room with its en-suite bathroom on the top floor of the house. It even had its own private balcony to sit on and look at the view. In the evening I had dinner with Yujie and her mother and father.

Over the years I have had the good fortune to meet Mr and Mrs Zhao on a number of occasions and for me it is an honour and a privilege to have come into contact with them. Their life story is symbolic of so much that is good and admirable in modern China.

Mr Zhao, one of a family of five brothers and a sister, was born and brought up in a small village in Hubei Province, just south of Beijing. His family of course experienced the deprivations of the Cultural Revolution and were poor. Seeking work, Mr Zhao and one of his brothers went to Beijing where they got jobs as construction workers on building sites. After two years of working hard and getting nowhere, they heard there were some more lucrative jobs available in Hohhot in Inner Mongolia so they moved there. After a few years they felt they had learned enough, and there was opportunity enough, to establish their own construction company which, over the years and with the help of two other brothers, they built up to be one of the biggest in Inner Mongolia. Not bad for some village boys.

In the meantime, Mr Zhao married Mrs Zhao, a woman from his home village and they had two children, Yujie and Renzheng. Mrs Zhao was a woman of integrity and often journeyed to Inner Mongolia to help with the family business. Yujie, Renzheng and Rende, their cousin, stayed in the village with their paternal grandparents. Grandfather Zhao was kind of a village wise man and deeply devoted to Buddhism. Had he not lived in the time of the Cultural Revolution, where people were forcibly prevented from bettering themselves, especially intellectually, it is probable that he would had been a man of eminence.

Despite their efficient business enterprises, the whole Zhao family are devout Buddhists, steeped in the spiritual heritage of an older China. Here, in the house in Hainan, Mr and Mrs Zhao have built a small temple and get up at 3am every morning to pray and chant sutras from Buddhist scriptures. I found it both intriguing and endearing that, on the large TV downstairs in the living room, they constantly had videos playing of the lectures of a charismatic man called Master Chin Kung. Born in Anhui in China, he moved to Taiwan in 1949, studied Buddhism and Philosophy, and then established centres of Buddhism all over the world. Mrs Zhao, in particular, always had an ear for what he was saying. When drinking tea in the living room I often just sat quietly and enjoyed watching this master and, although I didn't understand a word that he was saying, I could easily understand and feel his energy.

After resting for a few days, I spent time helping the young people – all English students – with their work. As they had not had experience preparing texts for a website I was able to give them some input on that and also, of course, to help them with writing English. We did a bit of sightseeing although I have to say I wasn't too taken with the island. Basically, it reminded me of war, as the landscape was similar to the scenes I knew from movies about the Vietnam War. Perhaps I was just missing Song Mountain and, now in China, I felt myself longing to be in the energy-field of the place I had come to love so much.

* * *

But first we had the New Year celebrations which were huge fun. It was a low-key affair with, of course, lots of food – especially the traditional dumplings which we all helped to make. Panky sadly missed these celebrations because her plane was delayed but when she arrived she provided an excuse to have a big welcome dinner party. Mrs Zhao had also organised a trip into the centre of the island which was enjoyable, but Panky had the same reaction to the island as I did – too much like the war-torn Vietnam we had heard and seen so much about in the late sixties and early seventies.

So when Meilin and Yujie decided that this phase of their work had been completed and that they now needed to be in to Beijing to continue with their project, both Panky and I were happy to leave and return to Song Mountain and the friends we now had there.

The Bollywood House

Yujie went directly to Beijing but Meilin flew with us to Henan because she had some business to attend to there and, as we were going to rent her house, there were various things to sort out.

Despite my anticipation, I was a bit disappointed when I arrived in Dengfeng. I had never been here this early in the year and, apart from being bitterly cold, it was quite bleak – grey and gloomy, just like England. Meilin had made what I had called the 'Posh House' reasonably comfortable and efficient. Panky immediately renamed it the 'Bollywood House' because of the abundance of coloured lights in all kinds of nooks and crannies – operated by an impressive control panel. Meilin adored this feature, turning the lights on and off as if we were on a stage set. I, remembering the trials of the previous house, was more impressed with the western-style bathroom.

We were touched by the frequent visits of the local villagers, especially Mr and Mrs Wang and Maiyen, who all came to greet us bringing gifts of fruit and food. They made me feel very much that I was coming home.

Then, having made sure we were well settled in, Meilin took off for Beijing. She had perhaps called Master Wu Nanfang on the way because soon after she left, he arrived accompanied by an extremely good-looking young Italian man who, in halting English, informed us that we were invited to come to dinner at the kungfu school that evening.

As we set off for the school I realised we might be in trouble because it was winter and it was already dark. There were no street lights in such a small village so unless the moon was close to being full it was difficult to see one's way. However, a few metres along the path, two young kungfu students appeared with torches to escort us to the school in safety. So thoughtful! We had an interesting, if pretty cold and distracting evening at the school. Cold because the temperature was already down to zero and there was no heating in the school, and distracting because our hosts, the master and the young man, were both so handsome that it was hard to focus on the actual conversation.

The young man's name was Naomitsu – a Japanese name, not Chinese, and definitely not Italian. This was a surprise. He told us that his father was Japanese and skilled in Japanese alternative medicines and treatments. On a lecture tour in Italy he had met Naomitsu's mother, an Italian student. They fell in love with each other instantaneously despite neither speaking the other's language. Naomitsu's father never returned to Japan, except on visits.

At the age of seventeen, Naomitsu left Italy and spent two years wandering barefoot, like a monk, in the southern Japanese islands, absorbing the heritage of his father's culture. He learned to speak some Japanese and worked now and then to finance his wanderings. He then decided to come to China and ended up in Dengfeng because of his interest in martial arts. He was now learning Chinese as well.

We were enthralled with this absorbing story told by this mesmerising young man. I felt a bit like I was in some ancient fairy tale. I love Japan, I love Italy and I love China and in Naomitsu these three ancient cultures converged. No wonder he had a special aura around him. What an extraordinary story!

We also had some communication with Master Wu Nanfang but, because Naomitsu was translating from one foreign language to another – not at all an easy task – communication was of necessity fairly limited. I also sensed that he was a silent, private kind of person and wasn't too interested in much casual conversation.

It was only as we were about to leave that I remembered to ask where Ibo, the young man who had lived in the flat I stayed in last year, was. I had registered that he wasn't around. It transpired that he was in Zhengzhou where he and two other western kungfu students had enterprisingly set up an English language school to earn the money to pay for their board and tuition. Apparently they left Dengfeng each Friday to teach during the weekend and returned on Sunday evening or Monday to train during the week. As it was now Saturday I was happy that I would be seeing him soon.

It turned out, however, that I would see him sooner than I expected because on Sunday evening there was a knock on the door and in walked Ibo and the two young western men whom Ibo introduced as Micha from Holland and Ali from Spain. Both spoke excellent English and were the teachers at their Big Ben Language School while Ibo was the business manager and 'recruitment officer'.

After a chat over some green tea and Shaolin cookies, Ibo asked if he could leave some medicine in our fridge because it had to be refrigerated at all times. He held up a plastic bag filled with ice in which he had carried the medicine on the bus from Zhengzhou. While being rather taken aback and concerned about the importance of this medicine, I had time to fleetingly consider the efficiency of the village grapevine. Somehow a kungfu student had learned that we had a fridge; this intelligence was communicated to Ibo in Zhengzhou and he had acted on the information by asking us this favour.

Naturally we agreed to house the medicine but I was really concerned about why it was so necessary. Then, for the first time, I heard Ibo's sad and shocking story – a story which would always be there in the background during my subsequent visits to China and which would, on occasions, even shape events.

* * *

Two years previously, at Ibo's graduation ceremony, he and some friends had overdone the celebrations and ended up in the local hospital with mild alcohol poisoning. I knew from my experience of living in Japan that Asian bodies lacked a particular enzyme which broke down alcohol when consumed, thus making them adversely susceptible to even small quantities of alcohol – quantities that a western person's body would have no difficulty in processing.

Tragically for Ibo, the young inexperienced doctor who treated him injected a highly damaging substance into his liver and almost destroyed it. Ibo spent the next year in hospital, often at death's door. He told me that various doctors had said that any normal person would have died, but Ibo's will to live was so strong that it kept him alive when medically he should have been dead.

He also said that when I had met him the previous year, he had only been out of hospital for one month. He had heard about the healing effects of Wugulun Kungfu – the exercises, the diet and the philosophy of ChanWuYi – and had joined the school in the hope that the healing process could begin. His progress was apparently up and down and recently his doctors had decided to put him on a course of Interferon to see if this could bring about a more effective cure. This Interferon, which Ibo had to inject into his body every two days, had to be kept refrigerated. Panky and I had no idea about this situation and were deeply shocked and saddened at this story.

It also became obvious that the language school business was for him not so much about paying for tuition but about paying for the very expensive medicine and hospital bills. His family – just a poor village family – were apparently deeply in debt from borrowing the money from friends and relatives to pay the previous year's hospital bills to save his life, so not only did he have to live with the constant ill health caused by a barely functioning liver, he had to find the money to pay for the ongoing medical bills and also face the prospect of getting a job good enough to earn enough money to pay back this huge debt. A very frightening and heavy burden for such a young person to carry.

Fortunately youth is quite resilient and after this disheartening story and many more cookies, the mood lightened and the guys regaled us with funny stories of their teaching efforts. They soon left, however, as they were obviously very tired.

When I went to bed I was still very much shaken by Ibo's story. Having had a ten-year-long serious illness myself, I knew exactly what it was like to have to work to support oneself and pay for treatment when one was sick and exhausted. I knew what it was like to have to draw on reserves of strength one never knew one had. I was luckier than Ibo, however, because, on returning to England after being away for more than twenty years, the free National Health System was there to catch me when I finally collapsed and was able to sort the problem out, free of charge.

This empathy with Ibo and his health problems probably created a bond which might not have otherwise happened. He would turn out to be one of the people who helped me the most to understand China and its ways. Because of his outstanding command of English, as well as his intelligence and awareness, he was able to explain many subtle things to me, thus increasing my understanding and enjoyment of this country, its culture and its people.

Spring Filming

I have mentioned Dengfeng's capricious weather system before. In the week after we moved into our Bollywood

House, the weather hit us with every nasty punch it could think of. We suffered rain, hail, biting winds and snow! My cavernous room – it was more like a small hall – was exposed to the winds blowing off the mountain and I was excruciatingly cold. The new houses in China are built with bricks made from concrete which retain the cold in winter and the heat in summer – hopeless – and there is no insulation in walls or ceilings and the roofs are mostly flat. There is no double glazing in sight.

Despite Meilin's instructions to the contrary, I moved into her room which was smaller and had one of those built-in combination heating and air-conditioning units. This and endless hot water bottles improved things a bit. Meditation in my magic spot was out of the question because of the bad weather, but occasionally I was able to make a quick visit there.

But then, having hovered around zero degrees for a week, the temperature suddenly, in twenty-four hours, shot up to about fifteen degrees and the sun came out to warm our frozen limbs. Within a week of this warmer weather, just about every tree in sight blossomed into exuberant white, pink and lilac flowers with yellow-green shoots on myriad branches hurrying to join them in a joyful spring dance.

Panky had already had long discussions with Master Wu Nanfang – via Ibo – as to the formatting of the documentary she was here to make. With the land awash with dancing blossoms it was obvious that filming should commence as soon as possible although the timing had to be calculated to avoid Ibo's trips to Zhengzhou as he was a crucial element.

I am actually quite amazed, when I look back, at how everything just flowed despite the communication difficulties. We all seemed to be so in tune with each other that everything just happened in an easy and creative way. Maybe Ibo's organisation skills also played a part. As before, I helped Panky with a script of sorts, but it was Master Wu Nanfang who came up with the locations and who stage-managed much of the visuals. His intimate knowledge of the area enabled him to pinpoint certain areas of compelling beauty to form the backgrounds for the action. The Shaolin Temple compound was the natural venue of choice and very early one morning we found ourselves bundled into the trusty van and driven off to sneak our way in.

I had never seen the temple grounds look so magnificent! A bright clear sky, fresh green spring growth and colourful blossoms presented a perfect, almost theatrical, backdrop for the film. We started off on an earth mound or small hill called the Sweet Dew Platform where the founder and first abbot of the Shaolin Temple, an Indian Buddhist monk called Batou, had had his residence and temple. Here he translated many Buddhist scriptures. Nothing is left of any building here except a base and some columns but it provides an excellent view of the surrounding compound.

Just as everything appeared to be ready for action, Master Wu Nanfang suddenly wandered off and proceeded to walk down the opposite side of the hill. Like little ducklings, we followed. It seemed that he had remembered an area of particular beauty and wanted to check it out. He took us into a hidden valley covered in blossoming trees with Wuru Peak and Bodhidharma's statue looming up on the other side. My camera finger was clicking frantically in an effort to capture something of the spectacular scene.

The master seemed to think it would be a good beginning to the film if he walked though this valley followed by his students and then climbed the stone steps to the top of the hill. He was right, of course, and the scenes were breathtaking. I stayed at the back out of the way and one of the photos I took looks like a picturesque Fragonard painting.

The main part of the action then started. Master Wu Nanfang wanted to explain Wugulun Kungfu and had brought three of his students – Hufei, Laochi and Wenju, his son – to demonstrate the forms while he gave a commentary. Ibo later translated the discourse to enable Panky to insert English subtitles in her film to explain what the master was saying.

Master Wu Nanfang demonstrating forms to his students

Once Panky and Master Wu Nanfang were satisfied with the shots we moved to another location where the master demonstrated the famous Dragon Form and then gave a short lecture on the nutritional and medicinal properties of various plants that could be found on the mountain side.

This was truly a stunning morning and I could see that Panky was itching to get her footage onto her computer to see what the visuals looked like on the big screen. We returned to the school for lunch, the following morning's film schedule was arranged and master and students retired for their usual afternoon siesta while we returned home: me also to have a nap and Panky to view her shots. I awoke to find her blissfully happy with the results which I of course had to immediately see.

The next morning a different location had been chosen: the grounds in front of the old gatehouse to the vanished temple where I was now meditating most mornings. Master Wu Nanfang first explained and demonstrated some Qi Gong movements and then did some very active sword and stick forms. Ibo told me that the stick he was using had belonged to his great grandfather, Master Wu Shanlin, the second Grand Master of this lineage. It was about a hundred and twenty years old. The sword which we examined minutely was spectacular, but, Ibo said, very new. It had been given to the master two years previously by one of his wealthy European students.

This was another stunning setting. In the immediate background was a carved wooden bridge leading to the ancient gateway, and behind it rose, amid other peaks and in imposing grandeur, the highest mountain in the Song Mountain range, Mount Shaoshi.

After lunch we filmed inside the school where Master Wu Nanfang gave further talks on the history of this lineage, illustrating his points with more forms. I reflected that Ibo was going to have his work cut out translating all these discourses – me too, as I would be doing the editing.

ChingMing Day

This day was, strictly speaking, part of the Spring Filming episode but so special was this event that it needs a section to itself.

ChingMing Day falls on the 5th April each year and is a national holiday during which people all over China visit the burial places of their ancestors to pay their respects and show that the ancestors are still remembered and cherished in their hearts.

Ibo had promised Panky that this would be a very special event to film. Actually, for me, it was a very special event to experience. It took both my appreciation of the Chinese culture and my dismay at the current destruction of so much of value, to another depth and dimension.

The Wugulun lineage has four Grand Masters: Master Wu Gulun; his son, Master Wu Shanlin; an adopted orphan, Master Zhang Qing He and, currently, Master Shi Dejian. All these masters were not only masters of kungfu but also embraced Zen Buddhism and the study and practice of traditional Chinese medicine. On this day we were going to visit the burial places of all the masters. The burial place of Master Wu Gulun, Ibo told me, was just outside the tiny ancient village of BaiYuGou which is where Master Wu Nanfang was born and brought up. I remembered Meilin pointing to it when we were on the top of Wuru peak and looking over to the other side of the mountain.

As usual, we got up very early, and by 7am we had all squeezed ourselves into a convoy of six vans. As I was one of the larger members of the group, I got to sit up front with the driver, and so had the best views and photographic opportunities during the journey. All the other smaller people, including Panky and all her film gear, were squashed into the rear seats. Wenju was driving and Ibo and Naomitsu were also in the vehicle.

I swallowed rather apprehensively when I realised we were going down that hair-raising pass which I had traversed before on the way to Luoyang. Wenju was still something of a novice driver and had very much a devil-may-care attitude to driving. I called him 'the kungfu cowboy' and had to trust that his reflexes were quick enough to get him out of any trouble! But I knew this was going to be a cling-to-the-door-handle type of ride with my brake foot stuck to the floor. About half way down there was some respite, however, as we suddenly stopped, climbed over the roadside barriers and walked down the hillside to what appeared to be a mound covered with paper litter.

In actual fact it was the burial site of the monk who had rescued Zhang Qing He as a baby and had brought him up. He had taught the child what he knew of herbal medicine and later sent him to Master Wu Shanlin to learn kungfu.

At each grave a ritualistic ceremony took place involving the lighting of incense, chanting and the burning of paper money to ensure that the ancestor was provided for in his heavenly domain. And, naturally – this was China – endless loud firecrackers of various sizes and decibel levels were lit to make sure all evil spirits were driven away. Or to give the kids a fun time…. That they loved playing with the crackers was obvious.

The second stop was at the grave of Zhang Qing He himself. We had to walk quite far through fields of wheat until we came to another mound covered with soggy paper. Now I was a bit curious: why the lack of a proper grave or tombstone or something? Ibo's explanation was surprising. Apparently people had traditionally buried their dead in the fields, to keep them close by and to 'stay in touch', as it were. But with the huge increase in the population, the government had forbidden this practice because every square metre was needed to provide food for people to eat. Many people ignored this edict and continued to bury their dead nearby, but no longer added the tombstones which would indicate a grave. Such a tombstone would be easily visible and roving bands of officials would destroy them and desecrate the graves if found.

A similar ceremony was repeated at this graveside but I was convinced that the young students were much more interested in setting off as many deafening firecrackers as they could – with deadpan faces – than doing all the pious rituals.

Zhang Qing He's grave was in the middle of lush green wheat fields which were, however, bordered on all sides by ugly metal and concrete structures involved, as far as I could make out, with the processing of gravel. Huge pyramids of gravel, crushed into various grades from fine to coarse, dotted the landscape and endless lines of huge trucks edged forward to be loaded with the stuff destined for the manic construction of buildings, highways and bridges in far away metropolises.

The origins of the gravel became obvious as we turned off the main road, already pitted with potholes, onto a dirt road that consisted mainly of ditches and trenches. Driving now resembled being in a boat – cresting a wave and then plunging into the trough behind it before rising up again onto the next crest. Wenju was completely unperturbed by this roller-coaster ride and happily chatted away or sang along with his favourite pop songs on the car radio.

The other vehicles either accompanying us or greeting us head-on on this rough road were huge ancient trucks dodging each other in both directions and laden with loads of gravel, rock or enormous boulders. Terrifying. The air rapidly became dense with powdered dust and we all started to cough as the particles entered out throats and lungs. My god! Ibo explained that we were now in a huge quarrying area with rock being dynamited out of the side of the mountain. This nightmare scenario was just one of hundreds of thousands of similar sites all over China as the government and big businesses relentlessly ravaged the country areas to provide the raw materials for their massive construction projects.

I was already in shock but started to get outraged when I realised that this 'road' was running parallel to the mountain on the other side of which, just a few miles away, was the Shaolin Temple,

SanHuangZhai and my meditation spot which were all supposedly in UNESCO protected areas. I asked Ibo how this devastation could be allowed to happen and he, as outraged as me, said that anything in China was possible provided enough money changed hands. Quarrying here was illegal but the officials who were supposed to control the area were getting nicely rich off the bribes they were receiving. UNESCO protection meant nothing if the locals had different agendas.

We passed through miles of dust-covered, jagged landscapes resembling a desolate background for an end-of-the-world type of movie, all the time dodging the thundering trucks with their huge, thick tires. At one point we stopped at a particularly devastated area – it looked like a moonscape – to view a new dam which was being built. I wondered how many villages were being drowned in the process.

Finally the traffic thinned out and the air got a little clearer and we turned right into another valley. Within minutes I gasped and whispered the word: psaolian – beautiful. After the horrific scenes we had just left, we now entered an exquisite valley filled with the yellow-green shoots of spring and hundreds of blossoming trees. Wenju heard my whispered word and said something to Ibo who then translated, saying that twenty or thirty years ago this valley was known to be one of the most beautiful in China and visited by many during the spring. This idyllic valley led to Master Wu Nanfang's village and I pictured him many years ago walking through the valley on his journeys into other areas. What must he feel like now, I wondered, to see such a delicately picturesque land so violently destroyed by the present madness? This, of all places, should have been preserved for posterity. I found it difficult to find some kind of equanimity between being so touched with the beauty of what I was seeing now and being so affected by the awfulness of what I had just been through.

We travelled further along the valley with its pockets of rustic charm interspersed with unsightly concrete houses and litter-strewn streets until we finally stopped at some fields of wheat. Here again we all piled out of the vans and walked through the fields to a clump of trees. This was the grave of Master Wu Shanlin, rather beautifully situated with the mountain behind it, and another ritual took place, ending of course with the firecrackers. This was a peaceful area and, while Panky filmed, I sat awhile to centre myself and absorb the silent energy.

Back in the vans, we drove still further into the isolated valley, now unspoiled by any signs of human inhabitation, until we finally stopped at an old stone wall with a gateway which led into BaiYuGou village. This was one of the first truly authentic places I had been to and I felt like I was stepping into an ancient China, unchanged for many hundreds of years, when we followed the master and students through the stone gateway past some villagers, three tethered cows, some goats and some squawking chickens alarmed at this sudden activity in what must be a very undisturbed life.

I was enthralled at seeing this historical place untouched by modern craziness. It was poor and dilapidated but charming and real. I loved it. It remains one of my most favourite places in China.

* * *

We followed the master and students through the village to a small field just outside where the ceremonial ritual for Master Wu Gulun took place. Not so many firecrackers this time – I think even the students were awed by the ancient silent feeling of the place.

After the ceremony, Master Wu Nanfang's wife took us to visit their village house. Like many old residences it was half built into the mountainside, making it warm in winter and cool in summer.

Until recently a surprising number of Chinese people still lived in cave dwellings – actually quite a few still do – which, although lacking in amenities, have the advantage of being naturally insulated against the elements. I thought ruefully about the concrete box I was currently inhabiting.

A small monument on the side of the road had been built to commemorate Master Wu Gulun, the village hero, who had escaped the ravaging of the Shaolin Temple in about 1870 and carried many of its secrets to this far away hidden village to preserve and protect them. An intense cacophony of firecrackers celebrated him and then we slowly made our way back to the vans to begin the journey home. I had much to contemplate.

I was roused from my reverie, however, when Naomitsu climbed into the driver's seat. I remembered Ibo saying that Naomitsu was a Formula 1 racing driver and laughing at him, saying that he was far too young to be a racing driver. Now I had my doubts because Naomitsu's driving was radically different to Wenju's and I realised we were in for an experience! Typically Italian, Naomitsu waited for no man nor vehicle and attacked the traffic with a studied concentration which made me pretty nervous. I soon realised, however, that he was totally in command of the vehicle and I quickly found the experience exhilarating rather than frightening. At one point we went round a bend and I could see the trucks ahead of us on this so-called road, really a rutted track. I counted ten trucks, and jokingly said to Naomitsu that this was going to hold us up. He took that as a personal challenge and one by one we passed every single truck along the way. No funfair roller-coaster ride could have anywhere near matched that ride.

When we finally reached the pot-holed main road it was smooth by comparison and we made it back to the school in double quick time – well ahead of the rest of the vehicles in the convoy.

This day really was a memorable event.

'Very Interesting'!

Soon after ChingMing Day it was time for Panky to leave – but Master Wu Nanfang had a surprise for us. Ibo was in Zhengzhou so the sparse information we were given left us rather mystified but it seemed we were going sightseeing. The following day, we were informed, we were going to visit a place which was 'very interesting'. More information than that was beyond the current translation expertise of anyone at the school.

Wenju was again driving which made us feel slightly apprehensive but fortunately he headed north-east instead of west so I knew that that terrible road to Luoyang was not on the agenda. I took my Lonely Planet Guide with me but, as I could not make out from the Chinese pronunciations and road signs where we were going, it was of no help. This road was in very bad condition too and apparently there was a lot of quarrying going on in this area which seemed to me to be in another area of the Song Mountain range. The scenery was pretty much desolate and the villages that we drove through were poor and ugly. When I was later able to ask Ibo about this area he said it was actually close to his home town and he spoke of how the government had forcibly moved people out of their traditional village homes in order to quarry stone from the mountainsides, and re-housed them in these ugly villages where they were isolated from all their previous neighbours and friends. So much damage done on so many levels.

Later Ibo told me that we had gone to a town called Gongyi which was on a tributary of the Yellow River. At that time, however, I had no idea were we were going but, after driving through this town, the area become much more attractive with green fields and a few trees. Soon we arrived at a huge parking lot where we disembarked and then followed the master and his wife to a small, compact, walled village complete with castle-like turrets.

119

Inside, the place immediately became 'very interesting'. As far as we could make out from the signs in questionable English, we were in an extended mansion belonging to a rich family who seemed to have been doing some lucrative trading. It was frustrating that we couldn't find out any more information about this strange but quite beautiful place, but things suddenly changed. Always expect the unexpected in China! I suddenly found myself accosted by three pretty young women who, in perfect English, excitedly introduced themselves as students who were training to be tour guides and, as they had never before met any westerners, they wanted very much to practise on us! This was a great opportunity for them, they said. Once again I was charmed by the lack of shyness in the Chinese, their energy and their willingness to take on any unusual challenge. Of course Panky and I were delighted. Finally we could get some idea about what we were looking at. The girls were fascinated by Master Wu Nanfang – they had heard about Dejian who was more famous in China – so suddenly all was excitement and energy. They were also thrilled that Panky was filming so much and delighted in imparting as many facts as they could – and their knowledge was extensive. Our visit turned out to be a very lively, enjoyable and informative one due to these charming, intelligent young women.

As Kangbaiwan is not really part of my Song Mountain story I am not going to go into details about this place but, briefly, the Kang family were a rich and successful family who, in the eighteenth century were trading salt made on flat land around this tributary, and other popular marketable goods like, of course, silk. With easy access to transportation along the Yellow River, the business prospered but then declined as successive heads of families succumbed to the lure of opium. (Riches and drugs – a story continuing to this day.) The mansion was really an extended village surrounded by stone walls and was an incredible record of life at that time – so much preserved, even children's clothing, books and playthings. I was especially interested in one of the first banks ever set up in China. Beautifully designed and presented.

Kangbaiwan is not mentioned in the Lonely Planet Guide but for those travelling off the beaten track in China it is well worth a visit. Chinese tourist websites do give information on how to reach it. It is, in fact, not that far from Zhengzhou and can easily be reached by bus and train.

Old and New

Having already spent a month in Hainan Island, it slowly dawned on me that my time in China was soon coming to an end. It was less than three weeks before I had to return to England. Leaving was also going to be a bit complicated because my return ticket was from Hong Kong rather than Beijing so I had to fly down south again. I needed to work this trip out.

Now on my own after Panky's departure I had time to reflect on my time here. I felt slightly frustrated because, in my mind, I had had expectations of meditating more but actually there seemed to be so many distractions that this wasn't happening. However, after pondering all this one morning I came to the conclusion that maybe this time other things were supposed to happen and I should embrace the incredible kindness and friendliness shown to me – and Panky – by so many of the Chinese people and western friends like Naomitsu, Micha and Ali. I had learned so much from so many special people and fascinating experiences that I should be much more grateful and go along with what was happening rather than trying to decide on what I should be doing.

And very soon Ibo came up with two more ideas! I had already called him an 'ideas machine' so I wasn't surprised.

He had been visiting our house every second day, often accompanied by Micha or Ali or both, to get his injections from our fridge, so we had had many opportunities to talk. One day he and Micha told me that they thought the school should have a website in both Chinese and English so that more people could learn about Wugulun Kungfu.

Knowing that I had helped Meilin with a previous website, Ibo asked if I could help him set up one for the school. He was very good with the technical side of computers but didn't feel confident about planning a website. As this was something I had had a bit of experience with, I was actually very pleased to be able to help and to maybe repay some of the gracious kindnesses I had received.

But time was short and there was a lot to be done. Ibo had been working hard translating some of the talks Master Wu Nanfang had given for Panky's film so, with the piece on ChanWuYi compiled previously, there was already a text of sorts. I could write more. Micha and Ali wanted to compose the practical information about tuition for westerners at the school. And between us all we had some stunning photographs. We sat down one evening and worked out sections, headings and drop-down menus so that we had a structure to work with. Ibo had, in the meantime, located a web-design company in Zhengzhou who had made some interesting and aesthetic websites. He asked me if I would go with him to Zhengzhou and meet the web-designers. This was one more interesting adventure to add to my now considerable collection of Chinese experiences so I of course agreed.

It was a pleasure to work with all these efficient young people and within a week I was amazed to find we had created an informative and visually beautiful website! The Chinese work very fast and seem to do things with a harmony lacking in western countries. I had thoroughly enjoyed the whole process and was happy to see that the school now had an efficient and very attractive means of reaching people who might be interested in, and benefit from, this special form of kungfu.

Master Wu Nanfang took us all out to dinner at the hot pot restaurant to celebrate.

SanHuangZhai Revisited

I now had only five days left before I would take the train to Beijing where I would spend two days with Yujie and Meilin before flying south to Hong Kong and then back to England.

Ibo then told me of his second idea. As I so very much wanted to stay at San Huang Zhai and do a meditation retreat there, he proposed that we go up there together and talk to Master Dejian and see if something could be arranged for my next trip to Song Mountain.

This was a perfect goodbye gift for me and the next day Wenju picked me up, drove us to the far side of the mountain and dropped Ibo and me at the start of that stone 'ladder' to the sky up which we had to climb.

As Ibo's health was still rather fragile we took things very slowly with lots of stops during which we talked about many things. As we were going so slowly, there was also time to notice things I hadn't registered before. One of these was the toiling climb of the workmen carrying bags of cement up to the monastery. As I mentioned before, the rocks for the building were hewn out of the mountain side but everything else, including the cement to stick the rocks together, had to be carried up the stair way. What a task! I expressed concern at these labourers undertaking such a strenuous labour but Ibo said they were used to it and were, in fact, treated much better than on other construction projects in China. I soon noticed that the men carried the bags only a short distance, deposited them on the side of the staircase and then went down again to pick up another bag. There must have been ten or twelve men doing this all the way up the steps so, in reality, they weren't carrying the bags for any great distance before having a rest by descending again. Ibo said they might do this heavy labour for a day but would then be switched to do something different on the construction site while others took their place.

The day was gorgeous, clear of fog for once, and taking things at such a leisurely pace I had time to savour the magnificent beauty of the mountain and the distant views we could see from so many turns of that tortuous staircase. I asked Ibo about the two nuns I had seen in the documentary and he told me a little of their story. Apparently the older woman, Yongyue, now ninety-two years old, came from a rich family who were also strong Buddhists, so as a child and teenager she had worshipped Buddha daily. Yonglian, now eighty-two years old, was her servant and companion. Yongyue's family wanted to marry her off to a rich man but she wanted to become a Buddhist nun, so together with Yonglian she escaped to a small temple – the site of this current huge construction project – on Song Mountain where they have lived until this day. An older version of youth rebelling against the status quo! Extraordinary!

As I slowly climbed, Ibo wandered off and practised his kungfu movements but finally we rounded the last turn and there was the monastery in all its glory. I was astounded at how much work had been done since I was there the previous year. A new feature had been constructed: a charming bridge over a small cleft in the rock and then the usual entrance hall from which more steps led up to the two levels of the main buildings. On one level were housed the living quarters of the women and the kitchen and dining rooms. On the next level was a temple. Both had expansive courtyards where one could sit and admire the views. The entrance way was not yet functioning so we went up the path we had been on before and then entered the first level where I could see Yongyue sitting silently in the sunshine and Yonglian standing near her gazing at the view.

When she saw me, Yonglian came quickly to greet me. I reminded her – via Ibo – that she had told me on my previous visit to return soon so here I was. She smiled and said she of course remembered me and was very happy to see me again. She took Ibo and me up to the temple which was now dramatically changed and impressive in its, to me, rather gaudy red and gold decorations and huge Buddha statues. She was obviously immensely proud of it all and led us both in the obligatory prayer ritual and graciously accepted my, also obligatory, donation. We then returned to the lower courtyard where she offered us tea and we had a nice chat. Unusually there were no people around so it was quite peaceful except for the dull noise of construction now a little way away. I asked how she felt about her tiny, lonely, silent temple now transformed into such a huge project with so many visitors and she smiled and said she was happy to see all the changes and even more happy to be taken care of in her old age because life had previously been quite difficult. I then asked her if it would be possible to stay there for a few days but she said I would have to ask Master Dejian as she had no authority to make these kinds of decisions. She said Master Dejian was meditating at the moment but would come for his midday meal soon. She invited us to go and see what else had been built and to return in about half an hour when she would give us lunch and we could perhaps talk to Master Dejian.

We made our way through the small quarry where the rocks were being hewn by hand out of the mountainside and then broken up into smaller pieces ready to be used for building. Because I was with Ibo, Wu Nanfang's kungfu student, we could enter the other side of the monastery which was closed to the public. We had of course been there twice before – it was where Dejian and his kungfu students lived. Again I was amazed at the progress that had been made since I was there the previous year. Now in evidence was a large flat area (created obviously from where the rock had been quarried) which was being cultivated as a vegetable garden so that the monastery could be more self-sufficient in food. The small building which Master Wu Nanfang had told me the previous year was being prepared for people to stay and do meditation retreats seemed to be finished and I really hoped I could stay there, even for a few days.

Half an hour later we returned to the temple area and Yonglian appeared with some bowls of food for us before disappearing for her own meal.

After we had taken our empty bowls back to the kitchen we saw Master Dejian in the courtyard also looking at the view. We went up to him, bowed with our hands together – like the Indian 'namaste' greeting – and Ibo politely told him of my request to stay there, at least for one night. A short conversation ensued and I was surprised to see Ibo's face darken with anger at Dejian's answer. The latter then swept off without a glance in my direction and entered the dining quarters. Ibo swore (he has a good repertoire of English swear words) and without saying anything set off down the path to leave. Bewildered I ran after him and asked what the matter was. At first he didn't want to tell me but then he finally said that Dejian had said, very rudely, apparently, that this 'was not a place for tourists'. I was definitely quite surprised at this reply. A polite 'no' would have amply sufficed. Ibo then stopped and said that he wanted to go back and confront Dejian about his treatment of us but I caught him by the arm and said if we weren't wanted it was time to leave. We silently made our way down the path until we came to a seating place where I made Ibo sit down to talk things over. He was obviously angry and upset on my behalf and, although a bit upset myself, I hastened to reassure him that it was not his fault and that maybe today had not been a good day for Dejian. In fact, I told him, I had been quite shocked on the expression on Dejian's face when he turned around before seeing us. It was an expression of anguish and I had fleetingly wondered if he regretted turning this silent remote place into a tourist circus. Perhaps it was this which warranted his condemnation of me as an unwanted tourist.

There was obviously more to the story but I couldn't get Ibo to explain further, so we silently made our way down the mountain side.

I realised then that my dream of staying there would never materialise. It was sad, because SanHuangZhai had been the inspiration for me to come to China. Since that day, I have never been there again – not because I didn't want to but, as age has overtaken me, I am no longer physically able to climb such a steep path up the mountain side.

Conclusions

That evening, as a gesture to Ibo, who was still quite angry after our visit, I invited him and Micha and Ali to a meal. Because food at the kungfu school was rather boring, the guys were always happy to go out and be fed! We discussed the events of the day and I said I wasn't really bothered. This was just the way things were. By the end of the meal I was happy to see that Ibo's mood had lightened and he was back being his usual humorous self.

Early next morning I went for a last visit to my meditation spot. Meditation is the best way to clear one's mind and see things as they are, not as one expects or wants them to be. Into my consciousness floated the following words of Osho:

Truth is not something separate from you: you are truth. It is your very consciousness, the very ground of your being. You need not go anywhere else to seek and search, to Kashi or to Kaaba. Not even a single step is needed.

Lao Tzu says: You can find it sitting in your own house, no need to go anywhere – because it is already there! When you go on a search, when you move into seeking, you go farther away from it. Each search takes you away from the truth that is already there.

And there are moments when you feel it, that it has always been there – moments of joy, love, beauty. Moments when suddenly the world stops: a beautiful sunset ... and you are gripped by it. Remember I am saying you are gripped by it, possessed by it, not that you possess it. How can you possess a sunset? The sunset possesses you, fills you; every nook and corner of your being is overflowing with the beauty of it.

And then one knows, deep down in the depths of one's being, it has always been there. Not even the words are needed; one simply knows without words – one feels.

Or, when you are in love... or when you listen to beautiful poetry... or the songs of the birds... or just the wind blowing through the pine trees... or the sound of water.... Whenever you allow yourself to be possessed you will find, suddenly, out of nowhere, truth has appeared, God has appeared, dhamma has appeared. You have touched something intangible, you have seen something invisible. You have been in contact with something eternal – aes dhammo sanantano –

the eternal law, the inexhaustible law.

Whenever you are in a state of harmony, everything humming, functioning in harmony, whenever you are in accord…. And these moments happen to everybody. These moments have nothing to do with churches and the temples and the mosques. In fact, it is very rare to find a person becoming enlightened in a church or in a mosque, in a temple.

Buddha became enlightened under a tree, watching the last morning star disappearing in the sky; not in a temple, not in a church – under a tree, watching a star. Must have become possessed. And the disappearing star, slowly slowly disappearing – going, going, gone. One moment before it was there, and now it was no longer there. And in that moment, suddenly something in him, the last citadel of the ego, disappeared too. Just like the disappearing morning star, his ego disappeared too.

That moment Buddha became enlightened. That moment he came to know dhamma, the logos, the tao, God, the cosmic principle of life.

Mahavira became enlightened, not in a temple – not even in a Jaina temple! There were Jaina temples in Mahavira's time. Mahavira was the twenty-fourth tirthankara of the Jainas – the twenty-fourth great master. Twenty-three masters had preceded him. There were Jaina temples, but he didn't become enlightened in a Jaina temple – the Jainas should note the fact. He became enlightened in the forest. Just sitting there, doing nothing, and suddenly it came. It comes like a flood.

Mohammed became enlightened on a mountain. And so is the case with everybody: Lao Tzu, Zarathustra, Kabir, Nanak – not a single person has ever become enlightened in a temple, church or mosque. Why do you go there?

Go early in the morning to see the sunrise. Sit in the middle of the night watching the sky full of stars. Go, befriend trees and rocks. Go, lie down by the side of the river and listen to its sound. And you will be coming closer and closer to the real temple of God. Nature is his real temple. And there, be possessed – don't try to possess. The effort to possess is worldly; the desire to be possessed is divine.

And so my conclusion was that it was the mountain that was the reality for me. Joyfully possessed by it, I would choose it for my inspiration and meditation. Master Dejian could keep his temple! After all, it was the mountain's energy that had been attracting spiritual seekers for thousands of years – a recent temple couldn't compete! Sitting here, under the tree, next to the water hole in front of the mountain was all that was needed. I was content.

4
A Wild Joy

AnYangGong Temple

Celebrate aloneness,
celebrate your pure space,
and great song will arise in your heart.
And it will be a song of awareness,
it will be a song of meditation.
It will be a song of an alone bird calling in the distance –
not calling to somebody in particular,
but just calling because the heart is full and wants to call,
because the cloud is full and wants to rain,
because the flower is full and the petals open
and the fragrance is released...
unaddressed.

Osho: The Guest

A Bit of Ancient History

Having done some research on this small rural area of China that I have somehow found myself living in, it is perhaps a good idea at this point to give a brief history of the place to put things in context.

The Yellow River valley of China is generally known as 'the cradle of Chinese civilisation'. The Chinese, of course, know something of its history but westerners may have heard of Luoyang – one of the most popular early capital cities because of its strategic position near the Yellow River and now fairly well-known because of its proximity to the Longmen Caves carved out of cliffs on the edge of the Yi River in 386 to 534 AD. Even more well-known is Xi'an because of its association with the recently discovered 'Terracotta Army' created by the first Emperor of China, Qin Shi Huang, to guard him when he died in 210 BC. Xi'an was also the beginning and end of the famous Silk Road – 206 BC to 220 AD.

But whereas records of China's early secular history are as comprehensive as one might expect for times so long gone, records of its early spiritual heritage – Taoism, Confucianism and Buddhism – are more sparse. This is due probably to long periods of religious suppression by various rulers and dynasties and the wholesale destruction of many spiritual texts and records at various times in China's rather turbulent history.

I am not about to give any scholarly dissertation on China's spiritual heritage but for the purposes of this book, I would like to briefly piece together a little of what I have learned about the early spiritual history of this area of Henan Province, just to give a background to my story.

A good place to start would probably be the fact that, of the five sacred mountains in China, designated as such as early as 470 BC, Song Mountain is the central and most important. These five mountains have both Taoist and Buddhist associations although Huashan, not very far from Song Mountain and also fairly close to the area of the Yellow River valley we are concerned with, is mostly connected to Taoism.

Lao Tzu (Chinese: Laozi) is traditionally regarded as the founder of Taoism although this is disputed by historians who claim that he is only a legendary figure. He is said to have been born in a small town, now the modern Luyi, in the eastern part of Henan Province between the fifth and sixth century BC. He was a scholar who worked as the Keeper of the Archives for the royal court of Zhou during the time that Louyang was the capital city, and gathered many disciples around him. He is mostly known for the story of how, when he tried to depart for distant lands, probably the Himalayas, he was stopped by an official, Yin Xi, who was in charge of the border crossing near Lingboa which is on the Yellow River not far from Luoyang. He was coerced by Yin Xi into writing down his teachings which became the world-famous 'Tao Te Ching'. After that he 'escaped' and disappeared through the Huangu Pass into the west.

My fantasy is that Lao Tzu travelled from eastern Henan – maybe on an ox – through the Song Mountain Pass which I have previously mentioned, into the area around Luoyang on the Yellow River. Did he perhaps stop at the site of what is now known as Zhongyue Miao? This Taoist temple is said to be the oldest temple in China and was built in the third century BC. It was constructed on a sacred site previously used by local people to worship the god of Song Mountain. The Chinese give different names to their temples depending on their origin or function. Miao in Chinese refers to an ancient ancestral shrine. It is thought that there was a local shrine dating back to perhaps the seventh century BC – a long time before the temple was built. Lao Tzu might then have cause to stop there! On one of the signs in Zhongyue Maio there is a reference to Lao Tzu but the English is so obscure that I could not make any sense of it.

With the royal court of Zhou being based in Luoyang, LaoTzu would have had an easy journey to Lingboa and Huashan.

A little more factual information exists about Chuang Tzu (Chinese: Zhuangzi) who lived between 369-286 BC near the present town of Shangqiu, Henan Province, on the eastern side of Zhengzhou. He is frequently mentioned along with Lao Tzu as a defining figure in Chinese Taoism and in fact expounded in length on the 'Tao Te Ching'. His book, 'Zhuangzi', is one of the most important Chinese Taoist texts.

Confucius, a contemporary of Lao Tzu, did not live in this area, but in Shandong in eastern China between 551-499 BC. He is slightly connected to this story, however, because another of the famous temples in the area is The Songyang Academy. This was once one of the leading schools for training classical scholars in Imperial China and was built during the Northern Wei Dynasty (386-534 AD). Here Confucianism was intensely studied by graduates of the school who would serve in the emperor's government as civil service workers. The huge cypress trees in the academy's courtyard are regarded as the oldest in China and are thought to be between three and four thousand years old.

In the first century AD our story picks up speed and a few more facts are known although legend still plays a large part of the history of this time.

The origins of Buddhism in China appear to start with the advent of two monks or priests from India arriving in Luoyang in about 64 AD. The Han Emperor at that time was Mingdi and it is said that he had a vision of a shining, golden man in the west. It was suggested to him that he had seen an image of an Indian Buddha. Mingdi immediately organised an expedition to India to find out something about this Buddha. In northern Afghanistan (possibly Bamiyan where there was a large Buddhist settlement) his officials met two Indian monks who were, coincidentally, on their way to China and were carrying many precious Buddhist texts. The officials invited them to come to Luoyang and returned with them riding on white horses. As Xi'an was the beginning, or end, of the Silk Road and close to Luoyang, the international route would have been well-known and relatively easy for travellers at that time.

By 68 AD a temple, named The White Horse Temple, had been built to honour the two monks and it rapidly became a centre of learning where the Buddhist scriptures were translated into Chinese and where many people came to learn about this new religion.

But it seems there is a bit of rivalry here, because not far away, on Song Mountain itself, another temple lays claim to being the 'earliest' Buddhist temple. FaWang Temple was built on the slopes of Taoshi Mountain in, apparently, 71 AD which makes it three years younger than the White Horse Temple. It too welcomed two eminent Indian monks with the unlikely names of Fran and Nimoten to come and stay and translate their collection of Buddhist scriptures. I wonder a little at more Indian monks being able to find their way there at that time given that The White Horse Temple had only just been built to house the first two monks – seemingly the first Indian monks to arrive in China – brought by the Emperor Mingdi! I can find no explanation for FaWang Temple's claim and I do wish that the various Chinese tourist boards responsible for promoting these significant and beautiful places, could get their collective acts together and produce some information in intelligible English for the many foreign visitors coming to appreciate these sites.

For the next four hundred years not much of great import seemed to happen with Buddhism in my little Chinese neck of the woods, possibly because Taoism was still so important here. Or perhaps because the capital of China moved somewhere else. As much of the spiritual activity depended on the emperor's patronage, it follows that different areas would become more active wherever the current emperor reigned. During this time Buddhism flourished in, and spread to, other areas such as Wutai Shan (shan is the Chinese word for mountain), where many important Buddhist temples were built. Other prominent places were the other three sacred Buddhist Mountains: Emei Shan, Jiuhua Shan and Putuo Shan. The famous Emperor Wu – a great champion of Buddhism – had established his court in what is now known as Nanjing.

Towards the end of the fifth century one more Indian monk, Batuo, having no doubt travelled via the Silk Road route, arrived in Luoyang just as the capital was moved back there from Pincheng (later Datong) in Shanxi province by Emperor Xiaowen in about 494 AD. Xiaowen immediately decided to build a temple for Batou and a site on Song Mountain, in the foothills of Mount Shaoshi, was chosen. In 494 AD work on the construction of the Shaolin (little forest) Temple began. Batou was installed and industriously began translating more Buddhist scriptures. (It has been said that were it not for the hard work of these translators translating Buddhist scripts into Chinese, many, if not most, of the Buddhist scriptures would have been lost – because Buddhism didn't really take hold in India, perhaps because the existing Hinduism was too deeply ingrained in the Indian psyche, and it was certainly not revered as it was in the more eastern areas of Asia

But why did Buddhism become accepted so quickly and comprehensively in China? At the beginning of the first century AD there was not much of a spiritual atmosphere in the country. The time was ripe for Buddhism. Osho explains the situation with so much clarity and insight that I will use his words:

> *The situation was that China had lived under the influence of Confucius and was tired of it. Because Confucius is just a moralist, a puritan, he does not know anything about the inner mysteries of life. In fact, he denies that there is anything inner. Everything is outer; refine it, polish it, make it cultured, make it as beautiful as possible.*
>
> *There were people like Lao Tzu, Chuang Tzu, Lieh Tzu, contemporaries of Confucius, but they were mystics not masters. They could not create a counter movement against Confucius in the hearts of the Chinese people. So there was a vacuum. Nobody can live without a soul, and once you start thinking that there is no soul, your life starts losing all meaning. The soul is your very integrating concept; without it you are cut away from existence and eternal life. Just like a branch cut off from a tree is bound to die – it has lost the source of nourishment – the very idea that there is no soul inside you, no consciousness, cuts you away from existence. One starts shrinking, one starts feeling suffocated.*
>
> *But Confucius was a very great rationalist. These mystics, Lao Tzu, Chuang Tzu, Lieh Tzu, knew that what Confucius was doing was wrong, but they were not masters. They remained in their monasteries with their few disciples.*
>
> *When Buddhism reached China, it immediately entered into the very soul of the people – as if they had been thirsty for centuries, and Buddhism had come as a rain cloud. It quenched their thirst so immensely that something unimaginable happened.*
>
> (…)
>
> *The conversion that happened in China is the only religious conversion in the whole history of mankind.*

Buddhism simply explained itself, and the beauty of the message was understood by the people. They were thirsty for it; they were waiting for something like it. The whole country, which was the biggest country in the world, turned to Buddhism.

During the next four hundred years, Buddhism reigned in the hearts of the Chinese: from the ordinary people, to the monks and priests, to the emperors.

But then came Bodhidharma! He was to dramatically shake up the Buddhist and Taoist status quo and turn the current spiritual climate in that area in a whole new direction.

Bodhidharma was unconventional in every way. His master, Pragyatara, was unusually a woman and it was she who told Bodhidharma to go to China. According to Osho, she *'told him to go to China because the people who had reached there before him had made a great impact, although none of them were enlightened. They were great scholars, very disciplined people, very loving and peaceful and compassionate, but none of them were enlightened. And now China needed another Gautama Buddha. The ground was ready.'*

Few factual records of Bodhidharma and his presence in China exist and Andy Ferguson, in his book, 'Tracking Bodhidharma', has done a sterling job trying to piece together fragmentary bits of information to make some kind of consistent record. He is quick to point out, however, that even the basic dates of Bodhidharma's arrival in China and his life there cannot be unarguably substantiated. He, however, favours dates recorded by the Chinese monk and historian called Daoxuan who placed Bodhidharma's arrival in China in about 463 AD and his death in about 531 AD.

For me it is interesting that Daoxuan says something similar to Osho: in recording Bodhidharma's importance and impact in China, he says in his 'Further Biographies of Eminent Monks' that *'All who heard him became enlightened.'* The phenomenon of an enlightened master is so vast that it not only affects those people who come into physical contact with him while he is alive, but lasts for centuries. Buddha, Lao Tzu, Jesus Christ and Bodhidharma are but some of the most obvious. This dimension of an enlightened master was missing in the Buddhism prevailing in China at that time, hence Bodhidharma's arrival there.

As a result of his in-depth research, Andy Ferguson says that Bodhidharma sat in his cave in Song Mountain during the years 475 to 494 AD. He then moved to the Luoyang area for maybe three years and then up the Yang-tse River to somewhere near Nanjing which is where the historical meeting with Emperor Wu took place. Placing this meeting at this time, instead of the more commonly accepted instance of Bodhidharma's first arrival in China, also makes sense to me because during this period of perhaps fifteen years Bodhidharma would have learned Chinese and would have acquired an aura of authority and stature because of his enlightened Zen teachings, making him more likely to 'stand up to' and quite summarily dismiss one of the greatest emperors in early Chinese history.

But Bodhidharma is, of course, most famous for the nine years that he sat in his cave on Wuru Peak, just behind the Shaolin Temple. During those years he somehow fused the prevailing doctrines that the Chinese were following – Taoism, Buddhism and Confucianism – into a new spiritual heritage, Chan or Zen. He also assured the continuation of the lineage of this new heritage by accepting Huike as his disciple and transmitting his teachings to him. Huike was the man who supposedly cut off his arm to declare his devotion to Bodhidharma and his intent to become his disciple.

After spending years living around Nanjing and travelling a great deal, Bodhidharma is said to have returned to the Song

Mountain area and to have died near Luoyang and been buried at KongXiang Temple. There is, however, the story that, three months after he was buried, a disciple found him walking westwards wearing only one shoe. Hearing this report, his tomb was opened and it was found to be bare except for one shoe! Perhaps Bodhidharma had decided to follow Lao Tzu's footsteps into the Himalayas!

Return to the Mountain

In mid-September, 2010, I flew back to China. I had kept in touch with Yujie and Ibo during the four and a half months I was in England. Yujie had left the company she and Meilin had formed and had gone back to teaching English and Chinese, working for an agency in Beijing. Ibo was busy with an influx of foreign students coming to the kungfu school. Not only was the new website out there online but I made a blog about the school with many photographs, and a YouTube channel using some of the video clips that Panky had made. Interested western kungfu students had begun to take note of Wugulun Kungfu and had started to make their way to Dengfeng and Master Wu Nanfang's kungfu school.

The Qatar flight from London to Beijing was excellent. Beijing airport was as stunning as ever and a welcoming Yujie was there to pick me up. Beijing is now one big traffic jam but still I felt so excited and so much 'at home' that even the clogged roads and rain felt good. Yujie had booked me into my favourite little room with the view of the Hutong area at the youth hostel where I had stayed before. We had some tea together and then she left me to have a very much needed sleep.

The next day was a bit of a business day. First Yujie helped me buy a mobile phone, now a real essential in China. Then we had a fantastic Japanese meal – Beijing is one of the epicurean centres of the world – and then she took me to a shop where I could buy western cosmetics. For future trips this would save me from having to carry them with me as they weigh so much. Then we went to the Bank of China to change some travellers cheques and finally the essential quest: to buy some English books. In Dengfeng there is absolutely nothing in English and I did miss having something to read in the evenings. Yujie took me to the biggest book shop in Asia. Incredible! It was a whole city block – not just a building. And it was packed with people. Despite the prevalence of the internet in China, the Chinese obviously still like their books.

Yujie was working the next day but she got a friend to pick me up at the youth hostel and take me to the train station to catch the train to Zhengzhou. He successfully organised everything – a real feat in this huge busy station. For a foreigner it is pretty alarming if you cannot read the signs and don't know where you are going – and also if you are carrying the amount of luggage I was carrying.

Having successfully boarded the quite comfortable train, I got out my little cards of Chinese words and phrases that I had made to help myself learn some Chinese, and started to study a bit – at which point the very nice guy next to me got interested and started to help me. His English was very hesitant to start off with but as time progressed he got more and more confident so we had a really nice companionable connection. He was a vet and also a mountain climber and had climbed Song Mountain many times. When I phoned Ibo as we neared Zhengzhou, he suggested that he speak to my companion and together they arranged that he help me with my luggage and take me to where Ibo was waiting. I doubt if I would have got out at the right exit without his help.

It was great to see Ibo again, looking much healthier than

before. He took me to a very good small hotel near where he, Micha and Ali had rented a flat to operate their English school from. We all had dinner together.

The next morning Ibo and I caught the bus to Dengfeng. This time I almost didn't recognise the countryside. During summer the whole of China had had a lot of rain which caused some devastating flooding but which also caused the landscape to explode into a riot of lush greenery. The scenery looked almost like a tropical jungle. About eight years previously China had started a massive tree-planting program to try to restore some of the damage done by poor farming methods and a decimation of the flora of the land. It looked like those trees had grown at least five feet since I was here in the spring.

When I arrived in Dengfeng, the clearness of the air and the majesty of the mountains caused my heart to soar in joy, a kind of wild joy! I was back in the place I loved more than any other place on earth.

* * *

Wenju, Master Wu Nanfang's son, met us at the bus station with the car and we decided to first go to the flat which Ibo had found and thought might be a good place for me to stay. It was in that 'concrete village' where I had lived previously and which I found rather barren so I wasn't too happy about it. I so much wanted to live closer to the mountain, preferably on it. We met the very charming landlady and she took us upstairs. Immediate change of heart! The place was absolutely beautiful. It was spacious, all white and clean and exquisitely designed, and, very important, had a nice bathroom with a western toilet, a shower – and heating lights in the ceiling. Not only was this the most beautiful place I had stayed in in China it was one of the most beautiful places I have ever stayed in in my life! And from the bedroom I could see the mountain – a bit blocked by buildings but still its presence loomed with silent power and joy.

In many families in China the son is expected to bring his bride to live with the family whereas the daughter goes to live with her husband's family. This flat had been especially designed for the son of the Shang family to live in but it seemed that he had other ideas and was not living at home. It was my good fortune that it was currently vacant; it had, in fact, never been lived in. Mrs Shang was very gracious and quoted me a price which, I later learned, was quite expensive in Chinese terms, but for me, used to English rental prices, ridiculously cheap. So the deal was struck with enthusiasm on both sides and I now had a very lovely home in China.

Master Wu Nanfang had apparently invited me to dinner so Wenju took us back to the school with its million dollar view of the mountain behind which the sun was just setting in a glory of pink and orange. I could not have imagined a better home coming.

I awoke very early the next morning and from my bed I was thrilled to see the mountain glowing pink in the sunrise. This would be my view each time I woke up – what could be better. The energy of this house was light and bright and quiet and somehow I knew that this time in China was going to be good.

But a lot needed to be done so I got up quickly, wrote a list of things that I needed and was soon on an early bus into Dengfeng. On the way, though, I had quite a panicky moment when I suddenly couldn't recognise where I was. It all looked so different. Had I caught a wrong bus? I then smiled to myself when I realised, when finally coming to a crossing that I knew, that the verdant greenery was so abundant that it hid the known landmarks. The previous times that I had been here were in late winter and early spring when it was cold and quite bleak and barren.

The day was spent getting my accommodation needs in order

and by evening everything was organised thanks once more to the incomparable Lui. Having a mobile phone made functioning here so much easier. I had called Ibo to ask him if he could contact Liu to pick me up at the big downtown supermarket. Within ten minutes Liu had arrived and I confess I had tears in my eyes when I greeted him. Such a beautiful person....

'Season of mists and mellow fruitfulness....'

Of all the times I had been here, this was the best. Keats's words kept surfacing in my mind because this time could really be described as 'mellow'– interspersed with a sometimes silent, sometimes wild joy.

Each morning, as I opened my eyes, the mountain was there to greet me. On some mornings it was clear and glowed pink in the sunrise; at other times it was shrouded in mists. As I sipped my morning tea I felt suffused with a well-being I had only before experienced when sitting at the feet of my Master.

In contrast to the bitter cold and searing heat that had been a feature of my spring visits, the temperature now was temperate and benign, perfect for relaxing and sitting silently in contentment. Although, to be honest, my initial attempts to visit my magic meditation spot resulted in a hasty retreat as the delighted midges descended on me for breakfast. But I found that simply sitting on my bed looking at the mountain, delicately tinged with the pink light of dawn, was equally magical. Meditation came easily and naturally. And the comfort and beauty of my lovely flat no doubt aided the process. The simplicity of it soothed my heart with its serenity and peace.

* * *

Here in this little rural area of China, people are still intimately connected to the earth and the seasons and I was happy to be drawn into their harmonious and rhythmical connections with nature; the Chinese season of 'mists and mellow fruitfulness' was a true delight for me. The first few days of roaming around revealed scenes of green with just a peep here and there of golden colour as a corn cob emerged through the leaves and apples swayed gently in the breeze. Tomatoes on shoulder-high trellises shone red, and orange pumpkins littered the fields in profusion.

And then suddenly everything changed! It seemed that each time I blinked or turned around something else had happened. Within a few days the fields morphed from lush green corn plants to bare soil already ploughed in lines for the next sowing. The corn cobs were collected and quickly the front gardens of each house, and the communal grounds in the village, turned gold as the cobs were laid out to dry in the autumn sun. I had to pick my way to the door of my house through a carpet of corn.

All day people turned the cobs so they got their full measure of sunlight -- and then, again suddenly, the neighbourhood resounded with grinding noises, from early morning until late at night, as small, one-man-operated machines did the rounds from house to house to grind the kernels off the cobs. So now there was a sea of corn kernels everywhere. Each house seemed to have its own supply of corn and nobody stole from anyone else. Amazing.

In addition to the corn, my landlady had a small cotton field in front of her house and she and her mother began harvesting the cotton, so in front of our house there appeared white fluffy clouds of cotton interspersed with the golden corn lain out to dry in the sun. The cotton was used as padding in hand-made quilts, a little village industry that occupied the long winter days.

I learned that most of the houses in the village had fields in the surrounding area in which food was grown. It seemed to be instinctive for people to cultivate any small patch of available ground for food. Again I think that the horrors of the not-so-distant past were deeply ingrained in the people, especially the older ones, and filled them with an urge to grow food so that they would never again suffer the terrible starvation of that time.

In front of the kungfu school there were large fields run by some kind of communal co-operative. It was here that the changes took place with bewildering speed. From one day to the next, the corn cobs were harvested by a small band of farmers, the corn plants were then pulled out and slung aside for small vehicles to pick up, and within two days the fields were bare and being ploughed in straight lines for the next sowing. The ploughing here was done by men pushing small mechanised ploughing machines – no tractors like we have in the west. Each man had his patch of soil to plough and, working in a paced harmony, they managed to plough all the fields, as far as I could see, in one day!

I did notice, though, that in one or two small private fields, the ploughing was done in the more traditional way: by oxen pulling a wooden plough guided by the farmer.

This way of life, so close to nature, was deeply nourishing and in a few days I moved from exhaustion to exhilaration. As mankind the world over is reduced to a computerised, technological existence, lacking any personal contact with nature, how can it continue to function with any health or grace? I remember watching one of Brian Cox's TV programs on the wonders of the universe when something he said brought dread to my heart. He said, 'If children never see the stars in the sky, how can they know where they come from or who they are?'

The moon waxed fuller and fuller as the fields turned from green and gold to brown and then, on the night of the full moon, the whole community turned out to celebrate the autumn festival, known all over China as 'Mooncake Night'. Candles shone in windows, people dressed in their party best and everybody visited neighbours or socialised on street corners (no drunken behaviour to spoil the pleasures) eating special cakes and apples and pomegranates. I spent the evening at the school and the kungfu kids ran round and round outside in excitement and I blissed out on their energy and the sight of the mountains drenched in moonlight.

* * *

The days now settled into a simple, mellow routine. As is often the case, the full moon brought a change in the weather and soon there was that slight chill in the air that heralded the deepening of autumn as it progressed into early winter.

The midges had now vacated my meditation spot so each day I made my way there to sit in silence with the mountain. The previous time I was in ShiLiPu, I had bought a bicycle which I had left for the kungfu kids to play with. I now reclaimed my vehicle and rode to the meditation spot, although on the way back, I had to mostly push the bicycle as the road was a bit uphill. I would then stop at the sesame-bun place to buy a hot bun for my breakfast and was interested to see these local small entrepreneurs developing their little business venture into something bigger and bigger.

They had a perfect site at the bus stop which was actually the last stop, a depot, so the buses and their drivers waited there awhile, as did their passengers. It was natural to buy a bun as a snack. My sesame-bun couple had started off with just their small barrow, keeping their supply of flour, oil and sesame seeds in a small cupboard which was part of the bus depot. But each time I returned they had enlarged their premises and had now built a small building to house their cooking facilities. They had strung up a piece of black plastic to give shade and keep off the rain and had added chairs for their customers to sit on. To complete this stage of their enterprise they had bought an icebox in which they stocked cold drinks. They always greeted me with beaming smiles and this time introduced me to their pregnant daughter who was helping them with the business. Fortunately my few words of Chinese enabled me to grasp some relevant bits of information.

On the way back to my house I usually stopped to pick up other supplies or charge my phone at the local convenience store. The proprietor, Mr Chao Feng Lee, was a good friend. In his shop he stocked many items needed for daily life and so I could buy many small things from him. He was also one of those Chinese who didn't panic when I tried to ask something – he would patiently try to interpret my hesitant Chinese and miming gestures and was good at guessing most of the things I needed. From him I bought wonderful free range eggs from a place I had visited across the valley near the open air mountain theatre. Here the chickens ran around happily scratching for insects in the ground. From him I also bought tofu, and local vegetables when he had them. Although he went to a market in Dengfeng very early in the morning, he also stocked vegetables grown by the local villagers which they brought in in little plastic bags. This meant that much of the produce I ate was home-grown and freshly picked that morning. I loved being so closely in contact with the sources of my food and I am sure that this is one of the reasons I got so healthy when I was in China.

Milk was the exception as it was not naturally part of the traditional Chinese diet. After asking Chao Feng a few times for one of the little cartons of milk for my tea, he one day produced a whole box of the cartons and somehow got across his idea that I should just buy the whole box and take it home, then I wouldn't run out too often! Brilliant. I was touched at his thoughtfulness and initiative. The box would have been too heavy for me to carry home from town but he could bring it for me in his van. (Milk in China is all UHT milk because most of the milk comes from Inner Mongolia.

I have never seen fresh milk as cows are not in great abundance – in my area, anyway.)

After a very late breakfast I would always have to do some cleaning because there was a lot of grimy dust around – borne in on winds passing over the coalfields to the south of the area. Then it would be almost time for a siesta, which was anyway a common practice in the village. They got up so early that they all had a quiet break in the middle of the day. In the late afternoons I usually went to the school and had an evening meal there. There was always a lot to talk about with Ibo and whatever western kungfu students were there. I could also practise my Chinese with the Chinese students and help them with their basic attempts at English. Ibo's health was much better which made me very happy.

Master Wu Nanfang was his charming open-hearted self. Everyone seemed to be happy and flourishing and there were more students, both western and Chinese. I liked to think that maybe Panky and I had helped with our publicity efforts. For the first time there were girls here, three of them. I loved watching them running around in their bright blue, red and yellow satin kung fu clothes. The boys only wore a drab grey.

One day Master Wu Nanfang presented me with a soya-milk-making machine! I had said once that I drank soya milk everyday in England so he decided to give me a machine to make it while I was here. He proceeded to show me how to use it – watched by the two little kungfu kids, Rouyi and Tian De, who stuck their little noses into everything. To be honest, I didn't use the machine after a few tries. Much too complicated and time-consuming – and cleaning it was a pain!

One small incident slightly upset the mellow routine. I was bitten by a rather nasty neighbourhood dog who seemed to sense that I was not a Chinese person and was therefore a threat to local security! So I had to go to a clinic in Dengfeng every three or four days to get an anti-rabies shot – at least I presumed that is what it was. That kind of explanation was a bit beyond the English skills that Lijuan had. She took me to the clinic the first time but I went myself for the follow-up injections. No problem at all. There was a very cheerful and competent nurse who actually seemed to relish the challenge of dealing with a westerner. I think I made her day!

As the autumn days slipped by I felt myself going deeper and deeper into meditation and, amidst the silence, often felt a song in my heart which I interpreted as being back on my path and in touch with my Master.

A Visit to the White Horse Temple

This temple holds a very special place in the hearts of Buddhists in China because, as I mentioned earlier in this section, it was here that the first monks from India – riding on white horses – arrived, bringing with them precious Buddhist scriptures. It is thus the first Buddhist temple in China.

As Ibo was having a few days off in a lull between foreign students arriving and leaving, he asked me if I wanted to go there because it is an easy bus ride from Dengfeng. I said yes, of course! But then plans changed because Master Wu Nanfang said he wanted to go the following Friday as it was a special festival day in the temple and he wanted to 'pay his respects'. So suddenly we were going by car with his daughter, Lijuan, and two young Chinese women who were staying at the school for a short time to do kungfu. It transpired that Master Wu Nanfang wanted Ibo to stay behind to work on the Chinese part of the website and that the tour guide honour was to be given to one of the young women who was studying to be an English translator.

She could have benefited greatly from observing Ibo in action because, despite her university studies, she didn't have a clue about dealing with Westerners, or how to translate unobtrusively. To this day I have only a hazy idea about what I was looking at, which is annoying as the temple was an important place for me to observe and understand. My translator had no Buddhist background so could not speak knowledgeably about the place and she pestered me with questions about my life etc. She was also very neurotic and kept on dragging me off whenever I wanted to look at something and take photos. This rather spoiled my enjoyment of this important temple.

Wherever we went, Master Wu Nanfang always 'knew' someone so we waited at the gates until a monk came and greeted us at the entrance to the temple. He took us through a back way past a pond (which looked more like a swimming pool) filled with the inevitable carp and some turtles. Later I learned that it was a custom for temples to have this kind of big pond to release turtles and fish rescued from the markets! Before entering the temple itself, one had to light some incense and make some prayerful bows in front of some beautiful large incense holders made of metal and filled with fine sand. Once inside, I managed to get a few very good shots of the day's special ceremony with my dear tour guide simultaneously telling me it was irreverent to take photos – despite the three hundred or more Chinese doing exactly that – and tugging at my sleeve in panic because Master Wu Nanfang had gone on ahead.

I had realised by now that most Buddhist temples had a similar lay-out and, to be perfectly honest, this got a bit boring after a while. This temple did, however, have a variation on the usual theme in that there were statues of white horses everywhere. Of course everyone had to have their photo taken with one of them and I took some classic ones of Lijuan who is generally very shy and unwilling to be photographed. But she seemed to like hanging onto the horse's head so I managed to get her to pose – and she looked gorgeous. The strict diet that the family and the kungfu students all follow means that many of them, although not all, have incredibly beautiful, flawless skin. Lijuan's skin is particularly beautiful.

One or two facts that I managed to pick up from various signs – when left alone long enough to be able to read them! – was that there was a surprising amount of travelling going on two thousand or so years ago. Of course there were the monks coming from India but there were also monks travelling from Japan. I found a statue of an imposing Japanese gentleman who had come here to study Buddhism and who had apparently become a very revered monk at this temple. Again I would have liked to know more and wished that Ibo had been there to give me more details.

Because of its Buddhist origins, the White Horse Temple is well-known for its international connections. On one side of the main temple compound there were two other Buddhist temples, each a 'gift' from their respective countries. One is a Thai temple but it was undergoing some reconstruction so we couldn't enter. The second temple, a gift from India, was completed in 2007, but it had none of the grace and exquisite craftsmanship which the Chinese temples usually have

So far the temple had been a bit of a disappointment, rather bland and boring, with the added irritant of the twittering translator – but then things changed. It was past one o'clock and I had been up since 5.30am, had had no breakfast and had forgotten to bring some water with me so I was wilting in the heat and wasn't too enthusiastic when Master Wu Nanfang appeared and announced we were going to see something else. We followed him to the other side of the main temple compound and over a bridge over a road –

into a fresh, green-tinted silence with magical vistas. I abruptly revived.

The feeling around this place was completely different from the main, tourist-ridden temple. Here all was silence and peace. As I was unable to decipher the sparse explanations given, I decided to just relax and feel the atmosphere and not be concerned with facts about what I was looking at. It was only when I got back home and got Ibo to give me some information that I learned that this was a 'private' temple for the monks and scholars that had lived at the temple for centuries, to meditate and study in. It was not a place where the public were admitted so the energy had remained undisturbed.

It was always great to go somewhere with Master Wu Nanfang because he knew so much that one always got glimpses of the unusual and unknown when one was with him. He took us further to a pagoda that was covered in scaffolding and he did a lot more of the burning of incense and the deep bowing. Here I felt a really unworldly silence and a kind of 'treading on holy ground' but as again no explanation materialised, I was quite mystified and could again only feel.

Later Ibo told me that this was the most important place, a kind of sanctuary, in the whole temple compound, where relics of enlightened people are buried at the base of the pagoda. The most famous relic, the one responsible for Master Wu Nanfang's deep bows and incense-burning, is a piece of bone from the body of Shakyamuni. Shakyamuni is one of the names the Chinese give to Buddha. So a relic of Buddha was supposedly buried at the base of this incredible pagoda. I am a bit sceptical about buried relics but not at all about the intense silence of this place. Thousands of monks meditating here over centuries had created an extraordinary atmosphere whether bits of bone were there or not. I would have loved to soak up more of this very special

155

energy but little hands tugged at my sleeve and I was carted off elsewhere.

Although the main temple had not interested me much, the private monastery was very special – but it paled to insignificance in comparison to the place I visited the following day when Ibo took me into an almost secret valley in my beloved Song Mountain to visit an old, poor, rather dilapidated nunnery.

A Taoist Valley Temple

It seemed that the more one got to know this area, the more there was still to know. I had heard of a small temple up one of the valleys between the mountain peaks that we could see from the school, but had never managed to get there. Ibo was annoyed that he had been denied the visit to the White Horse Temple so the following morning, a particularly beautiful one, he decided to play truant and suggested we go to this temple up in the valley. It was a bit of a walk so we decided to get a ride part of the way there because for sure someone on the road would stop as soon as they saw us. As cars were now becoming more and more prevalent, the locals were keen to earn spare cash by playing at being unofficial taxis. Within minutes a young man stopped, a fare was negotiated and off we went.

Our driver dropped us off just past the huge theatre complex where the spectacular open-air musical show, which I have mentioned before, was held each evening. We walked up a dirt track behind the complex, deeper and deeper into the valley which narrowed as we progressed. Soon it became almost a tunnel amidst tall trees, some deciduous but mostly pines, and thick shrubbery. Then suddenly we came upon a clearing on the side of which was a small stone temple – and equally suddenly I felt bathed in a cool, liquid energy which immediately took me back to the days when I lived in Osho's house in India. I felt myself becoming transparent and could barely move. Ibo said, 'Do you feel this energy? I want to sit and meditate.' We walked past the temple and a little further we found a tumbling stream with crystal clear water and some convenient rocks where we sat down and floated into a blissful silence, dimly aware only of the sound of running water and a few soft breezes in the trees.

When I finally surfaced I felt like I was hardly a body and when I looked at Ibo he slowly shook his head and whispered, 'What was that? I have never felt this way here before.'

We sat a while longer absorbing the magical quality of this primordial space and place and the words of the poet, Ikkyu, drifted through my mind: *'I can see clouds a thousand miles away. Hear ancient music in the pines.'*

We then decided to visit the small temple and climbed up the inevitable steps to a building so charming in its neglect that I had to smile. The steps up were new and ugly concrete but the entrance was of old crumbling stone and, entering the old gateway, the first thing we saw was a little pagoda with grass and plants growing out of its decrepit roof. There was nothing much else there except for some stone buildings surrounding the courtyard. Nobody appeared to be there but eventually an old lady emerged to greet us and then guided us into a small cave temple to worship at a dusty little altar hung about with threadbare, faded banners. On either side of us the cliffs rose high and sheer, and I felt like I was being cradled gently, embraced even, by the energy of the mountain.

I asked Ibo about the place and he told me that it was a nunnery called AnYangGong ('an' is the Chinese word for a very small nunnery) run by local village women who were dependent on the offerings (such as we had just made) of passing visitors to take care of the place. As it was far off the beaten track not many people came there. The temple apparently belonged to the government but as it was not an obvious source of revenue – like the Shaolin Temple – no attempt was made to take care of it and it was left to dedicated village volunteers to do what they could to maintain it. I was saddened at the hypocrisy of government and tourist boards because this place, and others I was yet to discover, were treasures and should be preserved.

I suggested to Ibo that maybe I could stay here for a few days instead of SanHuangZhai. My payments might be useful. He replied that, after the meditative experience he had just had, he would like to stay here for a few days too but we would have to move slowly as the local people might be a bit uncertain about a strange westerner. My personal 'ideas machine' then came up with a strategy to try to engage their trust: I should make a few more quiet visits over the next few weeks thereby slowly and gently letting them know who I was. Once they were familiar with me we could ask them about staying.

Then existence played into our hands when one sprightly old woman appeared and wanted her photo taken, warning us, however, that everybody always said they would come back with the photos but never did. Ibo assured her that we would bring her the photos and I took many of her because she was simply unique! And she of course provided me with a good excuse to visit again.

The next day I went into town and got the photos printed. I had to wait for Ibo to return from Zhengzhou where he was still running his English language school with Micha and Alia, but when he came back we again went up to the temple.

Again we sat on the rocks by the stream and meditated. The energy there was stronger than before and I had the same feeling of dissolving into nothingness, just floating on air.

Finally we made it into the temple. The old woman was delighted with the photographs and she took us inside the living area to meet two other women and offered us the boiled water from the stream to drink. We couldn't stay long this time as Ibo had to go somewhere but he was pleased that the 'getting to know Veena' strategy was working out well!

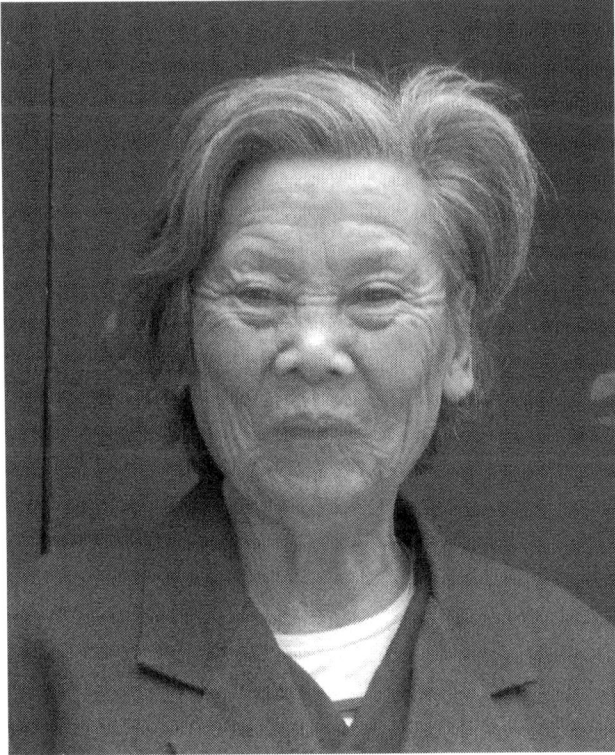

Old lady in AnYangGong

I decided that I would like to spend some time in the valley alone. As it was now autumn, leaves were taking on the expected vibrant orange and red hues and I wanted to try and capture a visual image of this so special place. There was no way I was going to flag down a local for a lift so I decided to try using my bicycle. It would mean pushing it uphill for the three miles there but at least I could freewheel all the way back home again!

I was pretty puffed by the time I arrived and my rather exhausted state engaged the attention of a visitor who had just arrived on his bike. He was an old guy, seventy-two years old, who spoke perfect English! Very surprising as the older Chinese people generally have no English at all. He told me he had been an English teacher in the local high school and had tried to hold on to his English skills even though he was long retired. Naturally he wanted to practise and so bombarded me with questions. I was so touched by his obvious delight at meeting me and being able to talk that I decided to abandon my meditation plans for the day and go along with his obvious enthusiasm. This took another interesting turn when he told me he was here to meet a man who was living in the monastery. (I thought it was a nunnery!) It all turned out to be a grand social occasion and I was given a very good lunch made by my wonderful old lady friend who I had photographed. Other ladies joined us, now getting more and more familiar with me and more interested because they could have some slight communication with me through my elderly but very much on-the-ball translator. They all knew Master Wu Nanfang and as I appeared to be associated with him in some way, they were even more relaxed and open.

After lunch I said my goodbyes and wandered off further up the valley to take some photographs of the place we had meditated in. As the valley is narrow with steep sides, the sun doesn't reach there often but at that time of the day the sun briefly peeped into the valley and illuminated the colourful autumn leaves giving me some great shots.

And the free-wheeling cycle trip home was exhilarating!

A few days after this experience, Master Wu Nanfang decided to oblige us with some old-fashioned story-telling. I so wished I could speak more with him because he knew the area so well and I would have loved to know more about it. But both his time and Ibo's was limited so it was a rare occasion when he relaxed and just chatted. That morning, in the hour after the early morning training session and breakfast, when the students were doing household chores, he brought a chair out in front of the school and Ibo and I joined him to sit and bask in the mild autumn sun. Everybody was in a cheerful mood brought on in part by the glorious day, and the boys sat around chatting or washing their clothes. Slowly they abandoned their activities and came closer to sit around us and listen to the master's stories.

About AnYangGong the master had the following story to tell. Towards the end of the 1800's, a doctor had a small house in that valley, more or less exactly where we had sat and meditated, and he soon grew to be very famous in the area as his skills were so great that just about everybody who came to him was healed. (I had the brief thought that his healing powers were helped by the energy field of that place!) Soon somebody decided to build a small temple in his honour, so painstakingly the local villagers began the task of cutting special stone in the area near the lake and carrying the rocks up into the valley to build the temple. The doctor had a cow, and so special was this animal that she decided to help with the building process because she could carry more rocks than an individual person. So for many months the cow joined the villagers – going with them down to the lake where they loaded some rocks onto her back and then walking back up with them as they climbed the foothills into the valley. And so the small temple was built. When the cow eventually died, the villagers buried her with great reverence and her grave is still marked with a headstone carved in her honour.

What intrigued me was Master Wu Nanfang's explanation of the dedication of the temple. Although it was built to honour the doctor, it was dedicated to the first woman on the earth who became a goddess. This was pure Taoism. I repeat Lao Tzu's words from the 'Tao Te Ching':

> *The valley spirit undying*
> *Is called the Mystic Female.*
> *The gate of the Mystic Female*
> *Is called the root of Heaven and Earth.*
> *It flows continuously, barely perceptible.*
> *Utilize it; it is never exhausted.*

Apparently the nine small statues in the first cave temple we had seen were enlightened women cherished by local Taoists. The statues in the second cave were local doctors revered for their skills in healing people.

Certainly I was deeply enraptured by this place and visited it many times during that and subsequent visits to the mountain. I never did stay there, however, because it would have been too much to organise and the primitive accommodation would have been too much for my ageing body to cope with. But every time I visit Song Mountain, AnYangGong is one of the very first places I visit.

Kungfu Kids

Each time I walked or cycled to the mountain to meditate, I had to pass the kungfu school so it was inevitable that my ties with the master and students would grow stronger. Ibo, Micha and

Ali were starting to look at a new plan for bringing more students to the school the following summer: a series of courses for foreign students to attend rather than people just randomly arriving at any time, which put quite a strain on everyone running the school. Having done a fair amount of this kind of thing in the past, I was able to help with a few bits of advice.

On a number of occasions I was also called upon to do a bit of PR work. For example, Ibo called me early one morning to say somebody from the government was coming and could I come to the school. Wenju would come in the car to pick me up. A westerner gave status to the school and I willingly put in an appearance as it was a little something I could do in return for the many kindnesses I was showered with daily. A fairly high-level official from the Dengfeng City Council had arrived, bringing with him a young graduate student who was from the apparently very prestigious Beijing Sports University and was doing a thesis on TaiChi and kungfu. He had seen this Wugulun Kungfu on the internet and wanted to interview Master Wu Nanfang about it.

On another occasion I was called to meet an extremely interesting youngish couple who had brought their little son to do some kungfu during his holidays. This couple were well-educated and, as far as I understood, had had rather prestigious positions in the local provincial government but had got so completely disillusioned with the politics involved that they dropped out and took religious orders. Ibo thought I could relate to their story – which of course I could – and, in addition, the woman spoke some English so she was excited to try her skills with a real foreigner. They stayed for about a week and we had many sweet and gentle times together.

Then there was the very important meeting with Andy, a good friend of Ibo's. Andy was a young businessman from Guangzhou in southern China but he had somehow found out about the kungfu school and came to visit because he was interested particularly in the health and medicine side of things. Andy had a degree in Business Studies from a university in Hamilton, Ontario, Canada, and had lived and worked in Toronto for a few years afterwards. He thus spoke very good English and was delighted to have the chance to recall his skills by speaking to me. Later on he was one of the people who helped me so many times when translations and other aids were very much needed.

* * *

Rouyi, the youngest of the kungfu kids, was training hard for an upcoming kungfu event but my other young friend, little eight-year-old Tian De, was moving in a different direction. By chance I found him one day drawing something with a pencil on a scrappy little piece of paper and I was amazed at his artistic skill. When next in town I bought him a drawing book and lots of crayons and coloured pencils. I don't think he had ever had the chance to use good art materials and what he produced was quite unbelievable. Ibo had also picked up on his skills and had a few days previously bought him a manual with instructions on how to make origami-like paper objects. Tian De had an amazing dexterity and control of his little fingers and was making really advanced paper sculptures. Having observed this further skill of his, I tried, when I went again into town, to find some more appropriate paper for him to use, preferably in bright colours. I could not get across to the young shop assistants in the local stationery/art shop to understand what I wanted so eventually I phoned Yujie in Beijing and got her to talk to the shop assistant and explain what I was looking for. It took a while but finally the coloured paper of the right thickness was produced. Tian De was ecstatic and, I am afraid, neglected his kungfu practice in favour of his creative endeavours, much to

Master Wu Nanfang's disapproval! For him kungfu was paramount!

I took a series of photos showing not only Tian De at work, but the relaxed evening scene: Master Wu Nanfang was in the background reading the newspaper, other kids were playing on the computer or sitting around chatting while Ibo came to Tian De's rescue because he couldn't quite put together the final pieces of the elaborate paper star he was trying to make. I also showed Tian De how to make a kind of snowflake paper cut-out and his second try was extraordinary – far more elaborate than anything I have ever made. I told the master that Tian De should be in an art school not a kungfu school. Needless to say that didn't go down too well at all.

I had noticed that something special was afoot because there was a lot of different kungfu training going on. I eventually found out that many students, including Rouyi and Micha, were practising for a special event which was soon to take place in a town called Yanshi, between Dengfeng and Luoyang. I gathered that, rather than being the usual competitive tournament, it was an all-day event during which local kungfu and TaiChi students demonstrated special skills. I was glad to hear that I was cordially invited to attend.

The day before the event, two Scottish guys showed up having seen the school mentioned on Micha's page on a website called 'Couch Surfing'. I had never heard of this but apparently this was a kind of social media site to facilitate budget travelling all over the world. People can connect with each other when travelling and stay with each other in family houses instead of going to a hotel. Cheap, and one gets to meet the locals which is much more personal than staying in a sterile hotel. One of the guys, Gary, was a professional photographer and he and his friend decided to come to the event as a chance to see some local colour. With Micha and Rhett, a Swedish kungfu student currently at the school, we were five westerners and even got an honourable mention and welcome when the proceedings opened.

For me the endless kungfu events were a bit boring but the high point was definitely Rouyi's 'performance'. Not only is he a gorgeous-looking little kid, but, at six years old, he is quite extraordinarily good at kungfu. This was his first performance in front of a large crowd and he was superb! Totally cool. No nerves, no mistakes. Quite unbelievable. Master Wu Nanfang said he thought he would be okay but never expected him to do as well as he did.

Gary and his friend were touring obscure parts of Asia and I reflected on how young people today, looking for something unusual, have to travel much further afield and push back the frontiers much more than I did when I started on my travels back in the beginning of the 1970's when even places like the then Yugoslavia were exotic unknowns.

* * *

Another significant event during this time was Master Wu Nanfang's search for a new place for his school. Despite the stunning views of the current site, the building was not at all fit for purpose: it was crowded, bitterly cold in winter and hot in summer, there was no place for students to eat and the training ground became a muddy pond whenever it rained (which was often) thus seriously interrupting daily training. The noise from the increased traffic on the highway was also annoying and not good for the silent meditative type of kungfu that was practised here. I had pronounced rather loudly that if more westerners were to come as a result of Panky's and my PR efforts, the facilities had to be upgraded! Quite a few western students had come and gone because they could not cope with the very primitive conditions.

This was a shame for everyone. Of course luxury was not the issue but having a shower and a halfway decent toilet was!

Ibo told me one day that the following morning the master was going to look at a possible place for a new school and had requested my presence to give my input on its suitability. The place wasn't far – we could see it from the school – and the master thought it had considerable potential.

The following morning Wenju took us in the van to the place. At first I was a little shocked because the building was just a shell of brick walls filled with farming rubbish but the site was stunning and very soon, as Master Wu Nanfang explained his ideas about it, I could see that its potential was huge. The rough structure was built around a large courtyard which would provide ample space for training and also space for growing vegetables. All the people in the area were farmers, including the master, and he was keen for the students to be involved in growing their own organic food. There was plenty of space for accommodation, food preparation and eating and for the small school which Lijuan ran. Also a guestroom! It was much closer to the mountain than the current school and totally silent. I was very enthusiastic.

The place was owned by a local and the rent was cheap, but all the building work would have to be done by the school, apparently a fairly normal procedure here. But in the end, just as a contract was to be signed, the deal fell through for no apparent reason. Master Wu Nanfang was pretty devastated and I asked Ibo repeatedly for an explanation for why things had come to such a sudden stop. It seemed even he didn't know.

Only two years later did I find out that the reasons for the sudden halt were due to a new and devastating development which was planned for this beautiful area. At that time nobody knew anything of these arrangements but the consequences were tragically obvious when I returned in 2012.

An Enlightened Great-Grandmother

One Saturday Ibo didn't go to teach in Zhengzhou because it was a public holiday so his language school was closed. He told me that he would like to go and visit another small temple in the mountains which a very special place for him. When I asked why, he told me he would tell me on the way there. I had to be content with that. He also said that he planned to take Rouyi and Tian De with us because they didn't have much chance of having outings as they were too young to go into town by themselves. I was delighted at the idea because they were so much fun when they played together. I offered to make a picnic lunch for all of us – the kids also didn't get many treats – so I dashed into town and bought a whole lot of goodies to supplement the sesame buns which would of course be the staple ingredient of our feast.

I had now learned another important Chinese word – zuba! – which means 'let's go!' so the next morning I took the little boys by the hand saying zuba! and we followed Ibo, carrying the picnic in his backpack, onto the main road. At the sight of me a local car screeched to a halt within seconds and the driver was happy to negotiate a fee to drive us to the mountain temple. It was much further away than AnYangGong and presented me with views of the mountain that I had never seen before. Turning off the main road we had to drive some distance along a small, potholed, single-lane road until we arrived at a ramshackle ticket office where an old man took our money after waiving fees for the kids. The driver was by now rather intrigued by us – he and Ibo had chatted unceasingly in the front of the car on our way there – and decided to visit the temple with us.

Ibo warned me that it would be a long walk but I didn't mind at all because I was really interested in his story. So he became a story teller as the kids played around us, relishing a change of scenery with small paths to explore and rocks on which they could climb to practise their kungfu moves. They were definitely showing off for our driver who, however, entered into the spirit of things and did some kungfu moves in response. All the men in Dengfeng know some kungfu moves! It was great for the kids to have somebody new to play with.

The temple is called the LianHua Temple – lotus flower temple – because it is in the centre of a circle of mountain peaks arising all around it. The peaks are the petals and the temple is the centre of the lotus flower. I later found the temple on Google Maps and whereas from the ground you couldn't see the circle of mountains and the central position of the temple, it is very clear from the air. The name is an apt one.

It is quite isolated and people have to walk a long way through mountain paths to get to it. I should have asked Ibo why it was built in such an isolated spot – but maybe in those days it was on a path that locals used to traverse the mountains and wasn't isolated at all at that time. Ibo told me that the path continues past the temple, climbs higher into the mountain and then turns east and descends back down past AnYangGong – a six-mile hike too strenuous for me.

Perhaps its isolation contributed to another aspect of Chinese temples which I find a bit strange: that often three 'religions' – Taoism and Confucianism and Buddhism – are worshipped in one temple. Apparently all three religions were, or are, worshipped in LianHua Temple. Maybe long ago the locals couldn't travel long distances to different temples.

The old traditions of this temple, as well as its history, have been lost because of the destruction of religious buildings and traditions during the Cultural Revolution but it is thought that it was built in the late Ching Dynasty, around 1900, just before China became The Republic of China.

This is the story that Ibo told me.

His great-grandmother lived in the LianHua Temple around 1930. Her name was Zhangshi which translates as 'a woman from the Zhang family'. Most women at that time did not have their own names – only the men. She often visited this temple to get away from her husband who was a very nasty man, an irresponsible gambler, who treated her very badly. During one of her visits, while she was meditating in the tranquillity of the valley, she had a vision. She saw herself visiting a Taoist monastery where she met a holy figure who pointed to a bowl filled with black, dirty, stinking water. He told her to wash her hands in this water. After she did so, the holy man told her that she now had healing powers and could treat and heal the sick, even stop bleeding.

From then onwards many people visited the temple to sit in her presence and to be healed by her. Her husband was infuriated because he thought she should be at home looking after him so he went to the temple and attempted to disturb the rituals and ceremonies and cursed all the people living and visiting there. His wife remained calm and refused to be disturbed by the husband or to return home to him. Within a day or two of leaving the temple he had a stroke and died.

When Zhangshi was about eighty years old she went into a very deep state of meditation – so deep that it seemed as if she was dead. She told her daughter, Ibo's grandmother, that she would enter this state and warned her not to disturb her. But her daughter was a village woman and not very intelligent so when she saw her mother like this she shook her violently and shouted at her to wake up. Zhangshi was brought back from her deep state but became paralysed and was confined to her bed, seriously ill. She was moved to a small village behind the well-known Yongtai Temple, called Shengshui, which means 'holy water'. Here she was cared for by her family for another three years. Just before her death she announced the exact day on which she would depart. More than ten thousand people from the surrounding area came to attend her funeral – so many that her son had to block the road because the people couldn't fit into the village.

In the LianHua Temple there are statues of ten women from the area who were said to be enlightened. Unfortunately they are not named but Ibo feels that his great-grandmother is the one third from the left because, he says, when he kneels in front of this statue he feels some very strong energy in his heart.

I was thrilled at hearing this very wonderful story. It made the place become so alive for me.

* * *

After a long walk we had to climb some stone steps and, arriving at the top, we saw a small valley, thickly covered in trees which, as it was nearing the end of autumn, were mostly bare of leaves except for one or two which still sported their glorious colours. Through the tracery of the bare branches we saw first an exquisite little pagoda and then, behind it, an astonishing gold-tiled roof shining almost blindingly in the sunlight. I had never before seen a roof like this.

The inner courtyard was in shadow, dark and silent and seemingly deserted until a very old woman came out to greet us – although she seemed more grumpy at our arrival than welcoming! The antics of the kids won her over a bit, though, and she nodded a 'yes' when Ibo asked if we could sit down and eat our lunch. I had brought plenty of food so there was more than enough to share with the taxi driver but the old woman declined to join us although she brought us some apples.

As we ate I looked more closely at the place. It was obviously much more prosperous than AnYangGong and all the roofs appeared to have been painted with iridescent gold paint which, as I said before, shone in the sunlight like only gold can. The doors to the main altar were intricately carved in wood – I had never seen this kind of carving in any of the other temples I had visited. On all sides the mountain loomed high around us. This was a precious gem of a building, and I again felt the familiar despair that such treasures were neglected and run-down, when for a mere fraction of the income enjoyed by the main Shaolin Temple – to which these places belonged – these beautiful buildings could be restored and preserved for the future.

After our lunch Ibo took me into a small side room to show me the ten statues of the enlightened women. The faces were rather primitively carved and, as is customary, were draped in different coloured cloth, now sadly dusty and threadbare where once, I am sure, they might have been quite luxurious. Ibo showed me the statue he thought was his great-grandmother and knelt in front of it. I withdrew as I sensed he wanted to be alone and went outside to play with the kids who were now getting a bit impatient to go home.

When Ibo came out of the small room we slowly retraced our steps, fortunately now downhill, through the valley until we arrived again at the ticket office and the car. I hoped our friendly driver had had as good a time as we all did.

Winter Approaching

The usually capricious Dengfeng weather behaved almost impeccably that autumn. There were none of those dramatic leaps and dips of temperatures that had hitherto made my time here very uncomfortable. My arrival was blessed with a comfortable English summer warmth which decreased gradually – gradually not rapidly! – to a pleasant autumn temperature with cooler nights. Only towards the end of November, as I reluctantly set my sights in a westerly direction, did the approach of winter gently make itself felt.

My fascinating trips and discoveries of so many hidden places around Song Mountain still left me with ample time to enjoy many solitary peaceful hours walking and meditating on the mountain. Even my little room had taken on something of a temple feel. It was blissful to wake up early, to savour my morning tea, to stroll down to my sesame-bun shop and have cuddly babies thrust into my arms by the friendly mothers out shopping. Sometimes I would wander away from the village, delighting at the first rays of the sun as it brushed the mountain in orange-pink splendour.

I was reminded of those early days in Goa, long before it became mostly the awful tourist trap that it is today, when there was nothing much to do each day except enjoy each little moment and each little task; for example, having the early morning cup of chai at the local chai shop and then the leisurely breakfast and then if you didn't feel much like doing anything it was totally fine and tomorrow was another day. Or else you made the huge decision to go and post a letter and that took up just about the whole day with all the little encounters and absurdities along the way.

In the small town of Dengfeng, things were rather similar. Even a simple task like opening a bank account could take considerable time, as I discovered when I decided to open two for future visits. The nice young woman at the bank, who spoke English, was never there when I needed her. (In India it was the same: 'She's out of station, madam, gone to village for cousin-brother's wedding.'!) After the third trip, she was finally there to help with all the formalities involved with opening two accounts as a foreigner. By now, most of the bank staff knew me on sight and I am sure that without their smiling support as well, the whole thing would have taken even longer.

On another occasion Ibo took me to a little design shop to get some business cards made. A very astute young guy operating Photoshop designed a card for me in no time, using a photo I had taken of the mountain in a morning mist. When I went to pick up the cards without Ibo a few days later, however, I saw consternation on the faces as I walked into the shop. The astute young guy quickly started hitting his computer keys and I saw some English words pop up on the screen: 'forgot it to do'. In China people don't phone much as there are very few landline telephones; rather they use 'qq' which is their version of Skype and they communicate online in this way. So my designer had written to someone somewhere who had obviously forgotten to do my cards.

Well, this was actually very fortunate because I had realised that morning that I should have written more on the card and had thought I would have to get another batch made. So the fact that they had not been printed was great but now there was no Ibo to translate so how was I going to communicate that I wanted to make additions to the card? I indicated to the young guy that maybe I could use his computer and wrote 'Can you speak English' to the invisible someone somewhere. The answer came back quick as a wink – 'incapable'! I laughed so much. The person was obviously using a computer translator.

But I was a little stumped as to how to explain what needed to happen but I drew a card and added a few words, showed it to my astute young guy who quickly understood that changes needed to be made and we worked together on the computer in perfect harmony until, very efficiently, everything got done to my satisfaction. When I returned a few days later, the cards were there waiting, beautifully printed. Quite amazing how it all happened.

Back to meditation.... I had got so laid-back that I had not even made it to Bodhidharma's cave this time. Going to the Shaolin Temple was always a bit of an effort as one's being was immediately assailed with the maniacal tourist energy that unfortunately is the feature of the temple except during the early mornings and evenings. Perhaps that was why I had avoided going there.

As my departure for England was sadly soon approaching, I decided to remedy the situation and made preparations to catch the first morning bus – 6.30am – to the temple. This would not get me there early enough to sneak in free but I would avoid the hordes of people for at least part of the day. I was so early I had to wait for the ticket office to open as all the staff were still doing their TaiChi exercises in the main entrance square. The whole area was cocooned in the arms of the mountains and everything was calm and serene. A very pleasant and healthy way to start the day. And I again marvelled at this place – it is so obvious why the ancients chose it to be a site for a shrine or temple.

It had been cold during the night and Ibo warned me there would be a cold wind blowing on the mountain so I had put on my thermal underwear for the first time. Mountain peaks are usually cold, I reckoned. There were only three of us in the little vehicle that shuttles between the entrance and the main temple building, and the friendly driver was chattering away to me, intent that I should find my way. What I couldn't explain to him and my travelling companions was that I had been to the temple many times before and didn't need any directions or help. Frustrating. What I wanted to do was to wander up to the area where the cable car starts to see where the best scenes of autumn leaves could be found so I could get some good photographs. But the driver – and the other two passengers – couldn't understand why I should be going off in this direction when the temple was in the opposite direction and were very insistent that I was going the wrong way! Finally the only way to escape these kindly people trying to help me to go to where I didn't want to go was to say the only words I knew that they would understand: Damo Dong – Bodhidharma's Cave. This meant a change of direction for me but as I was eventually going there anyway it was okay to do it a bit sooner rather than later. And my temporary friends were happy and satisfied at seeing me treading the right path!

The higher up the mountainside I walked, the more the panoramic view opened up vistas of red, orange and golden trees – none of my photos had a chance of capturing this beauty. So, abandoning the photographic project, I sat and meditated for a couple of hours until I realised that the promised bitter wind had not materialised and that the temperature had soared and that I was wearing thermal underwear which was rapidly making any further time there unbearable. I made a hasty retreat, even splurging on a taxi home to rid myself of the hot, scratchy underwear as soon as possible.

* * *

That evening, after cooking my own dinner, I went to the school to try to sneak a few quick minutes on the internet to send some emails. Ibo was in Zhengzhou but he had given me permission to use his room where he had now got his own internet connection set up to use the laptop which a dear friend called Mangala had given him, at Panky's request. The laptop was conveyed from our meditation centre in India by another friend who took it first to Corfu and then to London. I collected it from there, took it back to Somerset and finally delivered it to Ibo in China a month later. This laptop was probably one of the most well-travelled in China!

A Mountain in China

As I left the school I was greeted by a full moon in an almost clear sky – just a few white clouds drifting here and there in feathery mosaics across the sky. It was relatively warm that night, in contrast to the previous few nights, so I walked along the road in front of the school savouring the majestic silhouettes of the mountain peaks against the moon-lit sky. It was pure enchantment. I sat down at the edge of a field and felt flooded with such a deep silence that I thought I had gone deaf for some reason – but it was really only the silence of the mountain permeating my being. I felt so grateful for this experience. Never before in my life had I had such a deep connection with nature.

Slowly making my way home through the little village I realised that one of the reasons I could savour it all so much is that I was not afraid to be out alone at night. I would never walk around like this in England. I never felt fear here. There were no drunken louts, crazed drug addicts or sad, violent youngsters polluting the streets. The thought of returning to such ugliness after such incredible beauty here filled me with dread.

When I got home my charming landlady and her friend were sitting in the front of the house admiring the moon and we enjoyed a chat in my few stuttering Chinese words. We then all went for another walk in companionable silence around the concrete village which now took on a softened appearance in the light of the moon. The leaves had all gone from the trees so the moon was shining through the bare branches throwing hazy shadows on the path in front of us.

How could I leave? This was the home of my heart, my destiny.

* * *

But leave I had to. My only consolation was that on my way back to Beijing I would see my precious Yujie again. She had left

177

Beijing and had returned to live and work with her uncle and his family in a city called Shijiazhuang in Hubei Province and had invited me to stay there for a few days. Her uncle, Professor Zhao, was the fifth son of Yujie's father's family and had not joined the family construction business, but instead branched out on his own, gaining degrees in English, a professorship at a prestigious university and a flourishing speciality language school.

Shijiazhuang was just another ugly industrial city but seeing Yujie again was a delight and meeting her uncle, of whom I had heard so much, was a special event for me. Of course the fact that he spoke English made it easy to communicate with him but he impressed me profoundly with both his scholarliness and religiousness. He was a devout Buddhist and had an aura of meditation around him which felt very familiar and comfortable.

As I delved further into China's spiritual heritage – and Osho's possible part in it – he would, at a later date, be of immense help to me.

5
An Odd Wind Blowing

Early Morning on the Mountain

Within yourself, no fixed positions:
Things as they take shape disclose themselves.
Moving, be like water,
Still, be like a mirror,
Respond like an echo.
Be assimilated to them and you harmonise,
Take hold of any of them and you lose.

Chuang Tzu: The Zhuangzi

A Lasting Glow

Panky and I had been corresponding by email while I was away – whenever I managed to achieve some kind of internet connection – and I stayed overnight with her on my return to London. I was so glowing with the joy I had experienced over the past few months that she immediately became 'homesick' and decided she wanted to make another visit to Song Mountain. She had long had an idea about filming Master Wu Nanfang doing his other absorbing passion: calligraphy. We talked long into the night and before I left to return to the West Country a plan had been made. I would return to Song Mountain towards the end of March the following year when I hoped the worst of the winter weather would be over and she would join me there

On my return to the UK I had arranged to house-and-cat-sit for a friend for a few months before moving into a new flat, so during the next few weeks I happily occupied myself doing basically nothing except take the rather unique cat for long walks and catch up on the TV shows, Downton Abbey and Strictly Come Dancing. My blissful experiences from the previous few months stayed with me and I was even happier knowing that I would be going back soon.

The only worrying note that disturbed my silent, peaceful days was that Micha, Ibo's friend, contacted me to say that Ibo was again very ill. Of course this concerned me deeply and I discussed ways with him that I could send some funds to him because medical bills always added greatly to the stress of his health problems. Fortunately he was in the hands of an exceptionally good doctor who again managed to pull him through this crisis.

Time passed quickly and soon I was lugging my bags into Heathrow airport ready to fly eastwards – and home.

A Cold Welcome

As Yujie was now no longer in Beijing I flew straight on to Zhengzhou where Wenju and Ibo met me. Wenju was his usual effusive charming self and I was relieved to see that Ibo looked reasonably healthy (although I later found out he actually wasn't very well) if rather quiet. I knew that the previous few months had taken their toll on him, both physically and emotionally.

I also sensed tension between him and Wenju even during the drive back to Song Mountain. I started to have a bit of a premonition that maybe things were not going to follow on from the mellow peacefulness that had characterised my last sojourn here. As events turned out, I was right. This visit would turn out to be a rather fragmented time, suffused with undercurrents that I didn't understand. This and the extreme cold and heat made it difficult for me to maintain the meditative energy that I had come to cherish in the presence of the mountain. But, there was that 'expectation' again – and I quickly became aware that this was a time that I had to drop my preconceived plans and just go along with what was happening here and now.

The star act in the ensuing drama was the weather! I have seldom experienced such extremes of hot and cold, even in India. My optimism that winter would be nearly over by the time I arrived was dramatically misplaced. For the first two weeks it was freezing cold with a bitter wind blowing off the mountains and snow still lying frozen on the ground.

I hadn't brought my down coat and the car had no heating so by the time we arrived in ShiLiPu village I was frozen, barely able to move. Wenju took me first to greet Master Wu Nanfang who was, as always, charming and graciously welcoming, but the school offered no hint of warmth as it was as cold indoors as it was outside. There was a definite sinking of my heart!

Back in the UK I had corresponded a bit with Ibo about where I would stay this time. I wanted to return to my Zen flat – my landlady was apparently happy to have me back – but he thought I would be better off in the new, relatively luxurious house that Master Wu Nanfang had rented for the increasing number of kungfu students, especially western ones, coming to train. It seemed that my nagging about needing improved facilities had had some effect! After greeting Master Wu Nanfang, Wenju and Ibo took me to this new house which was actually quite impressive. Very well-designed and finished off. And there were three of the huge, plastic-covered sofas that the Chinese favoured as the ultimate in the latest furniture design. Design aside, for me it was bliss to have a proper comfortable place to sit down! Until now the only seating arrangements anywhere had been tiny little stools about a foot off the ground with seats about a foot square and only occasionally a back rest. Monumentally uncomfortable. In the school there was one sort of bench with a back but it was again low on the ground and as hard as a rock.

The new house also boasted a quite well-equipped kitchen – some of the western students liked to augment the rather basic food provided by the school – and a washing machine which could come in handy for me. These were all plus factors in the decision-making process.

I was given a choice of two rooms: the first one, upstairs and in the front of the house, had a view of the mountain and an air-conditioning and heating unit but no private bathroom; the second was at the back of the house with no unit and no view of the mountains but an en-suite shower and toilet. I didn't think it would be convenient to share facilities with a lot of boys and young men – I actually even didn't think it would be a good idea to share a house with them – but Ibo and Wenju were insistent that I stay there and set up a bed in the backroom for me, with a heater and some loaned bedding. I was exhausted by this time and went to bed immediately – decisions could wait for the morrow.

When the morrow dawned I was clear that I wanted to go back to my Zen flat. With a lot of youngsters around, noise was inevitable, but unless it was essential for me to put up with it I didn't want to. I preferred my own quiet, alone space. Naturally my decision met with a lot of opposition – Chinese hospitality demanded that I should be looked after! I tried to be as diplomatic as I could but remained firm, so eventually a team of little boys were called to move the bed, mattress, heater and my luggage over to my lovely flat, only a few hundred metres away, where I was welcomed by my landlady, her seventy-six year old mother and her ninety-six year old grandmother. Now I was really home.

Having given away all my household things when I left the previous time, I had to replace everything again. The first essential was a SIM card for my mobile phone so, before he returned to the school, I asked Ibo to call Liu, rather desperately hoping that he was still around. Happily he was – and he promised to pick me up in fifteen minutes to do the necessary shopping. He knew the routine by now!

Before leaving the previous time I had given him my English-Chinese dictionary (with the idea that it might be a translation help with other foreign passengers he might pick up) and he now proudly produced this from the shelf in the dashboard of the car. It was always useful – for example, this time I wanted to buy a chair. Showing Liu the word for 'chair' caused him to do an about turn and take me to a furniture shop I had never seen and I found a really comfortable chair. This sounds all pretty basic but things we take for granted in our western lifestyle often don't even exist in China and it takes quite a lot of imagination and effort to try to arrange something that works fairly efficiently, especially when you don't speak the language. It is then that a person like Liu, who was prepared to try to understand and help with my requests no matter how strange to him, is worth his weight in gold.

For example, mats to put on the floor don't exist but beautiful ones made from stripped bamboo, are used to put on beds. In the hot summer they are very cool to sleep on. Putting these mats on the floor, as I wanted to do, was something very strange for the locals to comprehend. I saw Liu blink a bit when I put the mats on the floor but he went along with it as just another strange thing this western woman did.

With my simple life more or less up and running now, I turned my attention to Panky's arrival. I didn't want to become too dependent on the school for the use of an internet connection so went down to the local dirty, smoky, noisy internet café where the family who ran it welcomed me back and proudly showed me how much their little boy had grown. As always, I was surprised at the lack of fear at strangers that Chinese babies have and this little one, after a few moments of scepticism, decided I was an acceptable addition to his small life and thereafter greeted me with great enthusiasm.

This lack of fear might be due in part to the way mothers in China traditionally look after their new-born babies. Apparently the first month after the baby is born is considered to be crucial to its life-long well-being. The new mother therefore spends all her time bonding with the baby. She never goes out, never watches TV or goes online, certainly never goes to work. Husband, parents and neighbours do the shopping and housework. The new mother just sits, in an almost meditative way, holding her baby close to her so that the baby is assured of her deep love and support in this strange new world it has entered. In the old days mothers didn't even wash their hair for the month in case they caught a cold. As the baby grows in those first weeks it starts to become familiar with its environment while all the time feeling secure that it has the total care of its mother, no matter what. At the end of the four weeks it is considered that the baby has understood its valued place in this world and can now start to interact with its environment.

The café was slightly warm as there was one of the old-fashioned coal-burning stoves which many poorer Chinese people have in their homes. This kind of contraption doesn't give off much heat but the family stays seated around it for most of the winter so it does provide some respite from the bitter cold. Food can be cooked on it and there is always a pot of hot water on it for making tea. On my arrival in the café I quickly chose a computer as close to the stove as possible. In this cafe I used their computers because it was too complicated to program mine into their system. I had tried that once and it was almost a disaster. By now, I was able to read the Chinese characters which navigated me towards an English search engine

I found an email from Panky giving me the time and date of her arrival in Zhengzhou airport in five days. She asked me to arrange for Liu to meet her at the airport and also to find a place for her to stay. I had already thought about the latter and had arranged with Master Wu Nanfang for her to stay in the guest room in the new house which had both a heating unit and a small en-suite bathroom. It would be very noisy as it was next to the communal room where all the boys gathered but as she was only there for twelve days I thought it wouldn't matter. She was there to make the film and the boys could be useful to her. Ali and Naomitsu, both of whom she knew, were living there and could help with any simple everyday translating that might be needed. I emailed her to this effect.

On a visit to the school the next day I found that Andy, Ibo's friend who I had met the previous year, had arrived to stay for three days. It was great to see him again. While Ibo was busy with some students I discussed my concerns about Ibo's health with him. He told me he had been up here in January to visit a Traditional Chinese Medicine doctor to do some training in stress reduction techniques which he wanted to learn to aid him in a new career. He had taken Ibo to visit the doctor and Ibo had received some treatment from him but hadn't continued with the medication. Andy thought it would be good for Ibo to go with him again to see the doctor. This happened and I was pleased to find that the doctor had recommended that Ibo stay with him for a month as he needed complete rest. The school was noisy and Ibo shared a room with a very young boy who was one of the rich kids whose family sent him to the school to learn some discipline. He didn't seem to me to be learning anything in this direction, rather he spent his time playing computer games on his very expensive computer which naturally fascinated all the other young boys, making Ibo's room as busy and noisy as a Beijing train station.

Before taking time off, however, Ibo was adamant that he wanted to help Panky with her filming and indeed it would be very difficult to do this without his help. Andy was only here for three days and had to return to his work in Anhui Province, south-east of Henan. I just hoped Ibo could manage to last the twelve days that Panky would be here.

In the meantime the temperature took another dive to below zero and I spent the next few days simply willing myself to survive. It was grey, gloomy, and bitterly cold with an icy wind making it too cold for the boys to train outside. With only a tiny heater, no insulation, no double glazing and a beautiful, big, uncurtained picture window which gave me a lovely view of the mountain and allowed a lot of light in, along with all the cold too, my room was almost as cold inside as it was outside. With a blue nose just peeping over the quilt my landlady had lent me (mine was far too thin) I gazed rather wistfully at the mountain but didn't dare venture out to visit it for fear of ending up a cold corpse on the mountainside. One afternoon I called Ibo and Andy and invited them to a meal at the 'hotpot' restaurant that evening because I just had to somehow be warm for an hour or two! We agreed that this kind of weather would make it difficult for Panky to film.

Dengfeng's weather system was, however, predictable in its fickleness and the day that Panky arrived, the sky cleared, the sun came out and the temperature shot up to a balmy fifteen degrees, so we were on course for a successful filming stint.

Digital Images

I went with Liu to meet Panky and bring her back to the new house. But it was to be a rather bizarre arrival for her as, just the night before, an incident occurred which gave me a rather different view of the apparently harmonious little village. Apparently the building of a second house next to the new school house had offended someone in the village for some reason and during the night this 'someone' had come with a huge earth digger and dug a deep hole in the shared drive-way up to the two houses, leaving only a narrow ridge for us to reach the house – easy for the lithe and agile kungfu students but hazardous for the likes of Panky and me.

As Panky had only a limited time here before she would leave to join her TaiChi group she was keen to get started with her filming quickly. There were some long discussions with Master Wu Nanfang who, as always, had some really good ideas both in terms of subject matter and locations. It transpired that the first thing that he wanted Panky to film was him giving a demonstration of how the Wugulun Kungfu movements were related to farming in the fields. In older times, everyone in rural areas was dependent on their own production of food so there wasn't excess time to spend on kungfu movements – unlike monks in the temples who had a lot of time to spend practising. In this way, many kungfu movements were incorporated into the farming activities. This was a topic very close to Master Wu Nanfang's heart and he was keen to demonstrate how this was done.

Now the weather co-operated beautifully and we spent a perfect morning in the fields with the mountain forming a stunning

Filming Farming Forms

backdrop. Apart from an occasional enthusiastic tree which had already sported a few green shoots, most of them were still bare except for a field of fruit trees covered in white blossoms. The hardy rapeseed plants were, however, already covered in yellow flowers which gave a much needed touch of colour to the still wintery landscape.

Master Wu Nanfang had brought three students with him:

Hufei, Laochi and little Tian De. With his artistic eye, Master Wu Nanfang knew that the small kid would add interest to the images. Certainly his presence added variety and an extra dimension to both Panky's film and my still photographs

It was very interesting watching the master demonstrate how to hoe and dig with an awareness of the right movements for the body. He showed how almost anything can be turned into a meditative process.

The next day or two were spent filming some of the kungfu lessons. Panky now had a tripod and she wanted to capture some of the forms again because when filming the previous time she had held the camera close to her body to steady it and the beat of her heart made the camera jump. So the forms were filmed accompanied by the steady beat of her heart!

On the third day I got a phone call from Ibo at 5am. Master Wu Nanfang wanted Panky to come right away because it was snowing and he wanted her to film him doing calligraphy through a screen of falling snow! Ibo said that he had already called Panky and she was getting her gear together and we would be picked up in ten minutes.

When we arrived at the school there was a lot of action as Master Wu Nanfang was setting up the scene on the covered veranda in the courtyard with a low table and his calligraphy paraphernalia. Again he had decided that Tian De was to be an accessory but I, now back in my role of wardrobe mistress (for many years I had designed and made 'costumes' for Osho's photographic sessions), saw that his clothes were extremely dirty. He looked like a sleepy little ragamuffin – not a cool kungfu student. I suggested to Ibo that we get him another set of clothes so while Panky set up her camera, shielded from the snow by two older students with big umbrellas, I raided the boys' dormitory. Tian De apparently didn't have another kungfu outfit and the boy who was nearest to him in size was much larger, so we had to roll up the sleeves of the top and the legs of the pants to make them sort of fit. All of this, plus his sleepiness and funny facial expressions, made for some rather endearing images and always creates a giggle in any audience watching Panky's film.

By the time everything was ready it had more or less stopped snowing but the sleet did add an interesting touch to both the film and my stills. Master Wu Nanfang was a consummate actor and the calligraphy episode certainly produced some great images for both Panky and me, even if we did practically freeze in the process.

The hot corn porridge that was then provided for breakfast was gratefully received even though I usually avoided it if I could. Master Wu Nanfang, high on the drama of the scenes just filmed, told us enthusiastically of his next idea. This was apparently to be filmed up one of the valleys in the mountain where there was a jutting outcrop of rock on which he wanted to do some kungfu forms. We would, however, have to wait for a clear bright day and he warned us to be ready for another early morning call because he thought that the colours of the early morning sunrise would add to the beauty of the scene.

He was right and I count the photographs that I took that morning to be the most stunning mountain photographs that I have taken in all my visits to Song Mountain.

* * *

The call came two mornings later but this time we had had some warning and were well prepared as Ibo had told us that the weather forecast for the following morning was dry and fine. This time we were awoken just after 4.40am and it was dark when the van arrived to pick me up. When we stopped at the new house, Naomitsu came out with Panky to join the expedition. Wenju drove us up into one of my favourite valleys and the sun was just peeping over Mount Taoshi, on the far side of Dengfeng, when we got out of the van. Slowly the mountain became illuminated with the glowing pinks and oranges of the rising sun and my camera-clicking finger went into overdrive.

Our first shots were of Master Wu Nanfang walking up a path towards the mountain, all bathed in the coloured sunrise hues. Then it turned out that he had decided to climb quite high up the mountain side in order to reach a jutting-out pinnacle of rock on which he wanted to do his kungfu and, after giving Panky very specific instructions about how she should film this scene, he set off accompanied by Naomitsu. At this point he wasn't really interested in me and my camera because doing the kungfu in this magnificent setting needed to be seen on film – a still photograph would not convey anywhere near as much. Ibo and Wenju had been instructed to help Panky climb quite high to give her a good vantage point.

So I was left alone to do my thing which made me very happy because I could really get creative with the shots I was taking. There was a small temple nearby and I climbed up some convenient stairs which put me almost on a level with Master Wu Nanfang on his rock. The early morning light was perfect, the mountain was at its most beautiful and the distant figure of the master, sometimes in his orange kungfu gear, sometimes in his brown monk's habit, provided some superb images.

He treated us to demonstrations of kungfu forms and a lot of sword forms sometimes with one, sometimes two, swords, festooned with their bright banners. He also sat and stood in meditation and even entertained us by lying down on this small outcrop imitating the pose of various famous lying-down Buddha statues!

We were all quite elated when we finally arrived back at the foot of this part of the mountain. Naomitsu had also got some fabulous shots from his vantage spot. Master Wu Nanfang, looking at playbacks and rewinds from various cameras, was well pleased with the day, as were we.

Next on the agenda, we quickly discovered, was a sequence of fighting forms to be filmed on an entirely different part of the mountain – just behind the atmospheric Taoist temple, Zhongyue Maio, one of my favourite places. Fortunately this expedition didn't warrant a pre-dawn start and at the respectable hour of 8am the next day we set off to the other side of Dengfeng. The plan was, apparently, to climb the small hill at the back of the temple and walk along a path to a clearing on another hill which Master Wu Nanfang thought would provide a further impressive scenic backdrop. The mountains here were more like rolling hills but they were picturesque in their own way.

From a small pagoda on the top of the hill behind the temple, the view was beautiful although nowhere near as awe-inspiring as the peaks near ShiLiPu. When I saw the master, the students and Panky take off along a narrow path on the ridge of a smaller hill for the filming session I decided I would remain on this high point and photograph the action from afar. Lots of scenic views! To be honest I was getting a bit tired of all this kungfu and wanted to do some meditation on my own. To that end, after having taken some really very good shots, I walked back down the little hill into the small forest at its base and sat there amongst the trees. Even outside the temple the energy was strong and so I sat in silence for a blissful half hour until I heard the film crew and performers returning.

* * *

My concern about Ibo was increasing as I saw that all this activity was really taking a toll on his body. As Panky wanted the following two days before the ChingMing festival day to transfer her film onto her computer, see the shots that she already had and decide what more she still needed in order to complete her documentary, I took Ibo off to dinner and urged him to go and rest with the Chinese herbal doctor as soon as possible. I felt he would collapse with all this action. I was alarmed to see that the whites of his eyes had turned yellow which, from my years in India, was a sign of liver dysfunction if not hepatitis. Panky was nearly at the end of her filming and there was another recently-arrived student, who had given himself the English name of Michael, who spoke good English and so could help out.

Ibo promised to talk to the master that evening when he returned to the school and the next morning phoned me to say that, with Master Wu Nanfang's permission, he had decided to go way for a month. The master could not have failed to see the deterioration in Ibo's condition and also knew Ibo needed to be strong and healthy to manage the influx of foreign students arriving in the summer months. Ibo said he wanted to leave a suitcase of personal things with me so came over to my flat an hour later. We put the bag under my bed and then I went with him to the bus stop and waited with him until the bus arrived.

Walking back to my flat I felt depressed. Not only would I miss Ibo but I was sad that such a young person should have to go through so much, more or less alone in the world. He did not want his family to know that he was seriously ill again. I vowed to be as much of a support as he would allow me to be.

* * *

I have mentioned ChingMing Day before. On 5th April every year China has a national holiday to allow everyone to visit the graves of their ancestors and pay their respects.

There were more students at the school this year than in the previous year so about six or seven vans with drivers had been hired to convey everybody to visit the same places we had gone to before. This was not as much fun as having Naomitsu driving! The trip followed more or less the same pattern as before so I won't repeat the details. I will just mention that, as well as feeling bad about Ibo, I could also feel an undercurrent of something strange on this journey that disturbed me but I could not understand what it was.

That evening Panky and I discussed her documentary and she said she wanted just a few more shots of Wu Nanfang to complete her footage. We agreed to meet in the morning to discuss this with him, take the final shots and then I would help her pack for her departure to Beijing the following day. Liu had of course been commissioned to take her to the airport.

A Mystery

On Panky's last day I got the usual phone call from her at about 7 o'clock: 'Are you up?' Arising even earlier than me, it was the routine for her to go to the sesame bun place and buy some piping-hot buns and then stop off at my flat to eat them with an English cup of tea. I had found some passable jam in one of the supermarkets which augmented the otherwise plain buns.

As she had decided what she needed for her final shots we then went together to the school. As usual the boys were practising their movements on the training ground outside and there was no hint of anything amiss until we entered the school expecting to see Master Wu Nanfang and photograph him. That he was nowhere around was not at first puzzling but two of the coaches, Yaofeng and Chengeng, instead of being their usual cheery selves, basically ignored us and hurried past us with Wenju without any greetings. We sat in the reception room to wait for the master but eventually Lijuan came in and told us: 'Shifu go away.' (Shifu is the Chinese word for master.) When Panky asked when he would be back the answer was: 'Maybe tomorrow.' She then left.

We were mystified. He had gone away? Without saying goodbye to Panky? He was meticulously courteous and surely would not have done that. He also knew she wanted more shots of him and, so keen was he on this documentary, he would not have jeopardised the completion of her footage. Then Wenju came in, intent obviously on something else, and when I asked him where the master was (I could manage that in Chinese) he hurriedly answered: 'Go. Pengyuo.' (Pengyuo is 'friend' in Chinese so I assumed he was saying that his father had gone somewhere with or to a friend.) We sat there a while longer but as nobody else came in we decided to go back to the new house and see if Ali knew anything. Naomitsu was training and we knew we must *never* interrupt a training session. On returning to the house, we waited until Ali appeared from somewhere but he didn't know anything at all.

Silently we made some lunch and then Panky reluctantly started packing, expecting all the time to get a call to come to the school to do the final filming. Nothing happened and I eventually went home for a nap. In the evening we went to the school for supper and things appeared quite normal with nobody seeming unduly concerned – but Master Wu Nanfang did not materialise. His wife was also not around. Wenju came with some presents for Panky but escaped before we could get someone to question him! Naomitsu either didn't know anything or wouldn't say anything.

And so we returned to our respective rooms and I promised to get up early to see Panky off when it was time for her to leave.

Wenju and some other boys from the school came to say goodbye but any questions about the master's whereabouts were skilfully evaded. Here the lack of English was a bonus to them as they only had to smile, bow and keep quiet! And so Panky left with Liu without knowing anything further.

To this day I have never discovered what actually happened; I got only a few hints here and there. Perhaps Ibo finally found out, but if he did, he didn't tell me so my only conclusion was that Master Wu Nanfang had some kind of sudden serious illness and spent some time in hospital. I did see him three weeks later, just before I left, and he was obviously weak and frail but no reason was ever given for this mysterious disappearance.

A Different Perspective

When Panky arrived she kindly brought some warmer weather with her and the daytime temperature, after previously hovering around zero, accommodatingly rose to and remained in the mid-teens for the twelve days she was here. Maintaining this benign level proved too much for the elemental forces, however, and on the day she left the restraints were removed and within three days the temperature shot up to and stayed at about forty degrees! Winter to high summer in a few days with no spring in between. Being hopeless in this kind of heat I soon became an inert blob barely able to function. My lovely flat was no longer a solace as the flat brick roof and concrete-bricked walls heated up and stayed hot thus effectively making my bedroom a brick oven. I actually got sick for the first time in China and finally asked if I could move into the new house, still with its large crater in the front, into the room with the air-conditioner where Panky had stayed.

The unbearable heat, the mysterious disappearance of Master Wu Nanfang and Ibo's continuing health problems made this an extremely uncomfortable time for me. Walking to the mountain in this high temperature was unthinkable – and it was impossible to sit in my meditation spot as the trees were still quite bare so there was no shade. The air-conditioned room gave me some respite, however, and was quiet when the boys were at school training. They were now training inside the school building as it was too hot for them to be outside.

The usual April rains had still not come and the air was so dry that my skin started to wrinkle up like an elephant's skin because it was so dehydrated. I had never experienced this before, even in all my years in India. Naomitsu, having been here much longer than me, seemed to have had some experience of this dryness and lent me a humidifier he had previously bought, which helped a little.

Fortunately, after five days of this punishment, the rain, along with crashing thunder storms, finally arrived and things cooled down enough to allow me to return to my own space which I was already missing.

But for the first time I wanted to go back to England! I would never have thought that I would feel that way but these conditions were too tough for me. There was, however, Ibo to consider. I was texting with him every day but the news was not good. Despite the Traditional Chinese Medicine doctor's ministrations his condition was getting much worse and then a few days later I was totally shocked to get a phone call from him saying he was outside my house and could he come in!

I flew down the stairs and let him in. He indeed looked terrible and my heart sunk as I helped him up the stairs which he could barely manage. I sat him down and gave him some tea. He told me he had decided to go to the hospital in Zhengzhou where he had spent so much time in the last few years because otherwise he thought he would not survive. He had already been in contact with his doctor there and she had told him to come immediately. I offered to get Liu and take him there by taxi and help him get to the hospital but he said I would be more of a hindrance than a help because he would have to take care of me a bit (true!) so he would prefer to go alone. He would, however, like me to go with him, first to the public baths and then to the bus station. While he got some other clothes from his suitcase he had stored under the bed I got out all my cash to give to him as I knew money would now be a major issue.

Apparently the public baths in China are like the ones in Japan where you can submerge yourself in a kind of pool as well as have a shower. When Ibo came out I was quite amazed – and relieved – at how much he had revived and I felt better about him going by himself on the two-hour bus trip to Zhengzhou. I knew the bus was air-conditioned which would help.

On my return home I phoned Andy who was fortunately still in Anhui on a business trip. He usually lived and worked in Guangzhou, in the south of China near Hong Kong. Anhui was only a six-hour train journey to Zhengzhou whereas Guangzhou was more than twenty hours away. I told him what had happened and he said he would take care of everything.

Would that everyone had a friend like this!! The next call I got was from him the following morning from the hospital in Zhengzhou!! After my call he had walked out of his office, packed a small bag, got on the next train going north and six hours later arrived in Zhengzhou. At the hospital he had found Ibo and then called me to report the results of the tests that Ibo had undergone. In one way it was good news. The tests showed that he actually did have hepatitis – not good – but that there was no change in the original liver damage so there should be no concerns there – good. Poor Ibo just had to be patient for the duration of the disease. It could be treated and he could get over it. Unless it is very serious, a person does not need to be hospitalised for hepatitis, but given Ibo's chronic liver condition the doctor felt it was advisable for Ibo to stay there so she could observe his progress. Andy arranged with the school to help pay for the hospital costs and, once he felt Ibo was in a stable condition, he jumped on a train and went back to Anhui.

* * *

My personal concerns were now basically about two things: firstly, surviving the punishing heat until it was time for me to leave. I decided to fly back to Beijing from Zhengzhou because I could not face the hot, noisy, crowded train stations in both cities, the five-hour train journey and then a final long taxi trip to the airport which is on the diametrically opposite side of Beijing from the south-west train station.

And secondly, continuing the English lessons I had started, before Panky arrived, for some of the senior students – particularly the kungfu coaches. I thought that it might be helpful for them to have some basic English skills to cope with the foreigners, especially if Ibo wasn't around. The senior students were very keen so I set up a class of about six students, meeting two evenings a week, and was helped tremendously by the young man I have mentioned before, Michael. His only English training had been in middle school and he was fascinated by my very different approach to teaching the language. As well as translating for me and the six boys, he felt he was learning a lot himself.

As I was using another air-conditioned room in the new house for a school room, the lessons also gave me a few cool hours.

I confess I was amazed at how Lijuan and the senior boys, the oldest being only twenty one, handled the absence of Master Wu Nanfang and his wife. Between them they efficiently carried on with the running of the school and the training and even managed to continue with the English lessons which were, however, often interrupted by a phone call from the school with questions or even a small crisis which meant one or other of them had to leave to deal with it. Really impressive. They had been well-trained!

* * *

There were a few other rainy days which cooled the temperature somewhat thus allowing me to go for a few walks on the mountain. Otherwise I stayed in my room, now sort of bearable with the humidifier from Naomitsu and a fan from Ali, meditating and basically marking time until my departure date arrived. I was in contact with Ibo every day by phone and his recovery, although slow, was constant so I was reassured on that point. I remember becoming quite tearful when he said he was 'the luckiest of the unlucky ones'. When I asked him what he meant he explained that he was unlucky because he had a disability that he would have to cope with for his whole life, but he was lucky because he had such a brilliant doctor who had made it one of her missions in life to keep him alive, and he also had so many good friends to love and support him. Again I was reminded of his courage in the face of his adversities.

Just before I left, Master Wu Nanfang returned, much to my relief. He looked frail, as if he had gone through some ordeal, but it was not my place to question, only to greet him with pleasure and to sit with him in a relaxed and friendly silence as there was nobody to translate. Silence was, I think, better than words in this situation.

Ibo recovered sufficiently to finally leave the hospital and came to the village for a few hours to collect his suitcase and computer and to say goodbye to me. He had decided, now that his health crisis was basically over, to go and convalesce with his family in their home on the other side of the mountain.

On the day of my departure, Wenju and Yaofeng took me to the airport by car. I actually wondered if the airport could function in the heat but the Chinese seemed to take it all in their stride and I flew out of China with no further dramas.

* * *

I could never have predicted that my trip to China would have taken the course I have just described. I went back there in a spiritual glow expecting to go further on my path of meditation, but instead got involved in some very down-to-earth, possibly critical, situations. And, unexpectedly, I felt the richer for it. I felt I had engaged with China as it was, with the people and their life experiences, rather than with a China of my own projection. I had encountered patient stoicism, courage, generosity, respect, love … and I felt honoured to have been accepted in the way that I had been and was grateful for this very real experience.

I had also learned something else: the extremes of the spring weather were just too much for me to cope with so my next trip would be definitely in the autumn!

6
The End of the Dream?

SanHuangZhai, Autumn 2013

Do you have the patience to wait
until your mud settles,
and the water is clear?
Can you remain unmoving
until the right action arises by itself?

Lao Tzu: Tao Te Ching

The Mountain, Bodhidharma and Osho

The green fields of England looked distinctly welcome as the plane came in to land and a drizzly rain all the way home to the West Country aided the start of the restoration of the dried-up, shrivelled tissues! A few weeks, however, were needed to get my rather exhausted body to function more or less normally.

Once operational again, and having caught up with family and friends, the looming question in my mind was, 'What now?' To return to China in the coming autumn was too soon – I had neither the energy nor the finances to embark on another trip. But the following autumn seemed so far away! How could I stay away from that mountain for such a long time?

Then two things happened almost simultaneously, setting me off on a creative path which was to hugely influence the next few years. Firstly, I got yet one more email from somebody asking how they could buy a copy of a small book I had self-published five years before. The book was about the twelve years I spent as Osho's tailor and hat maker, and told stories of what it was like to be a close disciple of an enlightened Master. With twenty-four pages of coloured photographs it had been expensive to produce and so I had not printed a second edition.

Secondly, I heard about somebody who had just published some ebooks via Amazon's Kindle Direct Publishing system. He was successfully selling two ebooks online and it hadn't cost him a penny to put them there. Investigating this program I thought that I could do something similar. And so I began to write another book, 'Glimpses of my Master', which also included the text from the previous small book. The more I got into it, the more I found that I had quite a lot to say, and soon I was spending happy creative days pounding the computer keys. Somehow the process fitted with my experiences I had had in China where, although very involved in the everyday life there, my innermost being was about meditation and my devotion to my Master.

As the weeks went by I started to have another idea. I enjoyed this writing lark so much that I thought that maybe I should also write about how I got to India and Osho – about the unique life-changing journey I made overland in 1970 from England to India through wild countries where westerners had hardly ever been. And then again, the China trips were also pretty unique so maybe I should write about them too. And so the final idea was formed: to write three books, a trilogy, about a person on the path.

This creative enterprise occupied me for many months and by February the following year I had self-published two books, available on Amazon as both ebooks and paperbacks. It was a fascinating experiment for me.

* * *

In the meantime I kept very much in touch (via Skype and telephone) with Ibo, Yujie and Andy and to a lesser extent (because of the lack of English) with Master Wu Nanfang and the kungfu school. Ibo, whose health was now very much better, was only occasionally at the school and was busy studying Business English as he had realised that his exceptional English language skills could land him a good job. Yujie, not finding the work in Shijiazhuang particularly inspiring, had gone to Hainan Island where she had got an interesting job as a business manager and translator for an English company there. Andy, while continuing with his regular job, was pursuing his studies in both Child Psychology and Chinese Traditional Medicine. I felt extremely fortunate to be in contact with such talented, enterprising young people.

* * *

But I was desperately missing China! There was an ache in my heart which I felt even more deeply as I finished the books and had time on my hands again. I longed to return.

Then, out of the blue, I got an excited email from a good friend in Bali, Bhagawati, with an attached article which astounded me and radically changed my perspective on why I was so enthralled with this particular place in China and this particular mountain.

I had gone there for no logical reason; I had simply followed a pounding feeling that I had to go. I could not do otherwise.

The article she sent was written for an online magazine published by the large Osho Centre in Delhi, India. The author had researched Osho's comments about incidents in his past lives and compiled them into one long document. Osho had talked quite often about such incidents but had also said not to get too caught up with them, so they had mostly passed me by. Reincarnation is not as strong a concept for westerners as it is for Indians, and, as I later found out, for the Chinese people – Buddhists in particular.

As I have mentioned, Osho had spoken at length about Lao Tzu, Chuang Tzu, Lieh Tzu, Rinzai (Linji Yixuan) and of course, Bodhidharma, and while in China, I had started to wonder how he knew so much about them. Yes, he read thousands of books but while he was alive there could not have been many books published in English about China, particularly about its spiritual heritage. Until 1975 China was a closed country and not many westerners had managed to get themselves there except perhaps for commercial purposes or tightly controlled tours. Having any kind of freedom to roam the country outside of the tight restrictions placed on a foreigner was almost impossible. Most of the books about China's spiritual heritage that I have looked at were published after 1975 – when China started to open up some of its closed borders to allow foreigners to spend time there. And there was of course no internet available when Osho was alive.

How then did Osho have such a deep understanding of Taoism, Zen (Bodhidharma) and Chinese Buddhism and be able to speak so authoritatively on them? Was he in fact drawing on personal experiences and an understanding gained from being in the Song Mountain area in another life?

The western Christian mind is sceptical, usually contemptuous, of the idea of reincarnation, but so strong is Osho's insistence on his actual memory of time spent in this area in another lifetime – as revealed in the following two amazing quotes – that I am convinced! Here are two passages in which he talks about Bodhidharma, a temple and the mountain. I have put names to the latter two – the Shaolin Temple and Song Mountain – because it is quite possible that he did not know the English equivalent of the Chinese names.

Osho says:

> *Beyond the mind there is only one laughter, but it resounds for centuries. The place where Bodhidharma became enlightened.... I have been to that place. He became enlightened fourteen hundred years ago and people have made a temple in his memory, in the place where he laughed for the first time. And the story is that if you sit silently in the temple, you will still hear the laughter.*
>
> *There is a statue of Bodhidharma. He was a very strange man. If he meets you in the night, you will never go out of your house in the night again! He had such big eyes that, if he looked into you once, that was enough for enlightenment! And his laughter must have been a great laughter because he has a very good, big belly. Even in the statue the belly has ripples.*
>
> *I had not time to sit there in the temple, but I know*

that if you sit there in the temple in the silence of the forest (Shaolin means 'little forest'), perhaps you may hear the laughter. Perhaps the mountains, the trees, the rocks around the temple are still vibrating with that great man. I have looked into the lives of many great people, but Bodhidharma stands apart ... very strange and very unique.

It is possible that his laughter was so infectious that the trees started laughing and the mountains started laughing. Although Bodhidharma is dead, they are still laughing; they cannot stop it. If you go with the whole idea, perhaps you may really hear it – or you may imagine it. But I have come across people who have heard it, because they have told me.

I had gone there, but I had not time enough to stay in the temple, because the right time is in the middle of the night – when he had become enlightened. And particularly on a full-moon night in a certain month, if you stay in the temple, in the middle of the night there is every possibility that either you will hear the laughter or you will start laughing.

Osho spoke many, many times about Bodhidharma sitting in his cave (on Wuru Peak just behind the Shaolin Temple) but this was the first time he had actually mentioned being there. And I had never before heard the following words:

I knew Bodhidharma personally. I travelled with the man for at least three months. He loved me just as I loved him. You will be curious to know why he loved me. He loved me because I never asked him any question.

He said to me, "You are the first person I have met who does not ask a question – and I get bored with all the questions. You are the only person who does not bore me."

I said, "There is a reason."

He said, "What is that?"

I said, "I only answer. I never question. If you have any question you can ask me. If you don't have a question then keep your mouth shut."

We both laughed, because we both belonged to the same category of insanity. He asked me to continue the journey with him, but I said, "Excuse me, I have to go my own way, and from this point it separates from yours."

He could not believe it. He had never invited anyone before. This was the man who had even refused Emperor Wu – the greatest emperor of those days, with the greatest empire – as if he was a beggar. Bodhidharma could not believe his ears – that I could refuse him. I said, "Now you know how it feels to be refused. I wanted to give you a taste of it. Goodbye."

But that was fourteen centuries ago.'

Given Osho's love for Taoism and Zen and, in particular, Bodhidharma, and given my love for Osho, I now felt it was a natural consequence that I should have such a deep connection with Song Mountain and the spiritual heritage it represents.

Winging Eastwards Again

The problem with Song Mountain was finding a place to meditate. Neither SanHuangZhai nor AnYangGong had, for various reasons, been suitable, and meditating on the mountain had its own

213

difficulties: the weather, the various biting bugs, the distance from my flat and the tourists for whom a strange western woman sitting alone on the mountain side was an invitation for loud exclamations, interrogations and serious photography.

I thought ruefully of the experiences of the vicar, Peter Owen-Jones. In the second documentary of the BBC series 'Extreme Pilgrim' he spent time in India meditating in a kind of cave in the Himalayas. The local Indians understood instinctively about meditation and, rather than disturbing him, they came with little gifts and joined him in his silent meditation. No such luck on Song Mountain!

I contemplated this problem deeply as I knew it was central to my return to China. Much as I loved my time spent there, it became meaningless unless I could meditate. Even knowing that it was a connection with Osho, as well as the thousands of years of spiritual search by thousands of seekers, that drew me to the mountain, I still had to find my own way of being there and my own way of tapping into the energy there in order to find my own path of truth. This needed a certain intensity of meditation and so far I hadn't found a place to support that.

But one day a faint memory surfaced. On my second visit I vaguely remembered Meilin taking me to a possible place to do a silent retreat. At the time, the place, a nunnery, was a construction site, undergoing major renovations so it was impossible to be there but the person she spoke to said that, when finished, there would be accommodation for outsiders to stay for a while. I remembered that it was on the east side of Dengfeng, past the Taoist temple, Zhongyue Maio, and that there was a reservoir near it. Minutely searching Google Maps I found what I thought was the place, so I made a screen print and sent it to Ibo to see if he knew anything about it.

At 6am the following morning I got an excited phone call from him! By an absolutely amazing co-incidence the nunnery was right next to the site of his new job where he also lived when not translating in various projects devised by his new boss. Our discussion resulted in his promise to go to the nunnery, called the Luya Temple, and talk to the abbess to see if it would be possible for me to stay there and meditate quietly. The answer came back very quickly, 'Yes!' Ibo also took some photos of the place and it looked charming – silent and peaceful. Ibo said that in fact there seemed to be only a few women living there, mostly village people, apart from the abbess and two or three nuns, who wanted a quiet retreat.

This all sounded excellent and I of course wanted to go immediately but then I would be going in the hottest time in the year. Impossible. I discussed the dilemma with Yujie whose clear young brain saw a solution: that I come to Hainan Island in July and stay with her and then go to Dengfeng in August which was the rainy season and should be cooler than the violent temperatures of June and July. I presented this suggestion to Ibo and he also thought that August might be okay, especially as the Luya Temple was on the mountain and cooler than Dengfeng or ShiLiPu.

Hainan Island would be hot but Yujie said there would be a lot of rain, even hurricanes in July, and her parents' large apartment had triple glazing and good air-conditioning. She also said that she was now driving her father's new car and she would be keen to go up to their mountain house at weekends where it was much cooler.

I decided to take a chance and found reasonably-priced air ticket to Hong Kong. From there a short flight took me back to Hainan Island where, despite the heat, I had a lovely restful holiday.

* * *

Disaster!

My attempt to do the silent retreat at the Luya Temple was a comical disaster! After two days I fled!

On my arrival in Dengfeng, Ibo checked me into his company's hotel which was awful! Noisy, dirty, full of cigarette smoke and hemmed in between two other buildings so no view from a window at all. I hated it. But Ibo was very busy with some foreign business people so could not make immediate arrangements to take me to the Luya Temple. Of course I needed his introduction. He also confessed that things there had changed quite a bit since we had made our initial arrangements. Firstly, the abbess who he had originally met and who seemed to him to be a woman of intelligence and spiritual integrity had left and the new, much younger abbess, although really nice, did not, in Ibo's opinion, have the same outlook as the first one. In addition, the nunnery had accepted twenty teenage orphaned girls who would stay there for their summer holidays. This had resulted in the addition of extra people being employed to look after them. Ibo had strong fears that the place was no longer a quiet peaceful place in which to do a silent retreat.

Finally the foreigners left and Ibo arrived in the company's fancy white Land Rover (he now had a driver's licence) and said that he wanted to go to the SanHuangZhai part of the mountain – on the west side of Dengfeng – because he felt stressed by his job (and no doubt my arrival which complicated matters for him). He parked by some trees and he said he just wanted to get out for a moment and feel the energy of the mountain. I got out too – and immediately had a feeling of becoming silently transparent. A silent ghost! I had had this feeling around Osho but never elsewhere; yet the energy of this mountain is powerful enough to create that space. It is because of this energy that I keep coming back here.

As had often happened before, we were both awed by the silence and power of this magnificent place and we then walked down to my old 'magic meditation spot' and just sat and absorbed the energy and beauty of the mountain.

* * *

The next day he took me to the nunnery to introduce me to the abbess and to make arrangements for me to stay there.

Oh dear! Alarm bells rang out loud and clear as we entered a door in the walled temple. I felt immediately that it was not the right place for me. I cannot put it into words: the energy was not bad, there was nothing wrong there, just it did not resonate with mine. After that softly pulsating, silent, still but alive energy of the other side of the mountain – an energy into which I could just melt and float away – the Luya nunnery felt flat and lifeless, despite the real friendliness and obvious kindness of the abbess and other people there.

I had no Plan B, however, and Ibo had three architects from Latvia coming the following day for a week to negotiate some deals with his boss and would be busy translating for the whole time. So I had no option but to stay there.

That day it wasn't too hot so my room under the roof on the third floor was quite bearable. Being in a sort of attic, there were only two small two-foot square windows at floor level, otherwise it was a concrete cavern. But it was okay. I unpacked a bit and rearranged the sparse furnishings – a bed, a chair and a rail on which to hang some clothes – after doing some intensive cleaning.

What was not okay was the fact that the squat toilets were on the ground floor and, contrary to what I remembered from my visit with Meilin, were not housed in individual cubicles but were nicely placed, four in a row, in the communal Chinese way. I would be sharing these toilets with the twenty visiting orphans and eleven nuns and sundry other persons living there. The cubicles I remembered seeing were for the showers but I couldn't even stand up in them as bizarrely someone had placed what looked like mattresses over the top of them. This was fine for small Chinese people but I had to stoop at an angle even to fit into them.

In early Indian days squat toilets were the norm and my legs were young enough and strong enough to squat and get up with ease. But these days it is a major effort and I need some support from a door handle or something to squat steadily and then lever myself up again! These toilet bowls had no support features at all.

I decided I couldn't face the problem at the moment and so decided to go for a bit of a walk around the place. What I dreaded happening did of course immediately happen! Everyone stopped and stared and I was the centre of everyone's attention. If one has been to countries where westerners are seldom seen, one knows how exhausting, even violating, it is to have every feature and every movement scrutinised by endless pairs of eyes. It was like this here. I tried to walk down the one side of the complex but was immediately met by a viciously barking little dog who defied me to pass him on the path. His barking alerted three geese on the other side of the path who set up an answering chorus of squawks. This duet was then enhanced by a third voice, a deep baritone from a large dog further on.

As the little barking dog was on a short chain and the geese were behind a fence, however, I successfully negotiated the path, only to be pounced upon by two ladies – not dressed as nuns – who grabbed me firmly by each arm chanting 'Aaaamitofu, Aaaamitofu, Aaaamitofu'! In the Song Mountain area the Buddhist god of choice is Amitabha so they have to keep on chanting his name as a kind of mantra to remember him.

These ladies dragged me into the main centre temple hall

which was amazing in its lavish decorations and the presence of hundreds of statues of deities adorning the walls from the floor to the very high ceiling. I have never seen so much decoration before although every Buddhist temple is abundantly supplied with statues. I of course had to do the obligatory bowing to the Buddha statue which was fine, I had done this many times before, and was then escorted round the hall having the hundreds of names of the deities shouted at me. The background to all this was an electronic music machine that loudly played a mantra – involving Amitabha – round the clock. When the German sannyasin singer, Premal, sings her mantras they are indescribably beautiful but blaring canned music on a 'loop' gets massively irritating very quickly. Added to this was the sound of one nun's sadhana; it appeared that she had to keep herself alert by incessantly banging a Buddhist temple 'instrument' which is a hollow piece of wood hit by another piece of wood making a 'clock, clock, clock' sound. Very intrusive if you are trying to be silent.

Shattered already by all this noise and by now desperately needing a toilet I got myself out of there, avoided the threat of a second large dog, retreated into one of the smaller side buildings with yet another deity and found an old dirty bed to sit on. There were no chairs in the whole place – just cushions to kneel on. When the aaamitofuing old ladies had disappeared, I again emerged and found to my relief there were some public toilets within a short distance. Here a slight concession to privacy had been made in that there were waist-high walls separating the toilet bowels which, while not ensuring much privacy, did give me something to hang onto.

The next ordeal was lunch. Only if one has spent some time in China does one know what an ordeal a mealtime can be. The Chinese eat an enormous amount. It still blows my mind when I see these thin, tiny people eating at least three times more than me! One serving bowl is more than my stomach can handle; they easily devour the contents of two or three. Did anybody ever measure the size of a Chinese stomach? Of course Chinese hospitality requires the hosts to load you with as much food as possible – otherwise they would be remiss in taking care of you. And I am much bigger than they are so logically I must eat much more than they do. And so the battle began! After one enormous bowl of very mediocre food I was full but everybody present was duty-bound to refill the bowl or, if I put my hand over it, to bring another bowl filled to the brim. And then their massive rolls of steamed bread had to be eaten. With half of one of those things I was full (they are dry and unappetising so are difficult to eat anyway) but now I had to fend off offer after offer of rolls. Finally the ordeal was over and I could escape to my room for a bit of peace and quiet to restore my shattered nerves.

The quiet was only temporary, however, because after the after-lunch nap there arose a cacophony of sounds outside my windows. I had thought there was only a bit of quiet wooded area outside, but no, it seemed like there was a major argument going on outside involving a lot of screaming and shouting amongst a lot of people. Only later in the afternoon did I find out that this was the 'bee family'. Outside my window, amidst the scraggy trees, were a lot of bee hives tended by a family of about eight people who lived there but whose meeting ground was an open space below my window. Here they passed the time of day and socialised with all and sundry who came up to visit the scenic area around the reservoir. I have mentioned how in India the locals would scream and screech at each other and it often sounded like they were having a massive argument when in fact they were only having a nice 'quiet' chat about the weather or their cousin's wedding. The Chinese peasant communicates in the same way!

Fortunately, after being in India for so long, I still never go anywhere without earplugs — the English chemist, Boots, has probably made a fortune from all my earplug purchases over the years! – so I was able to block out most of the noise while napping.

Of course after the nap I needed the toilet again so tried to make my way as silently and as inconspicuously as possible to the public toilets, only to have all attention focused on me again because of the barking of the dogs and the squawking of the geese as I negotiated my way between them, and the running orphans who were doing their daily exercise by racing round and round the central hall. In fact the place was like a small village with some kids playing around and everyone 'chatting' at high volume to each other.

I fled outside to the comparative quiet of the unattractive, litter-strewn farming area surrounding the temple and sat down on a concrete block to try and do a bit of meditation. Within five minutes this temporarily quiet space was rudely disturbed by one of the 'Aaaamitofu' ladies who, having seen me go outside, must have felt duty-bound to accompany me. She brought with her a hoe and proceeded to hoe the grass shouting 'aaamitofu' on every stroke and tried to get me to join in. After politely putting up with this for ten minutes I indicated that I was going for a walk and, even though it was very hot, walked up the road where I discovered the bee family and was introduced to their circle.

When I finally returned I experienced the only restful interlude in the whole day. Everyone had gathered in the central hall and were now chanting the amitofu mantra, with someone keeping time with the beautiful huge gong and someone ringing some bells. This was lovely and I sat on the steps and enjoyed the sounds. Peace was short-lived, however, as when the chanting was over, it was supper time and a repeat performance of the lunch time ordeal ensued.

Not only did the nuns live in the nunnery, there were, as well as the temporary twenty orphans who were actually the quietest group, a number of other women who appeared to live there – maybe about six of them and they all talked with (read 'screeched at') each other at a decibel level higher than my ears can easily deal with. As mosquitoes now joined the evening fray and it was impossible to sit outside in the cool of the evening – or go for a walk as the nunnery door was bolted shut at 6pm – I again retreated to my concrete cavern and eventually tried to go to sleep. But couldn't. There was something about the energy of the place that was at odds with mine and although I tried hard to centre myself and relax, I just couldn't.

At about 5am the next morning I decided to have a cup of tea. I had brought water, tea, milk, some sugar and a small electric kettle for the task of making that all-important early morning cuppa. But when I poured the water into the kettle I found to my disgust that the kettle was leaking – it must have been cracked or something – and water was streaming out of it almost as fast as I was pouring it in. So now the floor was covered with water and I couldn't make tea. And really, tea is an essential for me to start the day! I had just uttered a few choice expletives when there was a loud banging on the door (it was 5.45am) and someone shouting 'shiffana', the Chinese word for food. I cannot eat that early in the morning and the thought of another mealtime battle without the fortifying morning cuppa was more than I could bear so I, quite calmly considering how I was feeling, opened the door and said 'bu shiffana' – no food. The young girl disappeared only to return about five minutes later, again banging on the door and insisting on 'shiffana'. I again insisted on 'bu shiffana' and then crawled back into bed shattered – and it was now only six in the morning.

One thing was very clear: this was not my place. I felt as far away from my mountain as I would if I were back in England.

* * *

At around 8am I texted Liu, the taxi driver, and asked him if he knew where this temple was. He replied that he did so I asked him to come and pick me up as soon as possible. When he arrived I gave him the little present I had brought for him and then called Yujie in Hainan and asked her to ask him if he knew of a small, cheap, but passable hotel near the other side of the mountain for me to stay in – in the little village of ShiLiPu where I usually lived. At least there I knew where I was, could catch buses and get food for myself – and of course visit the part of the mountain I loved so much. My lovely flat would be unliveable in due to the heat and I also would have to buy all the household goods again – quite an expense – which I did not want to do as I would not be there for such a long time.

Apparently Liu did know of one and he took me to a very basic small place which was, however, clean and quiet and had air-conditioning. Coming down from the mountain it was noticeably hotter. It had its own disproportionately huge bathroom with a reasonable shower and western toilet. There was no doubt in my mind! Here I would stay. Liu had come up trumps one more time! I paid a deposit to stay from the following night and went back to the nunnery.

But now, as well as the nerve-wracking day ahead of me, I had to break the news to Ibo that I wasn't going to stay there and I knew he would *not* be pleased. He of course wasn't, so another battle ensued. He must have then called Andy who was in Harbin, in northern China, who then called me in the middle of lunch to find out what was going on and to no doubt try to talk some sense into me. He definitely wasn't happy at my change of plan and lectured me on the fact that Ibo would now lose face as he had made these arrangements, but I said it was my holiday and I couldn't stay in a place so unsuitable and uncomfortable just to make things convenient for everybody else.

However, I knew that losing face was an extremely important issue in both Chinese and Japanese life. To lose face means to lose one's dignity, social standing, honour and trustworthiness. I could not do this to Ibo but I also had my own agenda to consider so I asked Andy if he could see a way to sort the problem out – as someone who had lived in the west for ten years he could see both sides. He said he would talk to Ibo and call me back. When we again spoke he said he would talk to the abbess on behalf of both Ibo and myself (a kind of mediator!) and told me to find her with my phone at the ready. A long conversation ensued and, as the abbess was smiling and nodding, I concluded that Andy had successfully negotiated a way out of the problem! When I took back the phone he said that everything had now been resolved satisfactorily by putting the blame fairly and squarely on me, the stupid westerner, who hadn't understood clearly what Ibo had arranged!!

Well, I was fine with that so the abbess and I had a cup of tea together and we parted amiably to continue with the rest of the day's programs. I went for an unsatisfactory walk, sweating profusely in the ever increasing heat and had a hard time sleeping again that night, not only because of my own disquiet, but also because the room had become an oven and even the fan provided didn't have much impact anymore.

The final day was a bit easier – possibly because I managed to get some hot water for my early morning tea but mainly because I knew I was escaping. After lunch the abbess invited me to her room, for a 'chat', I suppose – with one of her sidekicks, a very sweet little nun. I then said I must go to my room. I had first said to sleep, at which point the abbess wanted me to sleep on the other bed in her room but this would be too public for me. So I then tried 'meditation' – Chinese word, 'datsuo' – so she said we should all meditate together. Well, I was fine with that and proceeded to close my eyes, sit still and meditate. I wanted to see what would happen.

It immediately became apparent that sitting in silence was something foreign to them. They could not sit still and were soon chattering quietly to themselves. Then one got up to close the curtains but three minutes later got up to open them again. Then a woman with a baby came in and there were more muffled chats with the baby playing around. Then they left and the two nuns at last fell silent and we meditated for about ten minutes after which they got up to stretch their legs – so I got up too! Major cultural differences here but it was all very amiable and heartful and we parted on good terms.

It was now crystal-clear to me that even with the best will in the world, Osho's ways do not mix with traditional ways. Perhaps it was because Buddhism, with its many rituals and ceremonies, was so prevalent here and I was steeped in Osho's Zen ways. Unfortunately, although Song Mountain was the birthplace of Zen, for which silent meditation is all that is needed for an inner transformation, it did not seem to be understood or practised here at all. Was this then the end of my dream of being able to meditate in undisturbed silence in the energy field of this mountain, the most sacred mountain in China? I felt sad that there was a distinct possibility that the answer was yes.

A Concrete Take-over

Concrete is for me the symbol of modern China. I have read somewhere that China consumes half the available concrete production globally.

Moving from the concrete cavern in the Luya Temple, I entered a similar cavern in the small hotel Liu had taken me to –

this one without even the small windows. Building cavernous rooms with ceilings at least sixteen feet high with tiny or no windows seems to be typical of this area. I had to keep the florescent light on all the time despite a window in the huge bathroom which allowed some light to filter into my room through the door. There were damp patches everywhere, alarmingly close to the air-conditioner, and I wondered what would happen if there was a real downpour. Would the fuses hold up against the penetrating moisture? It was reasonably quiet, however, and the air-conditioning was a godsend. I proposed spending my days writing on my small notebook computer and walking in the foothills of the mountains in the evening.

The proprietors of the small hotel (five rooms) and restaurant were predictably sweet and kind and the daughter even spoke a little English and asked for help with her 'homework' as she was training to be an English tour guide.

Construction in front of my landlord's house

I visited the landlords of my lovely Zen flat and found that, to my horror, they were constructing two buildings on the plot of land in front of their house. I had so much enjoyed looking out of the balcony window and watching them gardening on this plot of land, a green patch amidst the grey concrete, and wondered if I could ever come back here again as my view would be one more concrete building instead of the garden. I noted also that the flat was a furnace in this hot weather.

Their building was just part of a massively disturbing rise of construction in the area. It took me some time to put together snippets of information to form a picture of what was happening. It was a very ugly and distressing story.

In 2010, after much pressure from the powerful Shaolin Temple, many local 'spiritual' places had been designated World Heritage sites, making the Song Mountain area one of the leading protected areas in China and supposedly enhancing its tourist potentialities. But only individual places were protected, not the land in between.

Ghastly uninhabited ghost buildings

Entrepreneurs were quick to see this situation and exploit it. The results were appalling. On the first evening at the hotel I went for one of my old walks which took a different direction to my usual walk towards the mountain. I was shocked, devastated, at what I saw. Everywhere I looked I saw 'shells' of buildings, like 'ghost' buildings, being constructed at a phenomenal rate. I counted thirty-seven of these bizarre edifices from the one place where I was standing, and those were only the ones I could see. I had no idea what was happening here.

The next evening I went to visit Master Wu Nanfang at his kungfu school. The shock at seeing the school building – which he rented from a local businessman – was even greater. The building had changed almost beyond recognition and now sported a third floor and extensions on the side and front, the latter totally obscuring the extraordinary view which I had blissed out on so much for so long. I was so upset I could hardly take it in but Lijuan's English was not sufficient to give me any clues as to what was happening. Finally a young man named Wenzhe appeared and attempted to talk to me. His English was halting and basic but he told me that he was the new student manager. I could see he was very nervous at having to speak to me but his confidence grew as we conversed – it soon became apparent that he actually had quite a good grasp of the language but had had little practice at using it. This made it easier for me to help.

After a while I was able to piece together something of the greedy, ugly story. Apparently it had been decided by the government and the powerful money-grabbing Shaolin Temple to turn this whole area into a scenic park, anticipating a huge surge in tourism as result of the new World Heritage status. This would involve kicking out all the farmers and local people and destroying all the buildings already here to build five-star hotels and luxury apartments to take advantage of the stunning views of the mountain – and of course to make millions of yuan. The government would have to compensate the locals for the destruction of already existing buildings. The result was a manic dash by anybody who had some spare cash to quickly erect useless 'shells' of buildings or make additions to existing ones (bribing local council officials for planning permission) in the hope of receiving massive financial compensation when the time came for the government to destroy these buildings and start its new luxury construction project. It only took four to six weeks to build one of these 'shells' so they were going up phenomenally quickly.

I was deeply saddened by this information and wondered what Master Wu Nanfang felt about it. He joined me for the evening meal and I was happy to see him looking much better than when I had left the previous year. He was a bit noncommittal about the devastation around him and I soon learned why. Apparently he had finally found and bought a piece of land on which to build a new school from scratch so that it fulfilled all his requirements. The land was behind ShiLiPu village on the opposite side of this valley and would be quiet and secluded while still convenient to reach. I was very happy to hear that he would be out of this construction madness and away from the busy and noisy highway. This was, however, only a small compensation for the distressing scenes I had witnessed today and would be faced with each time I tried to go for a walk. Walking, in fact, became hazardous as it involved dodging endless trucks bringing bricks, concrete and other building materials down the once pleasant farm roads.

The same thing was happening on the other side of the mountain where the nunnery was. The destruction/construction there was largely the work of Ibo's boss's friend who had made millions from the construction of giant apartment blocks on the road leading up to the nunnery – and elsewhere.

Although this manic construction process had started when I was here before, the rapid acceleration had happened while I was away. Subsequent visits to downtown Dengfeng revealed what looked like a bombed war zone, with many buildings, sometimes entire blocks, reduced to rubble so that new buildings, mostly hotels, blocks of luxury apartments and shopping malls, could be built. Tiny little family-run shops, where I had bought, for example, pillows or mats, had totally disappeared.

Needless to say, the sadness that I felt at this mindless, money-driven destruction and construction was not conducive to meditation.

On a Brighter Note....

I was very happy to be able to spend time with Master Wu Nanfang and his family again. I was always mindful of the fact that they had welcomed me unquestioningly and hugely contributed to the very unique experiences I had had on my visits to China. For this I am forever grateful.

One evening we were enjoying a rather silent time together although there was sporadic conversation between me and a young American guy who was spending ten days at the school. I was telling him about SanHuangZhai and remembered that somehow I had never heard the full story of the two old nuns and their connection with the temple. As Wenzhe happened to come in at that moment, I asked him if we could talk to the master about this. I really wanted the story for my book as the little I had heard was quite extraordinary and, anyway, I truly loved Yonglian who had always welcomed me so graciously whenever I went up to the monastery.

It was my lucky evening because Master Wu Nanfang seemed to be in story-telling mode. Wenzhe was obviously a bit nervous at having to do some concentrated translating – he had never had to do anything like this before – but he rose to the occasion brilliantly and we were privileged to hear two wonderful stories, neither one of which, I am sure, has ever been told in English.

The first is the remarkable story of two Chinese women whose Buddhist faith was so strong that they faced censure from their families, dangerous parts of the country, soldiers of the Cultural Revolution and cold, hunger and privation to live in a small temple on Shaoshi Peak, the highest peak of the section of Song Mountain that could be seen from the school and ShiLiPu village. It is the peak on which SanHuangZhai is built.

Yongyue, now ninety-two years old, came from a rich family who were also strong Buddhists so as a child and teenager she worshipped Buddha every day. The family lived in Linying, near Xuchang, which is about two hundred kilometres south-east of Dengfeng. Yonglian, now eighty-two years old, came from a very poor family who were also strong Buddhists. She went to work for Yongyue's family and soon became the young girl's personal servant. Then, as often happened in the Chinese tradition, she became a companion and almost a sister to Yongyue, despite the ten-year difference in age. They lived and played together.

Sometime between 1940 and 1950, Yongyue and Yonglian visited a very small temple high up on Song Mountain. This was, however, not the only place they visited – they went to many Buddhist temples in the area, walking or travelling in a horse-drawn cart. But it was to Song Mountain that they were drawn.

Yongyue was allowed to travel alone as long as she had her companion, Yonglian, with her, as it was the custom for Buddhists to travel the country to worship at different temples, but her parents didn't know that, instead of going to the usual temples where they would have been safe, the two girls climbed up Song Mountain to the small temple that they had found, which was actually owned by the Shaolin Temple. It was a deserted place where very few people went, so it was quite dangerous. But this special, secret, little temple was the place that they loved and the girls decided that this is where they wanted to live. Eventually they settled there – telling Yongyue's parents that they were staying in another safer temple in case they were forced to return home.

With a Taoist monk called Mr Lou, who lived in one half of the building, the two women lived there until the Cultural Revolution started in 1966. Many temples and their statues and pictures were destroyed during this time. Even this small temple was almost completely destroyed – just the outer stone walls and part of the back of the temple were left. The two young women were forced to leave and returned to Yongyue's family home. But having lived in the beauty and solitude of Song Mountain for so long, they couldn't settle and so returned to a small village at the base of the mountain, almost directly below the now ruined temple. The village, called ShiYaHe, was situated next to a river ('he' means river) the source of which is very close to the temple high up on the mountain. According to Chinese law the two women registered as residents of ShiYaHe.

When the Cultural Revolution ended in 1975 they went back up the mountain and lived in the ruins of the temple. But the customs of the Cultural Revolution persisted and often during the next ten years the reserve militia – dedicated to destroying any remaining spiritual heritage – made them leave, but they always returned. During those times they attempted to rebuild parts of the building with Mr Lou who, because he was very old and frail, had been allowed to remain there. The young women lived in the front part of the temple worshipping Buddha and Mr Lou lived in the back part and practised Taoism. This division of one temple into different spiritual heritages is not uncommon in China. Mr Lou died somewhere between 1970 and 1980.

After 1975 China began to change rapidly. Many reforms were

brought in including the freedom of religion. So the two women were able to live in peace and without fear in their little temple on their beloved mountain. (Only those who have been there can know what a truly incredible place this is.) A few people managed to make their way up the rough path and always brought some kind of food with them as a gift: bags of rice or noodles or flour. The nuns had made a small vegetable garden and lived on what they could cultivate and whatever wild plants they could find growing on the mountainside.

In about 1988 a young monk called Dejian came to live at the Shaolin Temple. He had practised kungfu since he was a child but was keen to live and study at the so-called home of kungfu. He wandered over the mountain peaks in the area and often visited the nuns in their little temple. In front of the temple there was a small flat space where he practised kungfu. After meeting Master Wu Nanfang in 1990 he took him to this place and the young men trained together, now focussing on Wugulun Kungfu which Master Wu Nanfang had learned from his ancestors. In around 1990, work was started on the steps leading to the top of Shaoshi Peak – until that time there had only been a rough steep path.

Yongyue and Yonglian had by now been joined by two young woman initiates and had formed a small nunnery in their temple.

In the next few years Dejian had the idea to build a bigger and better temple as the site was such a unique one and, with the agreement of the two nuns, started making plans. Work began around 2002 and, although the temple is mostly finished, work is still in progress.

Yongyue was now very old but Yonglian featured in the BBC's documentary 'Extreme Pilgrim' in 2008 and went up and down the mountain two or three times a year. On one of the occasions that I met her, I asked her how she felt about having her tiny quiet temple turned into a major construction site and a major tourist attraction.

She smiled gently and said, 'I feel very lucky to have someone to look after us in our old age because it was always very hard living here. We loved it and would never have left, but often it wasn't easy, especially in the wintertime!'

Having met the two nuns I was deeply touched by their story. It was even more extraordinary than I had imagined. When one considers how women during the era of the two nuns' early lives were sequestered at home with limited chances of doing anything or going anywhere, the courage of these two women to live alone in such hardship was almost beyond belief.

* * *

And Master Wu Nanfang had yet another special story up his sleeve. How I wished I could speak Chinese because I was sure he had an inexhaustible supply of tales to tell!

He began his story by reminding us that of the five sacred mountains in China, Song Mountain is the most important. It is said that Shaoshi Peak, with the other lower peaks around it, resembles a nine petal lotus flower. Because the lotus is a sacred flower for Taoists, Buddhists and Zen Buddhists, this mountain became a sacred mountain for all of these three branches of the Chinese spiritual heritage.

Around 1870, when the Shaolin Temple was once again demolished, one of the monks, Master Wu Gulun, retreated to the small village, BaiYuGou, which I was fortunate to visit a few years before, to practise and preserve the secrets of the Shaolin culture. In order to pass on the secrets to someone he could trust, he married and had a son called Wu Shanlin who became the second Grandmaster in the Wugulun lineage. Wu Shanlin in turn had two sons: Wu You De and Wu Tian You, Master Wu Nanfang's grandfather.

A Mountain in China

Wu Tian You was born in 1910 and started to learn kungfu when he was six years old. As his father and grandfather did, he also trained while farming, using the using the typical movements and rhythms of working the land to hone his kungfu skills. Because he was strong and clever he became a kungfu master at the age of twenty-five.

In 1933 Wu Tian You built a kungfu school in Zhongyue Maio, the Taoist temple in Dengfeng, with the help of the Shaolin Temple and the Dengfeng local government. He taught many people and became a highly skilled and very much revered master.

Disaster struck, however, in 1936 when the Japanese, who had invaded China, bombed Dengfeng. People fled to the mountain and Wu Tian You went back to BaiYuGou village where he continued to farm with Wu Shanlin who had now also become a doctor and was treating people with traditional Chinese medicine. Many people retreated to the hidden village to protect themselves from the Japanese soldiers.

Towards the end of 1936, however, the Japanese crossed Wuru Peak and discovered BaiYuGou village. (I mentioned earlier that the village could be seen across the valley from this peak.) People immediately escaped from the village and hid themselves deeper in the mountains but they knew that the Japanese would burn their houses and possessions and that they would have nothing left when they returned.

Wu Tian You decided to come back to the village alone to see if he could persuade the Japanese soldiers to leave without destroying the village. With the soldiers was a Chinese man who had betrayed his fellow countrymen and was now in the pay of the Japanese. When Wu Tian You told this man that he was a kungfu master the man mocked him and challenged him to fight. Of course Wu Tian You won. The Japanese soldiers were impressed, and sensing a change in their aggression, Wu Tian You cooked them a wonderful meal and asked them not to destroy the village. They agreed and left, so the village and its inhabitants were saved.

Because of his courage, Wu Tian You now became famous and many students came to study kungfu with him. It was he who taught the orphan boy, Zhang Qing He, who later became the third Grandmaster of the lineage, and many other people about the Shaolin culture.

Wu Tian You became ill in 1950 and sadly died in 1960.

When the Cultural Revolution began in 1966 its members wanted to destroy all of the Chinese traditional culture so they came to Wu Shanlin's house in BaiYuGou and removed all his kungfu weapons (except his stick which he hid in the forest and which Wu Nanfang still uses today) and his Damo pictures but still he continued to spread the Wugulun Kungfu and Shaolin cultures. He and his students trained in man-made caves using tiny oil lamps so they couldn't be seen. At this time the Shaolin Temple was destroyed yet again and many local people were ridiculed and abused.

Wu Shanlin died in 1970 after which Zhang Quin He became the third Grandmaster.

With so much violence in China's history I think that very few of the incredible local stories of this area – and of course many other places in China – will be preserved. When this generation of people die, the stories will die with them. I am happy that I have had the chance to hear and record a few of them.

The Remaining Days

I had planned to stay in Dengfeng for only a month this time and already most of the time had gone by. Andy had arranged to take a train down from Harbin and spend three days with Ibo and me before continuing on to his home in Guangzhou in the south. I would fly back to England a day or two later.

Time went by tediously. It was too hot to go out during the day so I spent most of the time holed up in my concrete cavern trying to meditate – but meditation and concrete don't go well together. Ibo was so busy I hardly talked to him on the phone let alone saw him.

Wenzhe kindly stepped into the breach, however, by assenting to my request for some help in interviewing some of the local people for the book. One evening he came round and we visited first my great friend, Chao Feng Lee, the convenience store man, who had helped me out so many times by patiently trying to understand what it was that I needed. But I didn't know anything about him because, with nobody to translate, communication depended on smiles and miming which didn't go far. It seemed to me that he was not his usual cheery self and, if I understood rightly, this was because his wife had left him and had taken his gorgeous little boy, whom he adored, with her. The excuse was that she wanted to live on the other side of the village so she could be near her child's school.

I further learned from him that he felt badly that he could not provide for his wife as he should. Apparently his shop, which was on the ground floor of the building, belonged to his wife's father – who owned the whole building. Chinese custom dictates that the husband and his family should provide for the wife but in his case the opposite had occurred. It seemed he came from a poor family and had been working as a labourer building roads before he got married. I was so sad to hear this because he was such a nice man and worked from early morning to late at night, seven days a week, to make his convenience store a success. In all the times I visited ShiLiPu I had never seen the shop closed for more than two hours in the afternoon when he deservedly closed for the siesta time – sometimes! Very early every morning he went to Dengfeng to buy groceries and vegetables for the shop.

After talking to Chao Feng we then visited my first landlords, Mr and Mrs Wang. I had never had a good talk with them either and often wondered about their situation because, without seeming to work, they owned two big houses in the village and some land at the back which they farmed. To be honest, I am still not clear what their story is. It seemed like they were both from local families and lived in the village nearby but on the other side of the highway. Perhaps the story is that, as locals, they owned some land which was then sold to build the new modern village of ShiLiPu where they now lived. Perhaps this is how they got the money to build the

Maiyen and her brother

house where I lived on my second visit here – and where the older son now lives – and a very big new house next door. The younger son would have the second floor of this house when he gets married. It seemed that Mr Wang was still involved with some building projects in the village. His two sons worked for their uncle who had a road building company in Zhejiang Province and the daughter-in-law, Maiyen's mother, worked as a waitress in one of the local restaurants. Mrs Wang looked after Maiyen and her little brother during the day. Well, I couldn't get many details but they were a happy family and so sweet and hospitable to me.

* * *

Accessing an internet connection this time around was quite a problem. I didn't want to use the school's internet connection too often but my usual internet café that I had used in the past had disappeared! Apparently the authorities had raided the place and found that it was full of school kids playing violent computer games. This was obviously a lucrative source of income for the owner but his strategy was misguided because the government had brought in a new law making it illegal for internet cafes to allow school kids to play these games. My local guy, the one who was usually drunk, had, I think, felt he had a certain immunity because his café was well hidden in the depths of the little village on the other side of the highway from where I was living. There were not even streets in this old part of the village, only narrow passage ways between the houses. No vehicle could get anywhere near it. Unfortunately he still got caught out and the café was closed.

When the heat wasn't too bad I went to the youth hostel in Dengfeng and used their WiFi system. This had an added advantage for me because I often met some interesting western people who were staying there and it was nice to talk English with them and to hear of their travels.

Then one day I was surprised when the hotel owner knocked on my door and excitedly tried to tell me something. I really couldn't figure out what he was trying to tell me so in the end had to call Ibo. It turned out that the owner had decided to install an internet connection in his little hotel because he had heard from the young woman, who had now returned to Zhengzhou to continue her studies, that I needed an internet connection! So sweet! And sure enough within an hour some young guys arrived and installed a dubious-looking little machine in the passage outside the door of my room and presto, I had a WiFi connection! I offered money for the use of it but this was emphatically refused. I really never fail to be amazed at the way the Chinese do things.

* * *

Two days before I left Andy arrived from Harbin. It was great to see him again and we went to our favourite hot pot restaurant to celebrate. He had had difficulty booking a train ticket, however, and had to leave earlier than planned so it meant he could not come to the airport to see me off as planned.

As Ibo was too busy to take time off, I went alone to the airport with Liu. It was a very intense ride. It had started to rain in the morning and as we drove east the sky turned green-black – I had never seen something like that before. It was like night in the middle of the day. There were intermittent cloudbursts along the way with rain so dense I couldn't even see ten feet ahead, except when flashes of sheet lightning penetrated the curtains of water.

The weather reflected my feelings. I was confused and depressed. It seemed that it was impossible for me to create the right environment here to support silent, undisturbed meditation. Was a wasting my time pursuing this dream I had? To paraphrase Lao Tzu: the water was muddy and unclear and the right action had not presented itself. I did not know what to do.

7

A Most Blessed Mountain

'the whole range that goes for thousands of miles.'

This mountain is one of the most blessed in the world.
So many seekers, so many who are absolutely determined
to attain to their potential...
A thousand or ten thousand sleeping buddhas are trying to wake up.
This mountain is not a small place.
If it can contain ten thousand buddhas, how can it be a small place?
It is ten thousand mountains,
the whole range that goes for thousands of miles.

Osho: No Mind: The Flowers of Eternity

Those Ten Thousand Buddhas

My summer visit to Song Mountain had not been a great experience – to put it mildly. Not only had my attempt to do a silent retreat at the Luya nunnery been a comical disaster but the remaining days, enclosed in a concrete cavern with no windows, were definitely uninspiring. Of course it was my fault for going in the summer when I knew it would be very hot but I hadn't bargained on the nunnery attempt being so absolutely a failure. Then too, the horrific, greed-driven construction of those ugly ghost buildings in ShiLiPu village, resulting in the destruction of all that was sacred of this most sacred mountain in China had left me very disheartened. I seriously questioned if I was just chasing a figment of my imagination here and deluding myself about my connections with this place and I genuinely felt I would not return.

It took me a few months back in England to come to terms with the devastating effects this last visit had had on me But slowly the muddy water cleared and I started to feel that to turn my back on all that the mountain, the place and the people had meant to me simply because of one negative experience, would be cowardly. I still felt there were unanswered questions there. I still felt that there was something there for me to grasp. And I also felt that I didn't want to end my connection there in a negative way.

After months of deliberation and meditation I decided to go back one more time – if nothing else but to say goodbye and thank you to all those people who had been so graciously welcoming and helpful to me. And of course to meditate a little while on the beloved mountain again. But I would curb my impatience and return only in the autumn when the otherwise inhospitable climate would at least allow me to function comfortably without continually struggling to overcome the extremes of the capricious weather.

Having arrived at this decision I set about doing a bit more research for my book because one of the unanswered questions for me was still the mystery of those ten thousand buddhas. Why had Osho been so fond of using that phrase, of evoking that concept, and where, in the past history of China, was that concept hidden? My Chinese friends were familiar with the words but when I asked where they came from and what they meant, there was puzzled silence. Like us sannyasins, they had never queried the idea.

Searching online through all kind of obscure texts, I found that the first mention of the phrase and its relation to a cave was in about 366 AD. In that year a Buddhist monk had a vision of a thousand Buddhas bathed in golden light, which inspired him to build a cave housing images of a thousand buddhas. Thus began the construction of the Mogao Caves in Dunhuang, in north-west China. The caves later became famous world-wide because it was here that a scroll was discovered on which was written a well-known Buddhist scripture: The Diamond Sutra. The scroll actually had a date written on it – 868 AD – which makes it the earliest dated document in the world. The Diamond Sutra scroll is now housed in The British Library in London and is on view occasionally but not always, because the paper on which it is written is extremely fragile and extended exposure to light is harmful.

From the fourth century onwards, Dunhuang became a busy hub for the Silk Road as trade flourished between China and the west. The Mogao Caves and their artistic treasures were added to by an increasing number of monks who gathered there and it became a place of religious pilgrimage. It was thought that the presence of so many Buddha images would inspire people to meditate and further their quest for enlightenment.

It seems that as time went on, the original thousand buddhas became ten thousand buddhas and caves, like the Longmen ones, filled with buddha images, were created all over China and in other eastern Buddhist countries.

I was still not entirely satisfied. Why so many buddhas? Nobody that I asked had an answer to this and, in the end, after much reading, I felt that it was Osho who most clearly answered the question. He says:

> *In China there is one Buddha temple which has ten thousand Buddha statues, all Buddha statues. Wherever you look – the same figure. The ceiling has the same figure, all the sides have the same figure, the walls have the same figure. Ten thousand Buddha statues! Just think, sitting cross-legged in a Buddha posture and you are also surrounded by ten thousand Buddhas! It creates a geometry. From everywhere Buddha impinges upon you. From every nook and corner he starts surrounding you. You are gone. Your ordinary geometry is no longer there. Your ordinary life is no longer there. For a few moments you are moving on higher planes, at higher altitudes.*
>
> *That's what is happening here. While listening to me something is created – by my presence, by my words, by your attitude, by so many orange people around you. It is a situation, it is a temple. A temple is a situation. It is not just that you are sitting in a lecture hall. With so many people listening to me with such love, gratitude, with such silence, with such sympathy, with such rapport, this place becomes holy. This place becomes a teertha; it is sacred. When you come into this place you are riding on a wave, you need not make much effort. You can simply allow it to happen. You will be taken away, far away, to the other shore.*

It seems to me that Osho here is evoking, using, an ancient

concept – in this case the impact of ten thousand buddhas all together – to help us now in the twenty-first century. This is the essence and unique brilliance of his 'teachings': he takes the profound wisdom and understanding of the world's great spiritual heritages – Christianity, Hinduism, Islam, Hassidism, Buddhism, Taoism, Zen – and explains and interprets them in a way that you and I, living in this modern age, can understand and, above all, *use* to help us on our own spiritual path.

Buddha statues on the wall of the 'Ten Thousand Buddhas Cave' in the Longmen Grottoes, Luoyang.

He seems confident that the collective energy of many 'buddhas' – be they statues or human beings – can help to create the transformation necessary for the seeker on the path.

But I still had a practical query! Often with the phrase 'ten thousand buddhas' Osho would also mention a temple. My research revealed many caves – even a monastery in Hong Kong and a city in California – with ten thousand buddhas but never a temple! Where was this temple? The mystery would only be solved during the final days of my next visit to China.

Mongolian Moon

Shortly before leaving for China again, Yujie skyped me. Of course I had planned to see her in Beijing where she was now living, having started her own business: an agency to place Chinese students in western schools or universities. When I answered her urgent call she told me that the Thursday following my arrival was the mid-autumn Full Moon Day, an event celebrated all over China. I had celebrated that day two years previously with the kungfu students in ShiLiPu. She wanted to spend the day with her parents and asked me if I would like to come with her to Inner Mongolia, where they lived, for four days? What a wonderful invitation! I had so much enjoyed staying with her family in Hainan Island and would love to see them again so a trip to visit them and, in addition to see something of Inner Mongolia would be a great treat for me.

Then and there Yujie and I booked our flights. We would fly together to Hohhot but at the end of the visit she would fly back to Beijing and I would fly to Zhengzhou in Henan Province where Ibo would meet me and take me to Song Mountain.

As it was a China Air flight, we left from the Beijing Capital Airport instead of the domestic one. I had only arrived there five days previously! Flying west into Hohhot, the capital city of Inner

Mongolia, reminded me very much of Bamiyan in Afghanistan – with a barren kind of escarpment edging the city. And oh, the deep blue sky! And, when we walked out of the plane, the incredibly pure, clean air! In Beijing one usually feels that one is living in a grey soup, as the smog never really goes, so to sample this air – more pure than even Swiss mountain air – was an exhilarating. The whole time I was there I was constantly aware of the quality of the air.

Mr Zhao, Yujie's father, met us at the airport in his super new black Honda and I was momentarily taken aback when he got out and bowed in respect. Being devout Buddhists, Yujie's family members greet each other with a in this way, accompanying the bow with the greeting I had heard often before: 'Aaaaamitofuo'. Yujie later explained that this greeting by the Buddhist sect which 'worships' the Amitabha Buddha means: 'I wish you a speedy journey to the Clear Land'. Apparently, once you make it to 'the Clear Land', it is a very short and easy step to becoming enlightened. I am eminently happy to accept such a wish!

Hohhot has very wide streets as land is not an issue here and Russian-looking architecture, complete with onion-shaped domes, everywhere. And then there was a further surprise.... I was expecting a family gathering for this full moon festival but Mrs Zhao wanted to spend the evening at her favourite temple where they were going to celebrate the event, and had suggested that we join her. I was of course very enthusiastic about this unexpected idea, so soon we were on our way, negotiating rough roads full of potholes and puddles of water. We finally arrived at the very escarpment I had seen from the plane and entered the temple. It was only ten years old and was the inspiration of a wandering monk who, arriving here, had decided that it was the perfect place to build a temple. So he set about collecting funds and somehow everything happened and here was this quite magical temple set into the hills and shining with an uncanny light as the sun set and the sky turned a deep indigo blue.

It was lovely to see Mrs Zhao again and she had kindly prepared a very substantial snack for us as there would be some ceremonies before the evening feast and we had not had any lunch. After the meal, Mr Zhao took Yujie and me on a tour of the temple complex and then surprised me one more time by suggesting that I might like to meet the master whose inspiration the temple was. A very gracious eighty-four-year-old man greeted us as we entered the main hall and then we sat and had tea with him as he virtually interrogated me about meditation and my life with Osho. I think I might have been the first western person to go to this remote place – or at least the first one who was not just a tourist but was definitely 'spiritually inclined'. He sweetly concluded that, as I had somehow managed to get to this place, he and I must have a special connection. Certainly I felt very comfortable and at home there.

We missed some of the ceremonies by spending time with him but, after goodbyes, bows and lots of 'Aaaaamitofuos', we emerged into a cool, soft darkness illuminated by a spectacular full moon onto a terrace in front of the main temple building where people were slowly and meditatively pacing around fruit and moon cakes piled on a table. This was the same idea as the Hindu prasad: the food should be blessed before eating it. After many circuits chanting 'Aaaaamitofuo' we adjourned to the eating hall resplendent in the yellows, golds and reds of Buddhahood to sit down for the feast. Of course I now faced once again the problem of having piles of food thrust upon me due to the loving hospitality of my various hosts. With a loaded plate in front of me, I quickly whispered to Yujie asking how to say 'I am full'! I learned a new and extremely convenient word: bau-*la*. I used it to good effect and created much amusement among my hosts.

The temple master had offered me a place to stay for the night

(Mr and Mrs Zhao have a permanent room as they stayed often at the temple) but, because I was still feeling quite tired from jet-lag and was also anticipating the arranged trip to the Mongolian grasslands the next day, I politely refused. Back through, around, and over the potholes and bumps we somehow made it to the Zhao's apartment which, as I expected, was gorgeous. Mr Zhao has a construction company and knows how to build well but he also has a designer instinct and all his houses are beautifully decorated. I had an attractive room to myself, albeit with a rock-hard bed and bean-filled pillows which usually give me neck and back aches. I softened the bed slightly with some cushions I found on the chairs! Surprisingly I slept like a log.

Mrs Zhao gets up every morning at 4am and chants for three hours but as I was using earplugs I didn't hear her. However, as you can imagine, by 7am the household is always up and about so it was quite an early start to the day. After a quick breakfast, we set off for the journey to the Mongolian grasslands, or Steppes, as we call them.

Despite the early hour, the roads were crowded and I was suddenly thrown back into the Chinese road experience! In Beijing the traffic is so heavy that normal traffic regulations have of necessity to be followed if traffic is to move anywhere at all! But in smaller towns and rural areas, the disregard for even elementary traffic rules is total and absolute. Signs, lights, road line markings mean nothing at all; add motorbikes, scooters, bicycles and unaware pedestrians to the mix, and just the prospect of driving somewhere is terrifying! My nerves were predictably shattered and my brake foot practically rigid by the time we got to the outskirts of the city. Fortunately the roads then quickly emptied of vehicles and the escarpment edging the city turned into rolling hills which reminded me of the Southern Uplands of Scotland where I once ran a youth hostel in the god-forsaken Wanlockhead. Soon the land flattened out and I learned from Yujie that the main 'industry' here was agriculture and sheep and dairy farming. Hohhot is the dairy capital of China and certainly the only place I have I been able to find fresh milk and thus fully enjoy the Earl Grey and Assam tea I always bring with me. UHT milk is used throughout China as it has to travel vast distances.

And always that clear blue sky and the incredible pure air….

As we travelled further into the grasslands I was surprised to notice a lot of pylons and sub-stations seemingly carrying electricity in the direction of Hohhot and the other two towns we passed through. I was curious why. The main source of energy here in China is still coal and although I knew there were massive coal mines south of Inner Mongolia in Shaanxi Province, I hadn't heard of huge amounts of coal here. And there was certainly no obvious water source for hydro-electricity. Intrigued, I asked Yujie who actually didn't really know but her father told us the source was 'wind farms'! Well, it seems sad to litter this pristine countryside with wind turbines but, on the other hand, to have such a huge non-polluting energy source was quite something. China is usually condemned for its environmentally damaging policies but here was a huge non-polluting electricity project we know nothing about. The good is never trumpeted by the media – it doesn't sell newspapers! Solar panels are commonly used throughout China to heat water for domestic use – used on a far greater scale than in the west.

Past the pylons the land flattened and grew more barren until the only growing thing really was grass. The feeling of non-ending space was extraordinary, totally invigorating. I felt like I was plummeting back in time to a world sparsely populated, with human beings forming just a minute part of the vast whole. Huge majesty. Life-enhancing purity. Expansion.

Of course some tourism has found its way here in the form of occasional yurt-like structures in which to stay. In fact I would have liked to have spent some days in one of these beautifully designed yurts to fully savour the grassland ambience. What must the stars be like at night?

Mr and Mrs Zhao, having got up so early to do their chanting, said they needed a nap so they rented a yurt for two hours, leaving Yujie and me to explore the vastness further. We found herds of sheep and cattle moving amongst the grass – bulls these were, not cows, so I demurred when Yujie suggested I take some close-up photographs!

The silence! It was awesome to listen to and experience the utter silence that was there. We had had to drive on the necessary road so there were some vehicles passing through, but they were few and far between and in those long, long gaps was a kind primordial silence, unworldly, ancient, unsullied….

We found a small dam and sat and meditated at the water's edge, slightly hypnotised by the intense silence and the twirling of the wind turbines in the distance, until it was time to go and pick up the parents and start on our journey home. We took a different route back, much more hilly, which provided a suitably aesthetic backdrop to the twilight descending. As darkness fell the full moon rose, magically illuminating the stark terrain on either side of the road. Needless to say, the sleep that night, despite the hard bed, was deep and profound.

The next morning I woke up fairly late – around 7.30 – and found to my amazement that a man with a trowel and a bucket of what looked like cement was waiting outside my door when I opened it and, as soon as I had vacated the room (fortunately clothed), he rushed in followed closely by another guy who proceeded to move furniture and lay plastic covers everywhere. To be faced with this rather unusual activity when having just woken up and got out of bed was somewhat disconcerting, to say the least. And then I discovered, on going downstairs, that the beautiful living room was similarly covered in plastic and more men with cement-filled buckets were industriously slapping said cement on the windowsills.

Now definitely disconcerted I made my way to the kitchen to find parents and Yujie having breakfast. Seeing my face Yujie hastened to explain that today all the windowsills and frames were to be cemented. Apparently only two weeks previously the whole apartment had been fitted with super efficient double-glazed windows per kind favour of the local city council. Yujie told me that about six months previously, the central government had passed a law forcing councils to plough their finances into services for the people rather than building huge edifices like five-star hotels to further increase their own coffers.

Well, China is always full of surprises and one has to learn to accept whatever, so I buckled down to my breakfast without a word. Today, it appeared, was going to be a construction day and Yujie and I would be left to our own devices. There wasn't really anywhere to be, the furniture (gorgeous wooden handmade pieces) and floors were covered in plastic so we went off to do a bit of shopping and to visit some members of her extended family. We were then summoned to an excellent lunch at a nearby restaurant and I was surprised to find the workmen joining us around the table. I reflected that one wouldn't see this in England. This was a largely uneventful and peaceful day – actually very welcome as I was still suffering a little from jetlag. To be honest, I don't think anything could have topped the previous days so it was just as well.

The next day Yujie's father took us to the airport where we all said goodbyes and Yujie took off for Beijing while my plane flew me south-east to Zhengzhou. As the plane took off and flew over Hohhot I thanked existence one more time for giving me all these amazing experiences in this country and for the generous people I have met here.

Back to the Mountain

Having been very comfortably chauffeured around Inner Mongolia in Mr Zhao's nice black Honda, I was met at Zhengzhou Airport by Ibo and a business associate who was driving a brand-new black Toyota. This was apparently going to be a time of luxury cars for me! After an unusually luxurious drive to Dengfeng, Ibo checked me into his boss's Horrible Hotel for one night and then bundled me into a gleaming white Land Rover to go off to ShiLiPu to meet my landlords and negotiate arrangements for me to again stay in their house.

On the way Ibo told me that he had discovered that the hotel had formerly been an abortion clinic. With China's one-child policy more strictly enforced in the past than now, women who accidentally became pregnant were forced to undergo abortions, and abortion clinics proliferated all over China. This hotel had been one of them and I really felt it was not only the cigarette smells permeating the place that disturbed, but also the distressed vibes of suffering women and little dead foetuses. I shuddered at the thought.

Entering ShiLiPu, the positive energy of Song Mountain strongly prevailed and I felt immediately better as I got out of the car and was greeted by my very sweet landlords who seemed genuinely happy to welcome me back. Given all the construction that had been going on during my previous stay, I did want to check that the view of Song Mountain from the bedroom that I usually occupied was still unobstructed. This might have been an issue, but I was relieved to see that the crucial single-storey house in front of the window had not been added onto so, although third storeys had been built onto many other buildings, the view from the window was relatively intact. Negotiations complete, I asked Ibo if he could take me shopping for the many items necessary to set up this empty flat one more time and he duly whisked me around various places in Dengfeng to buy the basics. He dropped me off at the hotel, loaded down with a mound of packages, before heading back to work.

The next morning I discovered the boss himself wanted to take me to ShiLiPu (to see for himself where I was going to live, no doubt) and I had to load all my goods and chattels into his super-luxurious new BMW, white with a beige leather interior. Well, things were certainly different from the days of my little old basic bicycle.

I spent the day getting organised and in the afternoon Lijuan called to invite me for lunch at the school the next day. This would be the first time I would be visiting the new school and I was very curious to see what had been built.

But the most important thing first.... Very early the next morning, just as the sun was rising, I made my way to my meditation place in the foothills of the mountain. Here I again fell into the kind of meditation I knew was connected to my being in this special place. As usual the meditation went deep and I had the strange, and very welcome, sensation of everything inside falling back into a healing harmony. To continue with the car theme, I thought of a very good advert from a few years back which started off with a kind of robot made from all the parts of a car doing a bit of a dance and then suddenly it collapsed as all the car parts broke apart, flew into the air and then re-assembled themselves into a gleaming new car. I felt all the parts of myself that had broken into a jagged disharmony in the sad and sorry UK now re-assembling themselves into a peaceful and healthy whole.

Or, if a Taoist metaphor is more appropriate, Lao Tzu's image of the mud settling and the water becoming clear, beautifully described what happened when I was once again back in the presence of this magical mountain.

Protected by a Mountain Tiger

Later in the morning Wenzhe, the young English-speaking student manager who I had met during my last visit, picked me up in the old school van and we drove up to the new school. I was very impressed as we stopped outside. Master Wu Nanfang came out to greet me and he formed an aesthetic picture in his grey kungfu clothes against the tasteful blue-grey walls of his building. Usually Chinese buildings sport the traditional, often garish, colours of red and gold but Master Wu Nanfang had chosen this unusual, soft colour to blend in with the mountain behind.

Wenzhe told the master he would first take me on a little tour. We walked up the side of the compound and he pointed to the mountain, telling me that the fengshui for the site was particularly good because this part of the mountain resembled a tiger lying down and the school was built within the curve of its body so was well protected. In feng shui, there four main animals for each of the four directions or locations on a site: the dragon, the phoenix, the tortoise and the tiger – which is a symbol of protection. I confess that my imagination had to work pretty hard to picture the reclining mountain tiger but I knew from experience that the Chinese are very adept at discovering symbols in nature and mountains. I love the way they place such importance on these symbols as for me it shows their inherent awareness of their connection with their environment. This awareness is now rapidly disappearing, I know, but remnants surface every now and then, especially in the relatively untouched rural areas.

Wenzhe next showed me the well that they had had to bore because there was no easily accessible water on the small property. In fact, the water supply for most of the houses in ShiLiPu come from individual wells in the gardens of each property as there is no central water supply. The water was good but I tried not to think of how much the water table in the area was being drained – Ibo told me that many concerns about this had already been raised. In fact, due to the lack of rain this summer, the school's well had already run dry and they were now dependent on getting water from the old school building in the village. Each day they drove the van down to the old school and filled about ten huge plastic containers with water for cooking and drinking. (They boiled the drinking water.) Two or three times a week all the dirty laundry was hauled down there for washing and on Saturdays the students went there for showers if they didn't want to go to the public baths in town.

Then we walked into the courtyard of the school and I was again charmed by its aesthetic design – a far cry from the concrete monstrosity in which the family and students had previously functioned. But being so far from anywhere, they had had huge difficulties getting electricity and a phone/internet connection – essential for the business – installed. They had had to dig a trench to ShiLiPu village down the mountain slope – about one and a half miles – to bury the electricity and phone cables. The students did this digging themselves and Master Wu Nanfang had used this opportunity to demonstrate to them some of those farming movements Panky had filmed, incorporating them into their daily training schedule.

I was proudly shown the now very comfortable dormitories complete with air-conditioning and heating units to ward off extremes of temperature, and, finally, after all my nagging, decent toilet facilities. The kitchen, which had been a dark windowless hole in the previous place, was now a spacious, clean and well-lit room and Lijuan had a nice big classroom for teaching the students. Master Wu Nanfang could welcome his visitors in a very smart reception room – with chairs! No longer did I have to sit on that hard, low bench which resulted in an aching backside after only a few minutes and undignified struggles to get off it! Finally I could sit comfortably when talking to him and drinking tea. And last, but not least, the master had built what I knew he had wanted for so long – a very beautiful and peaceful meditation room. Of course it is wonderful to meditate outside, but in inclement weather a protected space is necessary.

I was so impressed at all the hard work the family and the students had done in such a short space of time – less than a year – to create such an attractive, tasteful and efficient complex to live and train in and I was delighted that Master Wu Nanfang had finally been able to create a fitting ambience for his very beautiful form of kungfu.

Missions to be Accomplished!

On this visit I had brought with me a very interesting book by an American author, Andy Ferguson, called 'Tracking Bodhidharma'. In it he attempted to trace Bodhidharma's movements through China and his connections with each place he apparently stayed in. Having read the detailed chapters about Bodhidharma living in the Song Mountain and Luoyang areas a number of times, there were a few more things I really wanted to see and explore.

I set off early one morning, therefore, to visit the Shaolin Temple yet one more time. This time my mission was to find a place I had surprisingly missed: Huike's house. I have mentioned before that Huike was the second Zen Ancestor, the one who cut off his hand to prove to Bodhidharma his worthiness to be a disciple. According to Andy Ferguson, this small building could be found on one of the mountain peaks opposite Wuru Peak where Bodhidharma's cave was. I had been up that peak with one of the kungfu students, who spoke a little English, during my second visit here, but he had not mentioned this place. Surely he must have known about it?!

Anyway, today I would find it so, after a quick walk around the temple itself, I set off for the this mountain which had a smaller cable car system than the one that goes up Shaoshi Mountain and leads to that long mountain walk to SanHuangZhai. This smaller system ended on a kind of ridge at the top of the mountain and from there I walked downhill a bit, past the usual sellers of tourist tat, until I found a large empty deserted space which had a sign, fortunately with a few words in English, pointing along another path. To my bewilderment I then came face-to-face with an ugly forty-foot-high wall, newly built with large concrete blocks. Horrors! What a desecration of a beautiful scenic area. To the left I saw a rough narrow path which I took, rounding the edge of the wall to view a messy construction site, at the far end of which sat a charming little house. Oh god! The Shaolin Temple intent on its horrendous preservation efforts once again. I don't have a problem with preservation efforts but they do it in such an insensitive, and inappropriate way.

I walked through the mess until I arrived at this little building. There seemed to be nobody around so I went inside and sat on an old rickety chair. With my eyes closed there was a feeling of timeless peace and silence and I quietly reflected on this second great Chinese Zen Master. He was the one to whom Bodhidharma had transmitted his Zen heritage. Local folklore says that, after Bodhidharma accepted Huike as his disciple, Huike built this small house to retreat to, both to heal his arm and to absorb the transmission of his master. As the small building is just below the crest of the hill it cannot be seen from the main valley and was therefore saved from being destroyed time and again as the buildings of the temple were. Consequently it is claimed that parts of the building are original remains from the time that Huike lived there. There was certainly still an ancient, rather charming, feeling to the small building.

Apparently around it a small monastery had formed and it was these buildings which had fallen into disrepair – the weather must be wild and inclement in such an exposed position – and which were now being rebuilt. I managed to make my way around the back of the little house, clambering over bricks and bags of concrete, to the top of the ridge from where I could see across the valley to Bodhidharma's cave on Wuru peak opposite. I imagined master and disciple waving to each other on a sunny morning!

Despite retreating at times to this hidden place, Huike travelled extensively in the Song Mountain and Luoyang area to pass on the Zen heritage he had absorbed from his great master.

* * *

To visit the next two places, I needed expert help so a few days after my visit to Huike's abode I went to see Master Wu Nanfang. With Lijuan's help I asked him if he had heard of the tomb of the mysterious seventh Zen Ancestor, Jingzang, which is apparently situated nearby, next to the Huishan Temple.

I say 'mysterious' because, according to Andy Ferguson, very little is known about this master. This in itself would not be too surprising but the strange thing is that he has an enormous tomb, bigger by far than anything in the Pagoda Forest in the Shaolin Temple and bigger, in fact, than Bodhidharma's tomb in KongXiang (which was the other place I was interested in). In ancient times the size of the tomb depicted the importance of the man who was buried there, so with such a big tomb, Master Jingzang must have been very important indeed. Yet there is almost no information about him.

Andy Ferguson had had great difficulty in finding this tomb and it took him three attempts to locate it before he found out that it was actually within the military area between Huishan Temple and the Wugulun Kungfu School. Obviously no tourists would be allowed into a restricted military zone. Ferguson eventually did manage to get inside the enclave and see the tomb, but not without great difficulty.

Could I manage to get there? Well, I had a secret weapon in Master Wu Nanfang, who knew many people in the area. When I asked him about the tomb he first expressed surprise at me knowing about it and then became quite animated and talkative. It was too much for Lijuan to translate but then she asked me when I would like to go? I was of course quite excited at this question – would I be able to go where no other foreigner except Ferguson had been? I replied that any time would do, to which Master Wu Nanfang said, 'After lunch?' Very much taken aback at the speed of arrangements, I of course said yes, so he got out his mobile phone, made a call (presumably to some military person) and then nodded his head. 'Okay, after lunch,' Lijuan translated.

So after lunch we got in the van, driven by Chengeng, now one of the two senior kungfu coaches, and travelled the short distance to the military barracks where the guards at the gate waved us through. No snarling dogs as in Ferguson's case!

The tomb is indeed large. And in relatively good condition. We were met by a military gentleman who was no doubt there to keep on eye on us but who also seemed to be on friendly terms with the master. They did a lot of talking but I could see by the consternation on both Lijuan's and Chengeng's faces that there was no way they could translate what was being said. I was of course frustrated but then I remembered that my good friend, Andy, from Guangzhou, was planning to visit me in a couple of days and I told Lijuan to listen to what was being said and then she could tell

Andy to translate it all for me. That resolved the issue and we had a relaxed time walking around the tomb and enjoying the afternoon in the shadow of the mountains looming close by.

When Andy arrived a few days later, Master Wu Nanfang was happy to tell him as much as he knew. Which wasn't much but still added one further intriguing facet to the wonder that is Song Mountain.

According to Master Wu Nanfang, Jingzang was a very famous and 'high level' Zen master. Master Wu Nanfang had unearthed a small booklet which contained just about all that is known about him and told Andy to translate it for me. Apparently China's only female empress, Wu Zetian – the one whose facial likeness is carved on the Losana Buddha in the Longmen Caves – loved to come up to Song Mountain from her court in Luoyang. She sometimes stayed at the Huishan Temple which had originally been built as a palace by a previous emperor, Xiao Wen, but was later converted to a temple. A Zen monk called Hui An, or Lao An, was much loved by the empress and, after living near Nanjing as a disciple of the fifth Zen Ancestor, Hongren, he came back to Song Mountain to spend his remaining days here at the Huishan Temple. Jingzang was Hui An's disciple and moved to Huishan Temple to be with his master.

Hongren transmitted his teachings to the great Huineng, the sixth Zen Ancestor, who later sought out Jingzang on Song Mountain and passed the teachings on to him. Thus Bodhidharma's Zen heritage continued.

* * *

I was surprised at what good condition the tomb was in, given that it is about fourteen hundred years old. Apparently this was due to the wealth of some of Jingzang's disciples who ordered the tomb to be built solidly of brick. As bricks were expensive and wood was cheap the usual method of constructing such a tomb was to make a structure of wood which was then covered with a layer of brick. By using bricks throughout, the tomb had great solidity and substance and, despite the weathering, it is one of the few original structures remaining in China. The strength and quality of these bricks can also be seen in the Brick Pagoda, also an original building, constructed in the sixth century near FaWang Temple on Taoshi Mountain.

Needless to say I was quite thrilled at being one of very few westerners to see and appreciate Jingzang's tomb and to discover one more hidden secret connected with my beloved mountain.

* * *

It seemed that Master Wu Nanfang was a bit infected by my enthusiasm for these historical tales because, after leaving Jingzang's tomb, he directed Chengeng to drive to a river on the other side of Dengfeng, interestingly flanked on both sides by strange rock formations. This, he said, was one of Empress Zetian's favourite places to come and rest in nature when she visited Song Mountain and the Huishan Temple.

And then, on the way back to ShiLiPu, the master suggested that he take me to KongXiang, Bodhidharma's burial place – or, rather, the burial place of his one shoe! Having searched for this place online I knew roughly where it was and knew it would be quite a long journey but Lijuan explained to me that the master loved going there and was happy to have an excuse to visit again.

The following day I got a call to be ready at 7am the next morning. Instead of the van, I was picked up in another luxury car belonging to the master's friend, and off we went.

We travelled on the highway to Luoyang, the same one Rende

had used when we had gone with Panky and Yujie to see the Peony Festival more than five years before. Then the road was deserted; now it was an almost perpetual traffic jam with all kinds of vehicles jostling for right of way. Frightening. The most obvious vehicles were huge car carriers piled high with new Toyotas or Hondas to feed China's now insatiable appetite for new luxury cars. I am sure vehicles this huge are not allowed on British highways. Between Luoyang and SanMenXia – more than an hour's drive – the scenery was just one endless industrial area filled with massive chimneys belching god-knows-what into the already polluted air.

I was getting a headache from all this dangerous driving and traffic pollution but fortunately we suddenly turned off the highway onto a pot-holed minor road back into rural China. The contrast was quite startling. Suddenly peace descended as we drove through a landscape of fields and trees and then onto a concrete approach road rising up towards a small rocky outcrop. This, I supposed, was Bear Ear Mountain although, with the best will in the world, I could see no bear and no ear in the rock formations. But this, I knew, was where Bodhidharma's burial place was. The approach road was quite long and soon there were no buildings and no evidence of human life until we rounded a bend and the gate house of the temple came into view.

Ours was the only car there and when we got out we were immediately enveloped in silence and fresh cool air. As far as the eye could see there were no signs of civilisation except a distant train line.

It was ethereally beautiful.

The master and his friend quickly made their way up the steps and through the gate house (to visit the head monk I later found out) but Lijuan and I lingered awhile to savour the ambience. It was an unusual but very definite relief not to have one's senses assaulted by all the trappings of our mechanised, modernised world. One doesn't realise how much they intrude until one finds oneself in a place where they almost don't exist.

Already refreshed and invigorated we climbed the steps through the rather picturesque gatehouse to find ourselves in a spacious area with the usual hall containing a Buddha statue ahead and a few low buildings on each side. The dominating feature was, however, a very tall, slender stupa obviously connected to Bodhidharma. The head monk later told us that they regard this stupa more as a memorial to Bodhidharma than a tomb, because there is no reason to think that he is buried there. He seemed to accept the story that Bodhidharma left for India. He also said that the original stupa had been destroyed and the one we were looking at was built in the fourteenth century.

Really nothing is known about Bodhidharma's last days but

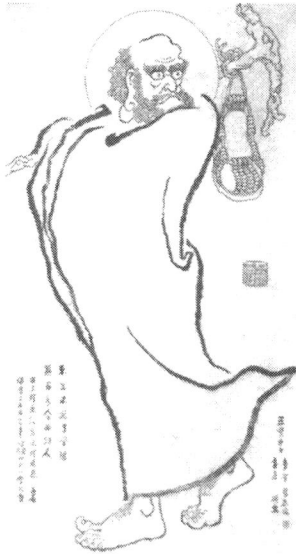

legends say that, after transmitting his Zen teachings to Huike, Bodhidharma told his followers that he was leaving to return to

India. It seems he stayed a while at a monastery, the Ding Ling monastery, which had existed on this site from about the first century AD, although it was later destroyed. Here he supposedly died and was buried. The twist in the story, however, is that about three weeks later, a monk who had spent time with Bodhidharma, met him on the road which eventually led to the Himalaya Mountains. Bodhidharma was barefoot but carried one shoe on his staff. The monk hurried back to the monastery to report what he had seen and, to check the truth of his story, it was decided to open the tomb. All that remained inside was a single shoe.

I remember Osho telling this story but he gave an interesting slant to the story. He said that an enlightened being had such control over his body that it was possible for him to make it look as if his body was dead. Osho said that this is what Bodhidharma had done and, once all the burial ceremonies were over, he simply stood up, got out of the tomb which probably wasn't yet permanently sealed, silently left the monastery and started on his journey towards the Himalayas and India. Osho said that Bodhidharma had done his work and now wanted to be alone.

Osho also mentioned somewhere that Jesus had used a similar process before he supposedly rose from the dead.

* * *

As with all Chinese temples, one moves from hall to hall, up the mountain slope until one arrives at the main hall where a statue to whoever the temple is dedicated, resides. When I climbed all the steps to the Damo Tian (Bodhidharma's Hall) I could see for miles. To the north and east the terrain was either flat or rolling hills (these are the Luoyang plains alongside the Yellow River) but to the west one could see the beginnings of a mountain range. I knew, from spending hours examining Google Maps, that these mountains were the very beginnings of the Himalayan range and felt that it was absolutely possible that Bodhidharma was heading in that direction after departing his tomb.

In front of Bodhidharma's Hall

In fact, another legendary figure was supposed to have done the exact same thing. Lao Tzu was apparently on his way to the Himalayas via the Huangu Pass when he was captured and made to write the Tao Te Ching. That incident reportedly took place near Lingbao, just a few miles from where I was now standing.

Legends ... but they do give food for thought.

We had a vegetarian meal with the head monk in his quarters but without a good translator I couldn't get any information from him. To be honest, I don't think there is any more information. We then spent more time just meandering around this silent and serene place – the ancients really knew how to choose the right locations for their temples and monasteries. I would have loved to have been able to stay there for a few days.

But return we had to and so back into the traffic fray we went. Even the rather dangerous ride home could not affect the impact of this special place. Somehow this visit brought together very strongly my connections, through Osho, with Bodhidharma, Zen and Song Mountain.

Fortuitous Flu

Having a cold in China was more or less inevitable and, sure enough, shortly after the visit to KongXiang, I succumbed. As this was nothing new I decided to just rest and wait for it to depart – usually in about four days. This time, however, it got worse instead of better and I soon developed a sinus infection which then went to my throat resulting in a bad cough, not helped by the dry, very dusty, environment. I soon became a bit nervous thinking that if this went into my lungs I would be in big trouble.

After about a week I went up to the kungfu school where Wenzhe became concerned at hearing my hacking cough. I didn't know that he was a qualified Traditional Chinese Medicine doctor and he offered to take me to a Chinese herbal clinic where he would get some traditional medicine to treat me. Naturally I acquiesced and he took me to a place I had never been before in Dengfeng – an absolutely amazing Chinese herbal clinic tastefully done out in wood and decorated with scrolls of Chinese paintings on the walls – and of course endless wooden drawers containing the various ingredients which a doctor would mix and blend for his patient. Wenzhe felt that he could recommend some ready-made remedies and he picked out a number of interesting-looking, beautifully-packaged boxes for me. I opened one to find eight round balls made of a whitish substance I didn't recognise and Wenzhe showed me how to crush the ball gently between my two palms thus cracking it open to reveal another round, sweet-like ball inside it. This is what one ate. It tasted very good – kind of earthy with a slightly sweet taste – and Wenzhe told me that the herbs were mixed with natural, organic honey which was the cohesive agent to enable the balls to be formed. So compact and beautiful. I felt I would be healed just with the care that had gone into producing the medicine.

Two days later, however, I was not better. Although the herbal medicine did clear my sinuses making it easier to breath, I felt that the throat infection was getting worse and descending into my lungs and I finally admitted to myself that antibiotics were necessary. But I had never been to a doctor in China before and I would definitely need help on such an expedition. My Chinese star of good fortune proved to be shining as brightly as ever, however, because just as I made that reluctant decision I got an unexpected call from Andy saying he was on the train to Dengfeng, would arrive that night and would come to see me in the morning. He didn't know about my severe cold but when I told him the situation he said immediately he would take me to a doctor the next day. He would be spending the night in Ibo's boss's hotel and would get details from Ibo. I had by this time lost track of Ibo's business comings and goings but it turned out that he was returning from Zhengzhou that evening too.

With Andy, I was in good hands. He took me to Dengfeng's main hospital, which turned out to be quite an experience – and often during the one and a half hours I was there, I thought that the managers of our British NHS should come over here and see how things should be done. The word 'efficiency' inadequately describes the process. Add the words 'caring', 'humane', 'humorous', 'expert' and you might begin to get the picture. Yes, the place was a bit shabby and not spotlessly clean, but the care and efficiency more than made up for that. And where it mattered ie taking a blood sample, the hygiene was impeccable.

I remembered Ibo saying that the hospital that he went to in Zhengzhou was not spotless but the care and expertise of those doctors that pulled him back from almost certain death on more than one occasion was truly remarkable.

We first checked into the office because you have to pay for the treatment in advance. Then we were directed upstairs to a long corridor with doctors' rooms all along one side. I relied on Andy's sense of appropriateness and followed him as he peered into the various offices until he finally made a choice. There were a few people in the room so we had to wait for awhile but it was interesting to watch how things were done. The doctor was sitting at his desk and he had a younger, maybe trainee doctor, sitting behind him watching. Two nurses sat opposite him and the patient sat on his right. When it was my turn I went and sat next to him and the youngish doctor was delighted to greet me with a few words of English – but a greeting was the extent of his English skills so I was glad Andy was there. The doctor did the usual doctor things, with the other patients looking interestedly on – no privacy here at all! – and then said he wanted a blood test and a chest X-ray done. My heart sank. In England it takes a week to make an appointment to get a blood test or an X-ray done and then another week to get the results and then another week before you can get an appointment to see the doctor to find out what treatment you need.

I expressed my concern to Andy and he looked at me in astonishment and told me that getting all these tests done would take about twenty minutes! He was right. We went to the other side of the corridor and entered a long room where there were five young nurses taking blood. I was able to immediately sit down in front of one young lady who efficiently pricked my finger and put the blood into a small test tube with my name and a number on it which she then placed on a table in the middle of the room. On the other side of the room were seven people in front of seven pieces of equipment and computers who were all analysing the blood samples which they took from the central table. Despite their concentration they all seemed happy and cheerful as they went about their tasks. Andy said it would take about ten minutes to get the results. In the meantime we could go downstairs to the X-ray department. There I was second in a queue but within five minutes had a chest X-ray taken. Andy told me to go up again and sit outside the blood test room (I was feeling a bit weak from the fever, I admit) while he waited there for the X-ray verdict. I had only been sitting down for two minutes when a nurse came and handed me the blood test results and then five minutes later Andy appeared with the X-ray report. I think the whole process took only fifteen minutes before we were back in the doctor's office. Unbelievable.

And I must not omit to mention the ambience. China is a communal kind of country and here on this floor it felt like all the patients were sort of embraced as one big family and people were relaxed, good-tempered and patient with each other. There was time for doctors, nurses and patients to communicate in a friendly way with no stressful time limits. In England a GP has eight minutes to see a patient and make a diagnosis and the ambience in the surgery is impersonal and stressful and often, in the case of my surgery, downright rude with a total lack of concern for an ill person.

Having examined my blood test and X-ray results and being satisfied that there were no complications in my condition, the doctor agreed that antibiotics in this situation would be helpful and prescribed accordingly. We then went downstairs to the pharmacy and bought some of the drugs. I was surprised, however, to find that the doctor had given me two prescriptions: one for allopathic medicine and one for herbal medicine to counteract, Andy said, the effects of the chemical stuff. Wow! I knew Ibo's doctor treated him with a combination of the two kinds of medicine and here was being treated in the same way. Apparently this is quite common. We had to go to a different place for the Chinese herbal medicine but it was just outside the hospital gates. The whole process took one and a half hours and cost me thirteen pounds.

By this time I felt like I needed to lie down and Andy found me a taxi and sent me home to bed. He wanted to do some things with Ibo in town.

Andy is studying Chinese herbal medicine himself so the next day he left to go and visit a herbal doctor on the other side of the mountain for a few days and I rested in order to allow the medicine to work. I was only given sufficient antibiotics for two days – usually in the west we need to take it for five days – so I was a little worried that it would not be effective but at the end of the two days I felt much better, the hacking cough had almost stopped and it was now up to the herbal medicine, enough for a week, to complete the healing process

With the body healing in the quiet and peaceful atmosphere of my lovely Zen flat I found it quite easy to meditate and I spent many silent hours just sitting on my bed looking at the mountain. I smilingly remembered Osho's apparently shocking statement when he said that he wished we would all get hepatitis when we came to India! Of course he didn't want us to suffer. What he meant was that a non-serious illness would slow us down so that we could begin to find our silent inner space undisturbed by the tensions and ceaseless frenetic activity of our western style of life. And I realised I had come here filled with the western mindset of purposes and missions to be accomplished and wanting to do things, and not in the least taking note that all this activity would scupper my attempts to meditate deeply. The flu had fortuitously enforced a slow-down!

By the time Andy returned I was practically better so I asked him if he would help me to talk to my landlady as I knew so little about her. He of course agreed and so we went downstairs to talk to Mrs Shang, her mother and ninety-nine-year-old grandmother. Mr Shang was away working.

Both Mr and Mrs Shang were born in Dengfeng, I learned, and both of their parents had been farmers – which is why they obviously loved working on their small plots of land in front of their house until they built the current houses on them last year. Mr Shang had had a trucking company for many years until he retired two years ago, built these buildings and bought a nice new car – a white Kia (Korean made) – enabling him to operate a private luxury taxi business. There are many visitors to this area now who would prefer this kind of prestigious private taxi to the usual company taxi like I use!

Mrs Shang works for the local village council as a social worker. She is the chairwoman of a local organisation which takes care of the women in the village. I now understood why she was so often out and about, mingling with the village women. I had noticed that on many occasions she seemed to be deep in conversation with them. When the local women have problems she will help them. In some situations she mediates in conflicts between husbands, wives, parents or children. She told us that many young parents are away in other parts of the province earning money – like the Wang brothers – and leave their young children in the care of the grandparents. Often problems arise from these situations.

Local women might have economic or health problems and Mrs Shang is responsible for helping them and arranging for them to get financial help from various government agencies – like our benefit system – and medical care. If the women are seriously ill she will arrange to get help for the families involved – perhaps care for children if the mother or grandmother has to go to hospital.

She told me that her daughter is a magistrate in Zhengzhou and I of course knew that her son was a policeman.

I was totally fascinated with her story. This was an insight into the way Chinese communities functioned that I had never been aware of before. I was also impressed at how socially conscious the whole family was. When I mentioned something to this effect she told me she felt she was contributing to the good of the people in the village and was following the ways of Buddha who asks his followers to be compassionate and help others.

I also thought how extraordinarily lucky I was to have unknowingly found myself living with such a generous, compassionate and socially conscious family -- people who were not concerned with making the big bucks but were helping to create harmony in their community.

I then asked Mrs Shang what was happening with the development of the local area. I was thrilled at her reply. She said yes, there had been huge plans to develop the area but that the project had stalled. I didn't get a very clear reason for this but the outcome is that all those ghastly ghost buildings were no longer being built, there would be no take over of the farmers' lands and nothing would be done in the foreseeable future. I asked her if she was pleased about this and she said she and all the local people were happy, but the greedy entrepreneurs who had lost money by investing in those ghost buildings were angry because the returns they had gambled on getting were not forthcoming. I saw Mrs Shang give a quiet smile about this and she admitted that she was pleased that those people, the majority not from the area, had lost out. This was very good news indeed and I told her how concerned I had been about the farmers and villagers and was so relieved that the area would be preserved for at least some time to come.

* * *

Andy said that he now had to leave and I thanked him profusely for all his help – not only with the whole doctor/hospital thing but also for the talk with Mrs Shang which had put to rest my concerns for this special area which I loved so much.

As I said goodbye to him it started to rain and the refreshing and life-giving downpour lasted for two days. By then I had almost entirely recovered and, when the rain stopped, I took a walk down to my meditation place and was ecstatic to see the farmers out in full force, hurriedly plowing their fields in preparation for sowing the winter wheat. Apparently the rain had arrived just in time to make planting a crop viable. I now understood that the reason for the lack of work in the fields was not because the land had been ear-marked for luxury tourist developments, as I had worriedly thought, but simply because there had not been enough rain to make the planting of the winter crops possible.

The farmers working on the land and the villagers going contentedly about their everyday life were all part of the harmonious essence of the mountain and its surrounds and I felt a great peace descend on me. This no doubt contributed to something that happened the next day during the siesta hour when all activity ceased and silence fell on the village as they all rested for an hour or so.

As I too was lying resting on my bed, not sleeping, not meditating, not, I suppose, doing anything at all, I suddenly felt a kind of electric shock go through my head and my brain stopped! I was actually very frightened because I thought maybe I was having a stroke or an aneurism or something but I tried to calm myself and observe as much as I could what was happening. Slowly I moved my fingers and then my toes and all seemed to be working well. My breathing and heart seemed to be functioning normally and I thought that if I were having a stroke I was sure I would be feeling something physically amiss. Still fearful, I tried to be as aware as possible. Maybe this was some different kind of meditative state? But it didn't resemble anything I had ever felt in my life – no bliss, no silence, no experience of anything at all.

I think I lay there for about two hours, just accepting and observing, but eventually I realised I had to go to the toilet! Well, this would indicate very clearly if something was wrong, but getting up and moving presented no problems at all. When I lay down again the 'brainless' state had more or less disappeared but the state of silence persisted. Osho had always said not to be attached to or impressed by out-of-the-ordinary experiences so when I later got up to make supper and go for my evening walk to watch the sunset, I decided to forget about what had happened and not dwell on it but simply go about my usual life with as much awareness as possible.

It was only many months later, back in England, that I came upon the following quote. Whether or not it is relevant to me I don't know, but I will print it here. It is at times like these that I do wish my Master were around so I could ask him about this. But, on reflection, I think he would tell me not to bother about it!

These are his words:

> *One of the most fundamental things to remember –*
> *not only by you but by everyone – is that whatever you come*
> *across in your inner journey, you are not it.*
>
> *You are the one who is witnessing it – it may be*
> *nothingness, it may be blissfulness, it may be silence. But one*
> *thing has to be remembered: however beautiful and however*
> *enchanting an experience you come by, you are not it.*

You are the one who is experiencing it, and if you go on and on and on, the ultimate point in the journey is the point when there is no experience left – neither silence, nor blissfulness, nor nothingness. There is nothing as an object for you but only your subjectivity.

The mirror is empty. It is not reflecting anything. It is you.

Laughing with Bodhidharma

On one of his now sadly rare visits, Ibo mentioned, quite off-handedly that a new youth hostel had been set up in the Shaolin Temple compound – up one of the valleys where there was a small collection of buildings for kungfu students to stay. This was news to me. I had always longed to stay, even for a few days, on the mountain itself but had, for various reasons, never managed it. And no woman would be allowed to stay in the Shaolin Temple itself – very much a male enclave! Now an idea started to form. Osho had said that if one went to the Shaolin Temple on a full moon night and meditated silently, one might hear Bodhidharma laughing. For me 'the laughter' would not necessarily be a 'ho ho ho' or a 'ha ha ha' but perhaps that blissful joy one feels in a state of deep meditation. So strong is the energy of an enlightened person that the trees, the rocks, the very mountain, becomes infused with his energy, and when the moon is full, an even more intense and powerful dimension is added. I could well conceive that the temple, with its Damo heritage, could be a powerful place on a full moon night.

Maybe I could stay at this little hostel on the night of the November full moon. When I later put the idea to Ibo he said yes, there would be no problem. He would arrange it for me as one of the monks there was a friend of his.

And so on the evening of the 17th November, Ibo drove me up the hidden valley and took me to the little hostel. Having had many bad experiences of Chinese hotels I wasn't expecting much – I was in fact steeling myself to put up with sub-standard conditions – but I was absolutely delighted with this charming place. It was obviously very new and my small room was well-designed with a spotlessly clean en-suite shower and western toilet and a heating unit. I immediately decided to stay another night – such charming comfort could not be dismissed! There was no problem with making another booking so this was all arranged and Ibo left quickly because he had to be back working.

As it was already evening I wandered down the road towards the main temple compound nestling in the valley to find a place where I could have a good view of the moon as it rose.

Without all the tourists the temple was a silent place – the only sounds being the subdued murmurs of the few people living there. I found a place to sit facing east where I assumed the full moon would rise, and softly descended into a peaceful meditation. Within a short time I sensed the dark cold evening becoming lighter and, opening my eyes, was rewarded with the sight of a huge golden moon just peeping over a mountain peak. The sky was totally clear so there was an uninterrupted view of the golden orb slowly ascending the heavens. After witnessing this impressive sight and taking a few photos, I again closed my eyes and fell into a deep meditation until I was finally forced to move before I froze into solid ice. On standing up I turned towards Wuru Peak and Bodhidharma's cave (couldn't see it of course) and bowed deeply in homage. It was then that I felt a sudden silent laughter bubble deep within me and tears rolled down my face as I stood, hands folded, in the silence, beauty and energy of the full moon night.

This space happily stayed with me during the night and all the next day as I wandered around the compound, again went up Shaoshi Mountain via the cable car, and climbed as high up to Bodhidharma's cave as this aging body would allow. The second night I again meditated on the rising moon and again felt deeply a familiar presence – maybe it was Osho, maybe Bodhidharma, I don't want to define or try to put words to it. Simply I felt deeply in touch with something....

* * *

And I was surprised a few days later when Master Wu Nanfang told me that the wonderful old nun, Yonglian, whom I had loved so much, died on the night of the full moon – as the moon rose, in fact. I felt so sad that I would never see her again but felt comforted and happy that I was actually very close by her on the mountain and possibly had a taste of that mystery that is the death of the body yet the flight of the spirit into the unknown.

One of the Most Blessed Mountains

After the full moon the weather changed dramatically and temperatures plummeted. Yujie suggested that I come to Beijing and stay with her for my last few days in China because she had efficient central heating. Many residences and hotels in China are 'plugged' into what Ibo describes as a 'heating grid' and on a certain date, this year it was 22nd November, the heating gets turned on for buildings all over China and the people get free central heating all winter! Then it gets turned off in February sometime. Incredible. You are limited to the times it is turned on and off but otherwise the heating is free.

She also said now was the right time to visit her uncle, Professor Zhao, in Shijiazhuang because her grandmother and her brother, Renzheng, and cousin, Rende, and their families were also staying there. Her uncle's flat was plugged into that heating grid so would be very warm.

She suggested that I take the new high-speed train line that had been built so astonishingly quickly from Guangzhou in the south, near Hong Kong, to Beijing in the north. The train journey from Zhengzhou to Beijing used to take five and a half hours, but now it takes two and a half hours, and to Shijiazhuang only one hour as it was about half way to Beijing. I was able to book this for myself as I knew where the ticket office was in Dengfeng and no English was required as I only needed to give the agent a date and time.

I was very happy to be able to meet the Zhao family again but sad to leave Song Mountain as everything here this time had been so infinitely fulfilling.

But before I left I wanted to visit Zhongyue Miao, the Taoist temple on the other side of Dengfeng, one more time. Despite the cold, the sun was shining brightly as I set off. When I arrived I was a bit surprised to see a lot of activity outside the temple. It seemed like people were setting up a market – making the usual noise! Strangely, though, after paying my entrance fee and entering the temple, I found it completely deserted and I was able to walk around very slowly and silently without the usual hassles from the locals and tourists. The latter are invariably sweet and charming, just curious, but sitting silently and meditating is not something that they understand at all so if I sit down for a while I am kind of a 'sitting duck' – fair game for interrogation by all and sundry.

The word 'miao', as well as meaning a temple or an ancestral shrine, also means a temple fair and Ibo later told me that I happened to visit the temple the day before the annual fair opened. This is apparently a very famous fair that has been occurring for hundreds of years and people come from all over Henan, even further afield, to visit it – and the temple is open to visitors free of charge for the ten day duration. Ibo laughed and told me it would have been packed from the following day onwards.

But that day the only people I saw were the Taoist monks, in their black gear and strange hats which contained their long hair tied into a 'top-knot', going about their business. They were totally disinterested in one lone westerner but I would have loved to have the chance to interrogate them about their Taoist beliefs and lifestyle; however, as none of them spoke English this was of course impossible without a translator.

A long-lasting, uninterrupted meditation in this so very special place seemed to me to be a fitting end to my time here. I felt that the mountain had imparted something of its mystery to me and had helped me go deeper and further on my own spiritual path.

* * *

The next day Andy arrived to say goodbye and to help me pack up and clean my flat. We then went up to the kungfu school for a farewell lunch with Master Wu Nanfang. While there, many of the senior boys, kungfu coaches and monks from SanHuangZhai arrived and I learned that they had been attending Yonglian's funeral that morning. How sad that I could no longer manage that incredibly steep climb up to the monastery. I would have loved to have been there.

The next morning, now ready to leave, I walked with Andy down to the bus stop where he would catch the bus to Luoyang and from there the local train to Anhui where he was fortunately still working. An hour later, Wenju came to pick me up to take me to the new train station in Zhengzhou where I would meet Ibo who was working there.

The new station was an eye-opener – China at its most modern. It was as big as many airports, roof soaring high on rounded arches, spacious, light and massively efficient: the trains all come through on the middle level, disembarking passengers get off and depart from the lower level, while embarking passengers arrive at the top level and descend to get onto the train once the departing passengers have left. No congestion, nobody in each other's way. And the train looked like something from a science-fiction movie with a 'nose' so long you could hardly see the carriages behind it. Also, unlike the Japanese bullet trains, the carriage and seats were spacious and comfortable. China certainly has some good designers and engineers.

The ticket collector at first refused to allow Ibo to descend the escalator with me (only passengers allowed) but he objected and finally the ticket collector relented. He told me later that he had said, 'How do you expect an old western lady to find her way down there and carry her suitcase onto the train? She is too weak to do that'. I guess being old and foreign has its positive aspects!

* * *

Yujie was waiting to meet me at the equally impressive, modernistic Shijiazhuang station and we took a taxi to her uncle's flat where Yujie's grandmother, Rende and Renzheng and their wives and babies were all gathered to greet me. I felt really touched to be welcomed into their family in this way. Later Professor Zhao came and told me we could meet the following day when he had time off. I knew he was a very busy man and was grateful that he had agreed to answer my questions which Yujie had told him about.

The next day we had a conference. Professor Zhao, Yujie and Renzheng all gathered to help me try to find some answers to a few remaining questions I had. My feelings were that Osho had played a large part in my coming to and connecting with Song Mountain, but, as well as the statements he had made about his connections with Bodhidharma, there were a few more indications in some of his discourses which I wanted to examine. In Dengfeng I had therefore prepared some questions which I presented to members present.

The first question was about the concept of the ten thousand buddhas and why it seemed to have so much significance, but my friends actually didn't really have an answer for this other than to venture the idea that it was a kind of symbol or metaphor signifying the idea that everyone has the Buddha nature within himself.

They provided a very satisfactory answer to the next question, however. I wanted to know if somewhere in China there was a temple of ten thousand buddhas as opposed to just caves which was all I had hitherto heard about. They all agreed that there was a strong possibility that Osho was referring to the cave temples in Yungang in Datong, near the mountain of Wutai in Shanxi Province. (Wutai Mountain also had had strong Taoist and Zen connections in the past.) I had never heard of these caves but later, looking online, I found out that the Yungang Grottoes were a remarkable collection of carvings of Buddhist statues carved both on the mountain side and in its interior. There is a similarity to the Longmen Caves but here the scale is much larger. In fact, the Yungang caves are hardly caves; rather, they are huge halls carved deep into the mountain and filled with statues of Buddha. So important are these carvings that the whole area was made a UNESCO World Heritage Site in 2001. On the UNESCO website we read:

'The Yungang Grottoes, in Datong city, Shanxi

Province, with their 252 caves and 51,000 statues, represent the outstanding achievement of Buddhist cave art in China in the 5th and 6th centuries. The Yungang cave art represents the successful fusion of Buddhist religious symbolic art from south and central Asia with Chinese cultural traditions, starting in the 5th century AD under imperial auspices. The statues of the Yungang Grottoes were completed in sixty-five years (460-525); this period marks the peak of development in Buddhist cave art of the Northern Wei dynasty.'

These Grottoes could indeed be the temple Osho mentioned so often.

* * *

Without knowing about the Yungang Grottoes, I had written the next question which, in the light of this new discovery, now seemed very relevant. I had been intrigued by the following story that Osho loved and often told:

'A MONK CAME TO SEE MASTER DAIZUI, AND SAID TO HIM. "MOUNT GOTAI AND MOUNT DAIZUI — WHAT ARE THEY LIKE? HOW IS MOUNT DAIZUI?
DAIZUI SAID, "SPEAK LOUDER — I AM HARD OF HEARING."
THE MONK REPEATED THE QUESTION IN A LOUD VOICE.
DAIZUI SAID, "IT IS LIKE A THOUSAND MOUNTAINS, TEN THOUSAND MOUNTAINS."

'A MONK CAME TO SEE MASTER DAIZUI, AND SAID TO HIM. "MOUNT GOTAI....

It was a great monastery. All these mountains were named after the master who had become enlightened, and because of his enlightenment a thousand seekers had gathered there. Gotai became enlightened and the emperor of China gave the name to the mountain where Gotai had become enlightened -- Mount Gotai. And the same happened with Daizui. When he became enlightened the emperor declared, "The mountain should be remembered as a memorial to Daizui and his enlightenment. It will be called Mount Daizui."

'A MONK CAME TO SEE MASTER DAIZUI, AND SAID TO HIM. "MOUNT GOTAI AND MOUNT DAIZUI — WHAT ARE THEY LIKE? HOW IS MOUNT DAIZUI?
DAIZUI SAID, "SPEAK LOUDER — I AM HARD OF HEARING."
THE MONK REPEATED THE QUESTION IN A LOUD VOICE.
DAIZUI SAID, "IT IS LIKE A THOUSAND MOUNTAINS, TEN THOUSAND MOUNTAINS."

It was a small mountain, but because of thousands of disciples moving on the golden path of becoming enlightened, Daizui said, "It is not only my enlightenment that makes Mount Gotai and Mount Daizui what they are, but thousands, perhaps ten thousands, are searching the same enlightenment."

This mountain is one of the most blessed in the world. So many seekers, so many who are absolutely determined to attain to their potential. A thousand or ten thousand sleeping buddhas are trying to wake up. This mountain is not a small place. If it can contain ten thousand buddhas, how can it be a small place? It is ten thousand mountains, the whole range that goes for thousands of miles.'

Neither Professor Zhao nor Renzheng nor Yujie knew of Master Daizui or Master Gotai nor the mountains named after them but I was convinced that these were the Japanese forms of the names, so it was natural that they wouldn't know. I was discovering that Osho generally used the Japanese form of a name, even if it was Chinese. The Japanese form is easier to pronounce! The puzzle was to link them up with the Chinese names. I had previously found online that, in a little-known book called 'The Book of Rinzai: The Recorded Sayings of Zen Master Rinzai', from the new English translation by Eido Shimano Roshi, there is a clear statement that Mount Gotai is Mount Wutai, or Wutaishan, as it is commonly known in China. 'Wu' means five in Chinese and 'go' means five in Japanese and 'tai' in both Chinese and Japanese means a terrace. The five mountain tops in Wutaishan are flat like a terrace rather than peaked.

I could not find any definite reference to who Master Gotai was, but in another small Chinese story featuring Master Dasui, another master, obviously a friend, was mentioned. He was called Touzi Datong. Perhaps this was the Chinese name of Master Gotai? I don't know if there is a Mount Datong but there is an important city, near which the Yungang Grottoes are situated, called Datong. The name of this city was changed from Pingcheng to Datong a hundred or so years after Touzi Datong died in 914 AD. Perhaps this is a connection?

Anyway, Osho, although correct in saying that many emperors 'gave' mountains to enlightened masters and named them after them, was, in this case, wrong because Wutaishan had been named almost as far back in time as Song Mountain and was obviously named after the physical formation of the mountains not a person. But Professor Zhao suggested that the mountain mentioned in the story could have been a smaller mountain in the Taihang Mountain Range (see below).

In Andy Ferguson's 'Zen's Chinese Heritage' he lists Master Daizui as the Japanese name of Master Dasui Fazhen (878 – 963), a Zen master who was born in Sichuan but who travelled extensively throughout China. He was born a few years after the death of Linji Yixuan (Rinzai), who died in 866, so it doesn't require much stretch of imagination to think that he might have travelled to this area to visit Yixuan's temple – called The Linji Temple – or monastery which is in the same area. This could therefore put Master Daizui and the unknown Master Gotai (Master Datong?) somewhere on the range of mountains of which Wutaishan is one of the most famous.

I asked Professor Zhao if the range of mountains that Osho refers to could be the range that stretches from the north of Shanxi, south to the Yellow River basin where Luoyang is situated, and finally reaching to the peaks known as Song Mountain in north-west Henan. He surprisingly replied that actually, according to the Chinese, this is indeed regarded as one mountain range – like the Himalayas – and is called the Taihang Mountain Range. He therefore thought it very likely that this is what Osho was referring to.

Professor Zhao, Renzheng and Yujie are all devout Buddhists and love this mountain range very much and have visited there often. The mountains are not far from Shijiazhuang which is actually situated almost in their foothills. Professor Zhao told me how the early Buddhists monks, after settling in the White Horse Temple in Luoyang, then travelled further to Wutaishan because this was the home of Manjushri (Chinese: Wenshu), one of Buddha's most famous disciples, and they wanted to make a pilgrimage to this mountain.

But I was puzzled. I asked my friends how these early Hindu monks knew about this mountain as no Indian people had ever been to China before. There were no books or internet connections! Yujie answered me with a look that I can only describe as 'pitying'! She said, 'You westerners don't understand about past lives. These Buddhist monks had past life memories of the mountain so, although they were born in India, they had memories of either being on Wutaishan or knowing about it. It was therefore easy for them to find it.'

Her comment absolutely silenced me! But, contrary to her

opinion about westerners not understanding about past lives, I was, in fact, surmising that Osho had a past life connection with this mountain range and was indeed talking about it from personal memory (he once said that enlightened beings had total recall of all their past lives). So without me voicing this to Yujie, she had independently confirmed my conjectures.

Given Osho's other stories about being on Song Mountain near the Shaolin Temple and walking for three months with Bodhidharma, I now feel pretty confident in saying that, with his comments on this story of Gotai and Daizui, he is referring to the Taihang Mountain Range and it is this range, which includes Song Mountain, that he calls 'one of the most blessed in the world'. I also feel that he is saying this from a personal experience of having been there. Bodhidharma supposedly died around 536 AD, by which time the Yungang Grottoes were complete – and the Longmen Grottoes in Luoyang were being created – the first phase starting in 493 AD and ending in 534 AD. If Osho was near Song Mountain or Luoyang in Henan with Bodhidharma – as he said he was – he most certainly would have heard about, possibly even visited, both places. Hence his love of so often repeating his concept of the ten thousand buddhas in a temple carved into a mountainside.

* * *

Like the early Buddhist monks, Osho, despite living in the twentieth century, had no internet connection and little access to detailed facts about China because up to and during his lifetime it had been a closed and inaccessible country. Maybe, therefore, his facts were not absolutely accurate (he often said he wasn't concerned about historical accuracy but rather about the point he was making) but what he says and how he says it, is enough to convince me that he was talking, with great love and insight, from first-hand experience of this area, albeit in centuries past.

For me he spoke on the early Chinese Taoist and Zen masters with such immediacy, such intimacy, such clarity, such authenticity that he created a longing in me to tread, if only for just a little way, on a similar path to the ones these luminous enlightened beings have travelled on.

Osho

Coming to Song Mountain has fulfilled much of that longing created by my beloved Master so many years ago.

* * *

Professor Zhao had one more extraordinary card to play. My third question was about Linji Yixuan. I had only a few months previously discovered that Linji Yixuan was the Chinese name of the Zen master whom the Japanese call Rinzai. As most of Osho's later discourses were on Zen he referred constantly to Rinzai but I had not found any Chinese link to him such as, for example, where he lived or if he had a temple or a monastery somewhere. When I started to ask my third question about Linji Yixuan or Rinzai, Professor Zhao sort of waved my words aside with his hand and said he would answer those questions when he took me to the Linji Temple the next day! I was stunned. After all my fruitless research I was now being told that Rinzai's temple was right here in Shijiazhuang and I would be taken there the next day!

We duly spent a serene and beautiful afternoon in this small temple with its attached monastery in which about twenty monks live. And certainly, as we slowly walked around, every now and then one of Osho's Zen stories popped into my delighted mind! It was very quiet and peaceful because not many people go there except groups of Japanese Zen disciples – but that afternoon there was almost nobody there and in the hazy light of the late winter afternoon it was a totally magical place.

It was to this temple that a Japanese monk called Myoan Eisai (Chinese: Rongxi) came in 1168. He spent only six months in China on this first trip, but returned in 1187 for a longer stay after which he returned to Japan and introduced the Rinzai school of Zen to Japan – as well as green tea, having brought some green tea seeds with him. He founded the Hōon-ji Temple, Japan's first Zen temple, in the southern island of Kyushu, but later moved to Kamakura where he founded the Zen temple, Jufuku-ji, in 1199 – ironically very close to where I lived for five years. The Shogun and the newly ascendant warrior class enthusiastically welcomed Myoan Eisai's teachings and Zen was therefore immediately accepted in

Japan and spread rapidly throughout the country, and then to the world.

And to end my tale….

There is a Chinese saying that when a wandering monk comes to a place in which he feels at home, he must dig a hole in the earth. If the hole fills up with water, then this is the right place for him to be. If the hole remains dry, he must move on. I feel that, as a wandering Osho sannyasin, I have dug a metaphorical hole for myself in the earth of Song Mountain and the hole has not only filled to the brim with water but has profusely overflowed – and continues to overflow – with a liquid deep silence, a fulfilling peace and a tremendous joy.

I feel infinitely blessed to have found my way, as have so many others before me, to this most blessed of mountains.

Appendix

References:
1) 'Zen's Chinese Heritage' by Andy Ferguson (Wisdom Publications, USA)
2) 'Tracking Bodhidharma' by Andy Ferguson (Counterpoint Press, USA)
3) Wikipedia and the internet
4) Various obscure Chinese texts translated for me
5) Osho: 'Bodhidharma: The Greatest Zen Master', 'The White Lotus', 'Tao, The Pathless Path', 'Tao, The Three Treasures', 'Zen, The Path of Paradox – and many other books by Osho.

Related Websites:
1) **www.3books.co.uk** – Veena Schlegel's website giving information about her books
2) **www.amazon.com/VeenaSchlegel** – to buy Veena Schlegel's books
3) **www.pankajabrooke.com** – Pankaja Brooke's film website
   www.vimeo.com/user1825120
4) **www.shaolinwugulun.com** – the kungfu school's website
5) **http://www.punyaweb.net** – Punya Kauffeler web design

Made in the USA
Charleston, SC
23 July 2015